A CULTURAL HISTORY
OF SEXUALITY

VOLUME 6

A Cultural History of Sexuality

General Editor: Julie Peakman

A CULTURAL HISTORY

OF SEXUALITY

IN THE
MODERN AGE

Edited by Gert Hekma

B L O O M S B U R Y

LONDON · NEW DELHI · NEW YORK · SYDNEY

Bloomsbury Academic

An imprint of Bloomsbury Publishing Plc

50 Bedford Square	1385 Broadway
London	New York
WC1B 3DP	NY 10018
UK	USA

www.bloomsbury.com

Hardback edition first published in 2011 by Berg Publishers, an imprint of
Bloomsbury Academic
Paperback edition first published by Bloomsbury Academic 2014

British Library Cataloguing-in-Publication Data
A catalogue record for this book is available from the British Library.

ISBN: HB: 978-1-84788-805-1
PB: 978-1-4725-5478-9
HB Set: 978-1-84520-702-1
PB Set: 978-1-4725-5480-2

Library of Congress Cataloging-in-Publication Data
A catalog record for this book is available from the Library of Congress.

Typeset by Apex CoVantage, LLC, Madison, WI, USA
Printed and bound in Great Britain

CONTENTS

PREFACE

A Cultural History of Sexuality is a six-volume series reviewing changes in sexual attitudes and behavior throughout history. Each volume follows the same basic structure and begins with an outline account of sexuality in the period under consideration. Academic experts examine major aspects of sex and sexuality under seven key headings: heterosexuality, homosexuality, sexual variations, religion and the law, medicine and disease, popular beliefs and culture, prostitution, and erotica. Readers can choose a synchronic or a diachronic approach to the material—a single volume can be read to obtain a thorough knowledge of the body in a given period, or one of the seven themes can be followed through time by reading the relevant chapters of all six volumes, providing a thematic understanding of changes and developments over the long term. The six volumes divide the history of sexuality as follows:

Volume 1: A Cultural History of Sexuality in the Classical World (800 B.C.E. to 350 C.E.)

Volume 2: A Cultural History of Sexuality in the Middle Ages (350 C.E. to 1450)

Volume 3: A Cultural History of Sexuality in the Renaissance (1450 to 1650)

Volume 4: A Cultural History of Sexuality in the Enlightenment (1650 to 1820)

Volume 5: A Cultural History of Sexuality in the Age of Empire (1820 to 1920)

Volume 6: A Cultural History of Sexuality in the Modern Age (1920 to 2000)

Julie Peakman, General Editor

SERIES ACKNOWLEDGMENTS

This series has been a long time in the making, mainly because it is not an easy task to bring together fifty-four international scholars, even when we were all willing and eager. Every one of us had other commitments—to our universities, other books, and/or to our families. I therefore appreciate those who came together to create this special project. I want to thank the editors of all the volumes; Peter Toohey and Mark Golden, Ruth Evans, Bette Talvacchia, Ivan Crozier and Chiara Beccalossi, and Gert Hekma for their sterling efforts in the face of my continual demands, and for helping to keep their contributors on track, especially when the occasional one dropped out with little warning. Huge thanks also go to all the contributors who freely committed their time and efforts. I also want to thank Tristan Palmer at Berg for all his support and Catherine Draycott from the Wellcome Trust Picture Library for making available the Wellcome images.

Julie Peakman, General Editor

ILLUSTRATIONS

CHAPTER 1

CHAPTER 2

CHAPTER 8

CHAPTER 9

CHAPTER ONE

Introduction

GERT HEKMA

During the twentieth century, the Western world saw some major changes in sexual practices and ideologies. The first and foremost was a heterosexualization of society—the monogamous heterosexual couple became the social standard. The older patriarchal model of marriage and family was replaced by a new version of couple relations that combined love and sex and demanded the equality of male and female lovers. The second change came with women's sexual emancipation, although it did not mean that men and women would be seen as equal in the field of sexuality. The old biological conviction that men are the more sexual and women the more loving gender persisted, creating many misunderstandings in heterosexual relations. The third development was the emancipation of homosexuality from a category of sin, crime, and pathology to something next to normal. The fourth development was an increased visibility of sexuality in the media, in the arts, on the streets, and elsewhere. Growing emancipation and visibility did not mean that puritanical attitudes changed that much—a fifth evident element could best be described as a lack of development in morals. Heterosexual coitus remained the norm, and other sexual pleasures were, in varying degrees, rejected. All over the West, it seemed that sexual liberalism was on the rise, but at the same time the number of moral panics, sex laws, and sex crimes and criminals continued to grow rapidly. Of course, these changes did not mean that sexual citizens did not pursue sexual pleasures beyond social norms or enjoy tabooed erotic possibilities.[1]

HETEROSEXUALIZATION

In the late nineteenth century, psychiatrists began to write about so-called perversions, often in close cooperation with the subjects involved, including many male homosexuals and masochists. The invention of the perversions—sadism, masochism, fetishism, exhibitionism, voyeurism, zoophilia (bestiality), nymphomania, homosexuality, lesbianism, pedophilia, necrophilia, and so on—was soon followed by a concern that many youngsters, who were seen as sexually indifferent or "polymorphously perverse" would deviate from the right road of marriage, heterosexuality, and reproduction. An effort was made to sexually discipline youth to prevent them from being seduced by sexual diversity. Psychoanalysis showed how difficult this might be, and Sigmund Freud developed an "Oedipal" model of sexual development that started with polymorphous perversity and that ideally ended with a monogamous, reproductive relationship with clearly defined male and female roles. Although Freud used the word *heterosexual,* coined in 1869, as counterpoint to *homosexual,* he mostly referred to *normal,* which meant that heterosexuality was not just statistically the most common sexual orientation but was in the first place considered socially normative behavior. This heterosexual social obligation was, in the case of Freud, intertwined with traditional gender norms for males and females. He was well aware of the many difficulties on the path to the Oedipal triangle, but saw it as fundamental to civilized society. Individuals would have to overcome their perverse inclinations to become healthy heterosexuals.[2]

Although the work of Freud and the early sexologists met with resistance as they underlined a psychic and social world of infantile pleasures and sexual diversity, the answer on how to prevent "perversions" would be developed over the century. Initially, the heterosexual norm remained unmentioned as such, but was rather explained as "natural," an understanding that was tied to the most common interpretation of Darwinism—that is, propelled by heterosexual selection. On the other hand, the perversions were depicted as unhealthy, dangerous, abject, or scandalous—activities no rational or bourgeois person would ever engage in. Only homosexuals could find supportive texts and examples in the margins of the mainstream. The media began to play a growing role in creating moral panics on sexual deviancy, starting with Oscar Wilde in 1895 and the Eulenburg circle in 1907–1908. Socialists used such scandals to put capitalism, church, and aristocracy in the pillory for their sexual degeneracy. The Freudo-Marxist ideals of sexual utopians like Wilhelm Reich and the progressive Soviet writers were monogamy, heterosexuality, and reproduction with the safety valve of divorce if such relations proved to be unhappy.

A general line in socialist thought was the facilitation of relations between boys and girls to enhance heterosexuality and to prevent perversion; the homosociality of bourgeois society would supposedly only breed sexual aberrations, and male bonding in particular. Sex education in schools and for adults focused on biological facts that always concluded with heterosexual morality. Regardless of how books such as *Married Love* (1918) by Marie Stopes, *Ideal Marriage* (1926) by Theodoor Hendrik van de Velde, and all kinds of anatomy books with realistic depictions of the genitals might have been regarded as scandalous in their time, the message was an idealization of the heterosexual couple—in Stopes's case combined with an ideal of planned parenthood. Socialists and progressives of all kinds were supportive of women's emancipation and propagated some sexual equality of the sexes, although both biological and feminist ideas on the differences between the sexes always complicated the struggle for gender equality. An exception to this heterosexual and marital morality was offered by a few anarchists who defended free love for both genders and sexual orientations and opposed state interference in intimate life.[3]

FIGURE 1.1: The traveling birth clinic of Marie Stopes that provided free advice on family planning by a certified nurse, 1920s. Wellcome Library, London.

One of the main catalysts of heterosexualization was a tighter control of youngsters both in the nuclear family and in education. Especially after World War II and the sexual revolution, the nuclear family became more insulated; family members outside of parents and children were put at a distance, while household servants disappeared, and the distance between workplace and home increased. Education was extended into and beyond puberty, and the school, more than the street or workplace, taught youth the lessons of life in this essential period of sexual awakening. The streets of cities and villages were typically places where ages and classes mixed, while the school was age-stratified and built on predominantly middle-class norms. Coeducation was another way to promote heterosexual norms and prevent the homosexual promiscuity of boys and girls among themselves. Other disciplinary institutions followed the same

FIGURE 1.2: An American soldier running to escape a thunderbolt in the form of the letters VD, representing venereal disease. Sexually transmitted diseases, as well as homosexuality, concerned military authorities. Color lithograph by F.O. Schiffers, 1946. Wellcome Library, London.

path of combating homosexual promiscuity. From the mid-nineteenth century onward, in prisons, solitary incarceration was preferred above group cells to prevent same-sex relations. The more repressive systems, however, used prison homosexuality as a way to control inmates by rewarding straight machos and punishing queens and punks who were used as sex objects by the first group.[4] In World War II, armies started to exclude homosexual men as risk factors for both mental disorders and treason.[5]

The old marital norm had been represented as a reproductive couple with a working husband and a wife responsible for the household and obedient to her spouse. Marriage was generally a dull affair in terms of love and sex and often a total dead end for women. The new heterosexual norm started with the idea of the necessity of sexual pleasure for the couple, and later it took on an ideal of sexual equality between husband and wife. Marriage changed from an affair controlled by the larger family and became more the choice of the partners, with parents losing influence over the young couple. In the past, marriage and sex came first, with the possibility that love might develop later. In more recent times, love has become the precondition for the sexual life of a couple, and marriage has become unessential. The development away from marriages arranged by, and integrated into families and ruled by gender inequality shifted to loving, equal, and more isolated couples whose primary aim was no longer reproduction—this was the major sexual revolution of the second half of the twentieth century. It also meant that same-sex marriages became more feasible—the first civil unions for gay and lesbian couples were introduced in Denmark in 1989, while marriage was opened up for same-sex couples in the Netherlands in 2001.

Ideals of romantic love were still largely asexual in the early nineteenth century and could be both homosocial and heterosocial. From then on feminists and socialists deployed this as a model for marriage and started to include sexuality—but only between males and females. The contemporary ideology—that love and sex should be combined—had been rather unthinkable in a past when love was about equal relations and sex about unequal ones. Until the early twentieth century, love and sex were considered opposites and not part of the same relationship. The deepest emotional bonds were often within, not between, genders. Boarding schools and fraternities created intimate friendships that some considered the foundation of public and political life. These bonds were valued above marriage because they were spiritual rather than physical. The new utopian ideals of socialists and feminists, who strived for better and more equal heterosexual relations, became normative with the sexual revolution of the 1960s. Multiple intragender attachments were replaced by single intergender ones. Apart from the gay worlds, places like the sports field now offer the main but meager possibility for men to experience homosocial intimacy, while women continued to have more opportunities to form special bonds, for example in friendships or female professions. Heterosexualization was building on the heterosocialization of society, and vice versa. Although there was no need to foster the sexual emancipation of women solely along heterosexual lines, this became the norm for reproductive and political-demographic reasons. While the change from marital to heterosexual norms may have been momentous, sexual diversity remained abject. Homosociality is now on the decline and heterosociality on the rise in most social fields.

The heterosexual couple who shared equality, and combined love and sex, became the standard in the Western world (as eulogized by Anthony Giddens as "pure relation"),[6] although patriarchal attitudes of men linger on in many intimate relations. This signaled a major sexual revolution. In the past, sexual relations were mainly between social unequals: male and female, rich and poor, client and prostitute, young and old. Even in gay and lesbian relations, which could have been the most equal, such power differences were the rule between butch and femme, queen and trade, man and boy (see later in the chapter). The inequality of the past was replaced by equality as the new sexual norm. The gender inequality of former days may have been shunned, but for various reasons, sexual equality remains problematic, firstly because gender traditions are deeply ingrained and do not change easily and secondly because it does not fit the sexual and social plurality which people experience and enjoy.[7]

Gays and lesbians experience more social and erotic equality than heterosexual couples do, as men and women in a relationship still have to overcome their gender differences. Gays can be seen as the great victors of this drive for equality. On the other hand, traditional heterosexual couples, sadomasochists, pedophiles, zoophiles, or prostitutes and their clients, and all those whose relations cannot fulfill the new norm of equality, lost out. Although the latter groups were never highly regarded, the sheer volume of hatred and legislation directed against them in recent years in the West shows how strict the new norm of equality has become—notwithstanding a long history of erotic inequality and also a general realization of how desire can flare up through social differences. Sadomasochists have a hard time getting their preferences accepted, and they do so by underlining that their practices are consensual—masochists agree to their own mental or physical humiliation. Consent is something child and animal lovers, and clients of prostitutes, cannot claim easily these days. The main accepted difference is ethnicity, although preferences for a specific race are frowned upon and can be seen as racist. The most amazing aspect of this sexual revolution is that it has gone so unnoticed and that theories of both

inequality and equality are dogmatic, unrealistic, and deny the existing variations in preferences that cannot be reduced to either theory.[8]

The greater stress placed on heterosexual pleasure led to a broadening
of the sexual repertoire. Although the twentieth century did not invent new
sexual practices, the general population engaged in a wider range of acts. Oral
and anal sex in heterosexual relations is increasing, male sexual violence of the
past is probably declining, and consensual violence among sadomasochistic
relations is on the rise—with men often being masochists. Over the generations, both men and women have more heterosexual partners before, inside,
outside, and after marriage, and more couples live unmarried, especially in the
Scandinavian countries. People also engage in a wider range of sexual acts,
with heterosexual coitus and self-stimulation being most common. The greatest winners of the sexual revolution are women, who in most sexual fields—
not unlike other fields of labor, education, or politics—have started to behave
more like men.

SEXUAL EMANCIPATION OF WOMEN

During the twentieth century women gained more sexual freedom. Feminism stressed a greater autonomy for women, and although sexual independence may not have always been a favorite topic for feminists because of the
strength of patriarchal and puritanical norms, some women used their rights
to promote sexuality. Loosening family obligations and a greater respect for
individual choices certainly helped women from the higher classes to create
some spaces for their sexual freedom. The garçonnes of Paris, the women of
the Bloomsbury group, the lesbians of Berlin, the female bohemians of New
York's Greenwich Village, women who lived as couples in so-called Boston
marriages, and so many others in different places could now find their own
sexual trajectories.[9]

Women still encountered many problems, whether they were promiscuous
or chaste. The rise of sexology and a growing visibility of sexual issues made
both men and women more aware of their sexual preferences. The growing
stress in sex education literature that both husband and wife should enjoy
marital relations favored women's heterosexual emancipation inside marriage
and beyond. Except for rare and individual voices, such as Simone de Beauvoir's
in the 1940s, there was a more widespread and shared assumption of women's
sexual autonomy in the late 1960s by feminists such as Germaine Greer and
Kate Millett. Over the next decade, lesbians and prostitutes would defend their
own sexual existence, although the mainstream of the women's movement
remained staunchly normal and heterosexual. The idea that a woman could

FIGURE 1.3: A fashionable young woman, exposing
her breast and lifting her dress to take off a stocking.
Bruxelles, 1920s, by Louis Icart. Wellcome Library,
London.

assume promiscuous practices, generally accepted for men, continued to be
suspect. Even today, few females show pride in their sexual conquests.

The main problem that women's sexual emancipation faces remains the
discrepancy between ideas of male and female sexuality, which date from
the eighteenth century.[10] Both biological and everyday conceptualizations
assume that women are less sexual than men or that men prefer sex and
women prefer love. This is attributed to the belief that women will become
mothers since they have a stronger interest in caring than in sexual desire.
Popular Darwinian and psychological views on males showed men as sexual
subjects, predators displaying mounting behavior, with females as submis-
sive objects. A more sensible explanation is that the sexual socialization of
girls teaches them not to be promiscuous or, in other words, not to sexually
explore. The gendered socialization that trains boys to be predators and girls
to be Madonnas may have changed somewhat in recent decades, but the
main structure has changed little. These opposing instructions for boys and

girls make heterosexuality a difficult endeavor, as sexual pleasure is complicated for a couple in which one partner has been taught to pursue his sexual
desires and the other has learned to restrain herself.

The majority of women fell under the heterosexual marital norm model, and
only a tiny minority escaped the demands of patriarchal and sexist ideology.
Like men, sexually assertive women had some options. Rich women migrated
to big cities or poorer countries where they faced less problems in living out
their erotic lives. Paris and Capri attracted both men and women with variant
desires. Poorer women could go to red light districts where sexual norms were
more relaxed and where many sexual specialties found a space—from prostitution and lesbianism to sadomasochism and transgenderism. French (oral),
Greek (anal), and Russian (sadomasochistic) sex were offered to men in Amsterdam's bordellos in the 1930s. Women could become prostitutes or find
other niches as bartenders, street vendors, or chamber maids. Many of them
were lesbians who sometimes invested money earned from sex work into bars
that welcomed queers and dykes. These venues offered a home to women striving for autonomy in jobs as nurses, shop assistants, seamstresses, actresses,
artists, or stewardesses. Since the 1960s, red light districts have become more
exclusively heterosexual places for straight men, and women and queers who
previously found a niche there have moved out and found other locations, such
as neighborhood bars, sex clubs, or gay streets. The profession of prostitutes
now attracts other groups of mainly non-Western women. With the multitude
of sexual transactions that are not clearly financial, the rise of sex tourism,
stricter state regulation, and the growing abjection of sexual inequality, prostitution in the West seems on the decline, while other sexual possibilities (more
for men than for women) broaden in discos, theme parties, or on the Internet.

The 1960s brought a major sexual liberation for women with the introduction of the birth control pill. Several other contraceptive methods had been
used, such as condoms, shields, or postcoital vaginal douches—the horrors and
fears of the latter have been forgotten by later generations. The pill was easier
to use, more effective, and became widely accessible. Although it was introduced as a family planning device, it immediately liberated women from certain
bodily constraints and made the sexual life of the married and unmarried more
carefree. Sometimes the pill's existence was used by men as leverage for sex,
and women then had to counter male sexual expectations without the excuse
of the dangers of pregnancy. The pill ensured women's erotic emancipation but
also contributed to a further heterosexualization of society, because it made
sexual relations between male and female adolescents more unproblematic.
Although concerns about the negative effects of the pill continue to be voiced,

it is still generally used. Efforts to produce a male counterpart were undertaken but were never widely accepted, indicating a continuing sexual inequality in which women are responsible for (non)reproduction.

The black, lesbian, and prostitute women who demanded their rights from the 1970s onwards, in and outside the feminist movement, paved the way for women who defended variety in female sexuality, such as sadomasochism and pornography. Feminists also ensured their sexual subjectivity and autonomy in the art world. They encountered fierce opposition, not only from patriarchal men, but also from mainstream feminism, which only accepted vanilla (nice heterosexual) sex. It led to the Sex Wars of the 1980s where radical feminists who opposed sadomasochism, prostitution, pornography, transgenderism, and sexual diversity stood up against those who defended such pleasures and transgressions and were seen as having internalized male norms. The battles were fierce but have abated, while the uneasy question of how to deal with sexual diversity still stands.[11]

Today's generation of young feminists defends sexual pleasure but mainly in its heterosexual and marginally in its homosexual variations, accepting and rejecting in different degrees the issues of promiscuity, pornography, prostitution, pedophilia, bestiality, public sex, and sadomasochism. All these variations and their presence in mainstream media have led to concerns among women and others about the oversexualization, or pornification, of society. Such critics complain that many women, and especially girls, develop low self-esteem because of media representations, especially in soft porn and video clips, and then feel obliged to wear sexy clothing or undergo surgical changes. The presumed oversexualized culture makes innocent girls the victims of male predators who feel empowered in their hegemonic masculinity by the same imagery. Some women even feel proud to be promiscuous and defend their behavior by seeing it as their sexual autonomy, but their critics charge that they are only confirm masculinist norms.[12] The complaints of these neofeminists seem to be overdone, as most young people lead rather unadventurous erotic lives and are in effect often afraid to show erotic interest and generally believe that sex is only allowed in loving relations. The sexual overexposure is moreover mainly located on television channels and Internet sites that the users access of their own choice, and is, except for small talk and insults, absent in most parts of public life—it is not on the streets, almost completely absent in education, health care, sports, and the family. Additionally, religion and politics provide mainly negative messages about eroticism. What these youngsters need is not puritanism or taboo on sexual imagery that often teaches them erotic basics but better education in schools on sexual citizenship and media use.

The general approach of the neofeminists and their many male supporters looks very much like the perspective of evangelical Christians who now defend sexual pleasure and discuss extramarital sex no longer in terms of sin, but in terms of a lack of self-esteem.[13] Their terminology also resembles the terminology of late nineteenth-century psychiatrists who differentiated perversion from perversity (the primary versus secondary interest in sexual variation) and sex as marital obligation from sex as diversion. Much may have changed, but the prejudices against gender and sexual diversity remain strong. A younger generation of feminists stands up against an older generation that still has a broader, but not so loudly voiced, view on erotic variation. The boundaries become drawn increasingly closer around the couple that may enjoy, in the privacy of their bedroom, coital sex spiced up with oral and anal sex, sexy clothing, a bit of female-friendly soft porn, and perhaps some gentle flagellation. On the other hand, what is now discussed in terms of "instrumental sex," the new term for promiscuity, continues to be rejected. The new ideology of sexual equality, promoted by socialists, social-democrats, and feminists to various degrees for more than a century has become generalized, and the short episode in which some feminists defended sexual diversity and took a more instrumental approach to sex seems to have passed. "Slut" and "whore" remain terms of abjection among almost everyone.

Notwithstanding all the debates on the boundaries of sexual pleasures, women have gained the greatest advantage in the sexual changes in the twentieth century. While up until the 1960s girls were expected to remain virgins until marriage, both pre- and extramarital sex became lesser concerns from the 1970s onward. Recent surveys indicate that women masturbate more, have more heterosexual and lesbian sex, look more at pornography, engage more in various sexual variations, and feel less guilty about sex.[14] Regarding most practices, the percentages of sexual activity for women are lower than those of men, but the gap between them is closing. There are some remarkable exceptions where women are overtaking men. In a recent Dutch survey, 40 percent of the women claimed to have used sex toys while less than 30 percent of the men did so.[15] Women emerged from patriarchal control to find a measure of sexual autonomy, but various social institutions and heterosexual norms still limit what they are allowed to do and what they allow themselves to do.

HOMOSEXUAL WORLDS

The first homosexual rights movement was established in 1897 in Germany, and now all Western countries have many LGBT (lesbian-gay-bisexual-trans gender) institutions. Most countries had laws against same-sex practices, and even in countries that did not, such as France, homosexual men were still persecuted and discriminated against, particularly for public indecency or loitering. Since the 1960s, most laws against homosexuality have been eliminated, and the European Union now forbids discrimination on grounds of homosexuality. In 2003, the U.S. Supreme Court declared the remaining sodomy laws unconstitutional—212 years after France had abolished them. There were no legal rights for homosexual men and women in 1900, but now they exist all over the Western world and are even enshrined in the South African constitution. In some countries, such as the United States, the incorporation of laws that protect gays and lesbians still has yet to be realized. In the U.S. army, for instance, the so-called "don't ask, don't tell" policy means that the army is not allowed to ask about sexual preferences, and gays and lesbians are not allowed to speak out.[16]

Germany, in particular Berlin, was the capital of (homo)sexual sciences, homosexual rights movements, and gay culture at the beginning of the twentieth century. Magnus Hirschfeld, who was the founder of the Scientific-Humanitarian

FIGURE 1.4: Magnus Hirschfeld also was one of the founders of the World League for Sexual Reform (WLSR). Presiding table at the final Brno congress of the WLSR in 1932. This organization existed from 1928 till the mid-1930s and had no successor after World War II. From the left: Norman Haire, Magnus Hirschfeld, J. H. Leunbach, unidentified man, and Dr. Weisskopf, the congress organizer. The blackboard behind Haire announces a film—for physicians only—about "The Gräfenberg Ring," which is one of the first intrauterine contraceptive devices. Wellcome Library, London.

Committee (the homosexual rights movement), was also the editor of the *Annual for Sexual Intermediaries,* a prolific writer of sex books, and an expert witness in many court cases. From 1919, he was the director of the Institute of Sexual Sciences and, up until his death in 1935, the pivotal queer of Europe. Several gay organizations coexisted in the 1920s and both competed and cooperated in the fight against antihomosexual laws and attitudes. They published dozens of journals and organized parties, while many bars catered to a variety of homosexual clienteles. This vibrant gay culture (and to a lesser extent lesbian and transgender cultures) attracted an international public. Writers like Christopher Isherwood, Stephen Spender, André Gide, René Crevel, Yvan Goll, and many others described Germany's gay life or Hirschfeld's Institute of Sexual Sciences, which was for most foreign guests a museum of exotic curiosities. Both Paris and London had also developed a vibrant queer subculture by that time, but both suffered from antihomosexual biases that prevented the development of a homosexual movement and culture comparable to those of Berlin and Germany.[17]

FIGURE 1.5: Ads for Berlin homosexual bars of the 1920s. In: Institut für Sexualforschung Wien (Hrsg), *Bilder-Lexikon der Erotik*, Bd I: Kulturgeschichte, Wien/Leipzig: Verlag für Kulturforschung, 1930.

All over the Western world, the most important queer locations for encounters were public toilets, parks, railway stations, and streets. Here the queers, often seen in gender-inverted terms, had sex with each other, but mostly sought out young men who were heterosexual and in itinerant professions: bell-, farm- and schoolboys, soldiers, sailors, servants, construction workers, or police officers—as we know so well from the life and work of Oscar Wilde, Marcel Proust, André Gide, Jean Cocteau, Joe Ackerley, Jean Genet, and many others. These effeminate men (fags, sissies, or queens in English; *tantes* or *folles* in French; *Tunten* in German; *maricones* in Spanish; or *nichten* in Dutch) had a homosexual identity while their male sex partners had no such identity. They were the passive partners of active and masculine heterosexual men, the latter enjoying such sex in the absence of women who were unavailable because of demands of virginity. Another large slice of gay sex life was between adult and adolescent men, or male youths. The gender dichotomy was even more pertinent for the lesbian world, where dykes (masculine lesbians) had no sex or relations with each other but only with femmes (feminine lesbians). The main setback for dykes was that women were considered to be nonsexual, although definitions of sex were so narrow that lesbian sex was not always seen as such, because no penis was involved in the act. At that time, the main theory of sexual desire implied that desires could only be inflamed between opposites, such as a passive, fag, or sissy with an active macho. Desire was based on inequalities of gender, age, and class: male with female, masculine dyke with feminine femme, active with passive, young with old, rich with poor. In most cases, homosexual affairs were occasional and comparable to contacts in prostitution: the one partner paid the other. Often the queer paid the straight, but in some cases the money or services would flow the other way, from heterosexual men to fairy hustler boys. Payment could consist of money, a bed for a night, a dinner, drinks, or gifts. Queers and straights met each other in the aforementioned public places and only rarely in gay bars.[18]

Karl Heinrich Ulrichs (1825–1895), called "the first queer of the world,"[19] even made a theory of this gendered and sexual opposition. According to him, uranians (his term for homosexuals) were "female souls in male bodies" who longed for real men with "male souls in male bodies." Urnindes, or lesbians, were "male souls in female bodies."[20] These gender-inverted souls were, according to him, the spiritual counterparts of hermaphroditic bodies. Equal sexual relations—both homo and hetero—were unthinkable but became the social norm in the 1960s when gay men started to engage in sexual relations with each other, as did lesbian women. Gay men (more than lesbian women) then started to deny their gender inversion and to defend their masculinity, and so-called lipstick lesbians began to replace the butches of former days.

It was only in the 1950s, with ideals of social equality, that the sexual border traffic between queer and trade declined. Now, gay men had sex with each other, were no longer considered sissies, and saw themselves as masculine. They rejected all signs of the formerly celebrated effeminacy and used psychological theories that defined homosexuals as just the same as heterosexuals, being only different in sexual partner choice. The meeting places shifted from the old haunts in public places to the semipublic subculture of bars, discos, and saunas. These were more exclusively homosexual places where gays and (to a lesser degree) lesbians met each other and looked for stable love. Homosexual relations could no longer be compared to those in prostitution, as the fixed friendships of gay men and lesbian women started very much to look like marriage. Nonetheless their supposed or real effeminacy would continue to haunt gay men.

Lively debates in sexology on sexual variation, vibrant queer cultures, rich gay literature, and homosexual rights movements that actively but unsuccessfully battled against criminal laws faced their greatest setbacks in the 1920s and 1930s with the rise of communism and Stalinism in the Soviet Union, of fascism in Italy, and of Nazism in Germany. The fascist regimes of Franco in Spain and Salazar in Portugal had similar effects. Other European countries saw a tightening of rules and regulations, and queers (mainly those who loved younger men) faced, from the 1930s on, castration as possible punishment for wrong desires and practices now deemed criminal. With the victory of the Axis powers after 1939, the only remaining gay movement was the Swiss Der Kreis. The Nazi regime created one of the cruelest persecutions of homosexuality, with 15,000 homosexual men incarcerated in concentration camps, half of whom would perish. The Soviet regime instituted antisodomy laws in 1934 that made homosexuals a prime target of Stalinist persecutions. In both cases, the effects of criminalization that targeted a largely invisible group went beyond the concrete numbers of criminal persecutions, because legal and penal institutions were the ultimate manifestations of disciplinary measures that built upon others such as education, medicine, and the social control of families, landladies, neighbors, political organizations, or churches.

After World War II, homosexual emancipation took off again, this time with more success. It started in The Netherlands, Germany, and the Scandinavian countries and spread to France, Belgium, and the United States. After the war, the United States became the main locus of the gay movement because of its status as a major empire and because of the development of sexology. Paradoxically, the United States saw not only the most dramatic developments, such as the Stonewall riots, but was also the country to experience the least success among the Western countries. In 1951, the homosexual movement created its first cross-national body, the International Committee for Sexual Equality, whose main members were from Western Europe and North America. It faded away in the early 1960s, but was revived in 1978 as the International Gay Association (IGA), renamed in 1986 ILGA to include lesbians and again in 2008, adding bisexuals and transgenders to the subtitle.

The first proposals for sexual reform came from England, where the Wolfenden report (1957) suggested a broad decriminalization of homosexuality and prostitution. Partial legal changes were enacted in 1967, and other countries would follow suit, or had already preceded England (Sweden, for example, in 1944). Soon, many more countries decriminalized homosexuality, with the United States finally doing so in 2003 through a landmark decision of the Supreme Court that declared sodomy laws unconstitutional. At the moment the European Union does not allow legal prohibitions against homosexuality in its (candidate) member states and demands antidiscrimination laws regarding gays and lesbians in labor relations.

The legal changes were a result of social changes—movements to increase individualization, democratization, and secularization all sped up the drive for homosexual emancipation. Antiwar, black, hippie, student, and women's movements set an example for the gay and lesbian movement. Gays and lesbians came out of the closet and burst into the streets, most notably in New York in 1969 with the Stonewall riots following the 1968 Summer of Love. Homosexuality changed after 1970 from a sin, crime, and disease to something akin to normal. Gays and lesbians came out to family, friends, and colleagues in unprecedented numbers. They joined the subcultural movement but soon emerged aboveground to begin the march through particular institutions. They created their own media and caucuses in various professional groups from churches, universities, trade unions, political parties, and companies to armies and police forces. In the 1980s, the disaster of AIDS struck among gay men, killing thousands of them. Many feared that the epidemic would lead to a backlash against the gay world, and it did so, as seen in the form of moral panics and the closing down of saunas and dark rooms (places in bars and discos where gay men had sex) by authorities. The Cuban authorities introduced forced hospitalization of AIDS patients, and the Swedish introduced obligatory registration of persons with HIV, who had to regularly report about their sex life to their physician. On the positive side, there came

FIGURE 1.6: AIDS prevention poster for gay men
of the Black HIV/AIDS Network of the Terrence
Higgins Trust, 1990s. Wellcome Library, London.

a greater acknowledgement of gay rights in the field of relations, insurance,
pensions, health care, and housing. Lesbians demanded such rights at the same
time for similar reasons but also to safeguard situations where couples had
offspring.

With the introduction of the legalization of gay and lesbian partnerships
starting in Denmark in 1989, and later with the opening of marriage for same-
sex couples in 2001 in the Netherlands, the feeling started to emerge that gays
and lesbians were becoming equal to heterosexuals. The gigantic step forward
from outcast to insider made many queer and straight people believe homosexual emancipation had reached its summit. But it has been more a legal
than a social change. Society has remained heteronormative—that is to say,
heterosexuality has been increasingly more strictly applied as the norm and
homosexuality seen as a second-rate choice. The most common way to enforce
the heterosexual norm is the continuous promotion of straight examples, and
the eternal insults of "fag," "homo," and "queer," against boys and men who
fail to show gender-appropriate or heterosexual behavior or characteristics.[21]

For girls and women, the main comparable insult is "slut," used more than "dyke." The most extreme examples of antihomosexual prejudice and physical violence, including murder, continue unabated even in the most gay friendly places. Dutch research showed that the acceptance of homosexuals comes only with the condition that they should behave normally—that is, they should show neither unmasculine nor sexual qualities and should remain invisible. There is no discussion about the acceptance of heterosexuals. Western countries assert that they are open and democratic societies where no distinctions are made between the various kinds of sexual citizens. Yet heterosexuality remains the norm, with conditions established for gay men and lesbian women, where being accepted often exists more in theory than in practice. Queerer variations in sexual, gendered, and cultural practices and behaviors face even greater intolerance.

VISIBILITY

In the late nineteenth century, when eroticism became a central topic of literature, and sexology opened up the study of perversions, sexuality became a popular topic in print. Serious publishers issued medical books that less respectable publishers ransacked in order to create popular versions and translations. There were books and pamphlets on sex education that discussed free love, sexual variation, prostitution, venereal diseases, contraception, and family-planning and visualized the human body, including the genitals. Photography made new mass-produced pornography available. The media followed suit and started to pay attention to sexual issues, often related to major scandals, such as those of Wilde and Eulenburg, but also to petty sex crimes. The latter became one of the major attractions of the yellow press. With some ups and downs, the media interest in erotic themes grew, and in most cases as soon as countries became liberated from right or left dictatorships, sex exploded in the media, from more serious material to straightforward pornography. This occurred in Germany, Spain, and most former communist countries of Eastern Europe. The commercialization and commodification of sexuality happened not only through the sex industry but also became a regular feature of advertising, as eroticism was used to sell all kinds of products, from perfumes to cars and houses.

Any time a new medium was invented, especially after the sexual revolution, it was immediately used for eroticism. This can be seen with the introduction of television, super-8 movies, video, and the Internet. When a new medium is introduced, puritanical organizations protest and governments make regulations or restrict access, while the industry exploits sex to promote its new products. Yet the more sex a new medium offers, the quicker and broader it is spread and accepted. All media have been intensively used for the portrayal of various forms of sex, usually heterosexual. The more the media production is controlled by private persons, the wider variety of sexual pleasures can be shown. So television remains much more heterosexual than the Internet where sites, blogs, and profiles offer a chance to expose the most obscure variations of sexuality. The sexual variety of the media stands in stark contrast to the heterosexual monoculture of social life, where sexual variety remains, by and large, invisible.

The strong presence of sexual imagery through history has given rise to concerns of both conservative and religious groups alike, as well as some socialists and feminists. They believe that porn can lead to corruption of high Christian morality, family values, the pure working-class ethos, and children's innocence or that it will promote the sexual abuse of women by men. After

FIGURE 1.7: Sex shops in the Amsterdam Red Light District, one of the few places that exhibit explicit imagery. The alley in between the shops has windows for sex workers. Although Amsterdam still has visible sex displays in this district, this kind of material has been restricted and the city is also limiting the number of windows. Photo: Gert Hekma.

the first ascent of antiporn laws in the late nineteenth century, there have been regular moral panics and efforts to contest such imagery. An important wave of antiporn fights occurred in the early 1980s when so-called radical feminists like Catherine MacKinnon and Andrea Dworkin not only combated porn but also joined forces with Ronald Reagan's Republicans, participated in the Meese Committee, and helped formulate antiporn measures. They did so with the slogan "Porn is the theory, rape the practice" of Robin Morgan. However, many feminists disagreed with them in this decade of the Sex Wars. Nowadays the strongest opposition is directed against child pornography, because it involves child sexual abuse (see discussion later in this chapter). The other new panic concerns violent or extreme porn, which is often sadomasochistic material.

The visibility of sex may be enormous in some public arenas, but sex is often only privately accessible (e.g. via the Internet or television). When it comes to certain areas, anxiety about oversexualization or pornification tends to be unfounded. Far too little attention is paid to sexual issues in other social fields such as education, labor, health care, sports, families, religion, or politics. Most of the attention, moreover, goes to heterosexual themes and images and little to sexuality outside this norm. When institutions pay attention to the erotic, it is often more negative than positive in its response: warnings are given against abuse, venereal diseases, unwanted pregnancies, harassment at the workplace; it remains a taboo in sports, families, and health care. Sexuality in the political sphere mainly relates to scandals. Conservative politicians tend to use their opposition to gay marriage, abortion, and prostitution to attract voters. In sports, health care, and among family and friends, many contacts are physical and intimate, thus bordering on the erotic, but the most common and easy way to deal with them is often repression or denial, rather than a positive approach. There is little concept of sexual pleasure as something to be learned and cultivated and no concept of sexual citizenship among politicians, because they see sexual life as private and natural rather than as something essential to social functioning. There is no concept of how eroticism could benefit work or educational relations. The outspoken anxiety about pornification may originate from some real concerns, but to generalize it to a general social problem is mistaken.

PERSISTING PURITANISM

The liberal laws of the nineteenth century that originated with the French Penal Code of 1810 were contested by socialists and Christians alike at the end of the century. Even social liberals followed suit and joined the struggle against immorality. Biblical perceptions that sex was for procreation in marriage, Darwinian ideas that the struggle for life needed a strong heterosexual investment, and psychiatric ideas on sexual degeneracy and perversion all put an end to a liberal age that had relied more on tradition than on law to control sexual practices. In the twentieth century, laws would be the final resort in exerting sexual control that routinely relied on medical and psychological interventions aided by social taboos and regulations on a local level. While the period around 1900 saw many new legal initiatives to control sexuality—for example, regarding age of consent, pornography, contraception and abortion, homosexuality, and sex in power relations or in public—such efforts were doubled in the 1930s in both legal and social fields, by the Nazis and their allies on one hand, and by the communists on the other. Other countries at that time started to use psychiatry to combat what they saw as sexual deviance by castrating sex criminals or to select recruits for the army or other workplaces. After World War II, the United States introduced sexual psychopath laws intended to punish more serious sex crimes. In practice, however, the laws were generally implemented for lesser crimes, since lust murder and rape could already be dealt with through existing laws.

With the sexual revolution, laws were again abolished or restricted. After the invention of the pill, few countries continued to oppose contraception, while most countries started to allow abortion under certain broader conditions. Homosexuality and pornography were decriminalized, and divorce was made easier. This liberalization did not mean per se that persecution decreased. After the sex laws in England were liberalized in 1967, the number of persecutions for remaining crimes, such as public indecency, rose. The period of liberalization was also of a short duration. The concept of sexual violence was soon extended from rape to sexual harassment. Recently the European Union (Council Directive 97/80, December 15, 1997) demanded in labor relations that the company has to prove its good practice rather than the plaintiff proving the company guilty, which is a reversal of normal judicial procedure. What has become defined as the sexual abuse of children was extended, age of consent went up, and penalties became stiffer. Stalking became a crime in several countries. Some jurisdictions now forbid the release of unrepentant pedophiles, and the UK wants to follow persons convicted for sex with minors for up till six years after their release—a measure unprecedented for any other crime.[22] Sex tourists can now be prosecuted back home for acts of pedophilia committed in another country, where such acts may not be a crime. The same legal clamp down is apparent regarding child pornography, where criminalization has tightened from prosecuting the production and the sale of the material to the prosecution for possessing or viewing it. During the sexual revolution, some considered such material as educational, but since 1980 it has become illegal. In the recent past, legislators have only seen harm in the production for the children involved, but now it is believed that such material will also lead to sexual abuse of other children. Virtual pornography is thus being forbidden in the European Union, while the U.S. Supreme Court blocked such legislation because of the freedom of expression. It fits with the contemporary ideas of the United Nations Educational, Scientific and Cultural Organization (UNESCO), some states, and many nongovernmental organizations that children's rights include protecting them against sex while still not providing access to sexual knowledge. Children are defined as those under 18 years. They are defined as potential victims, not as sexual agents.

A few places have legalized prostitution, like the Netherlands, Germany, and some Australian states. Other abolitionist countries have gone in the opposite direction and attempted to eradicate it altogether, such as Sweden, which criminalizes clients who pay for sex. In many U.S. jurisdictions, clients who have been caught with prostitutes are obliged to follow aversion therapies, paid for by heavy fines, where they learn to respect women and where former prostitutes insult and humiliate them. Even the Dutch may go from legalization back to criminalization; the city of Amsterdam has closed down its zone for street prostitution and now has the intention to restrict the scope of its Red Light District. New laws on bestiality and animal pornography are the newest addition to the series of further restrictions on sexuality in countries that praise themselves for their alleged freedom. Iacub and Maniglier have indicated that the percentage of persons in prison (currently still growing) in the United States and France for sex crimes has gone from about 5 percent to some 20 percent between 1970 and 2000; because there are broader definitions of what constitutes a crime, more sex crimes have been added to the law books and harsher penalties have been imposed.[23] The extent of sexual liberation that has supposedly taken place since the sexual revolution is thus debatable in these countries.

Criminal prosecution of certain sexual behaviors is used as the ultimate way to handle tabooed sexual practices, but most disciplining was, and is, being done by social institutions such as the nuclear family, the school system, the media, the health care system, and the legal system. Although most people consider sexuality a private affair, such institutions often deal with unwanted sexual practices and desires in subtle but often strictly heterosexual ways.

OTHER PLEASURES AND DISPLEASURES OF SEX

In the twentieth century, masturbation moved from an act that endangered bodily health to a helpful device to learn about sexuality. Until the sexual revolution, children were warned about the dangers of solitary sex, because it would exhaust the body and lead to all kinds of maladies and weaknesses, or, as Freud saw it, endanger couple-sex. Since the sexual revolution, however, masturbation no longer constitutes a major problem, although it is still not considered a topic to be discussed in polite society. Masturbation is on the increase, certainly among women, and also among men who find it easier and less problematic to please themselves (sometimes with the help of pornography), rather than to engage with partners who may be unwilling or prefer other acts. The fears of Freud proved to be true. Along with individualization, modern society witnesses an onanization. Solitary sex competes with coital sex for being the most common sexual practice.[24]

Venereal diseases have remained a major problem. In 1910, Salvarsan was developed as a new cure for syphilis, which replaced mercury and its frightening side-effects. Penicillin proved a new major breakthrough in 1940 and initiated a period of forty years in which people could have sex without much concern—if they had access to antibiotics. In the early 1980s, a new deadly disease starting in the United States led to devastation among sexually active groups, primarily gay men in the beginning, but then spreading to drugs users and hemophiliacs. AIDS was transmitted by blood and semen. The patients died very quickly, but with new therapies introduced halfway through the 1990s, the disease changed from a mortal to a chronic illness. In the mean time, the epidemic has spread all over the world, now affecting heterosexuals in Africa or India, rather than only gay men in the West. It remains a major concern because safe-sex guidelines are not always followed.

Another major problem is the persistence of sexual violence throughout the world, notably the rape and sexual harassment of men, women, and girls by (usually male) perpetrators, known and unknown to the victims. Families have been known to force their female relatives (usually daughters) to behave how they see fit, which often means disregarding their sexual autonomy. In some countries, so-called honor killings regularly occur in which male family members (usually fathers or brothers) murder female relatives who have consorted with partners of their own choice. These have become a major concern. Violence also continues to be directed against sex workers, gays and lesbians, transgenders, and other sexual minority groups—sometimes by the institutions

FIGURE 1.8: Window of Mr. Rob, an Amsterdam Leathershop. The man is wearing red rubber with a gas mask attached to a tube that can be used for various fetish sex plays. Photo: Gert Hekma.

of the state. In the infamous Spanner case, British courts condemned a group of gay men for consensually engaging in sadomasochistic practices, and the European Court of Justice supported this judgment. Persisting and widespread puritanism, hypocrisy, and deeply ingrained heteronormativity impede sexual citizenship rights for all those who deviate from social norms.

On the other hand, there have been major periods of sexual liberation, such as the 1920s. In Paris, London, New York, and above all in Berlin night life was flourishing. Paris was the city of light and the arts, while Berlin, due to the enormous German inflation, became a place of cheap pleasures, the sex capital of the 1920s. After the Roaring Twenties, the 1930s became a decade of the threat of war and the rise of totalitarian regimes, first in Italy and subsequently in the Soviet Union, Germany, Spain, and Portugal. Both the left and the right were puritanical and restricted sexual rights—for example, on abortion and homosexual sex—although the German Nazis allowed certain heterosexual pleasures.[25] After the war, many nations witnessed a short period of sexual fervor that was soon dampened in favor of a work ethic directed at rebuilding societies that had been devastated by the war. Only in the 1960s did pleasure receive a central place again, soon to be marginalized by concerns over sexual violence and AIDS. Although most people have the feeling that they are now freer than any earlier generation, evidence indicates the opposite, as seen in the rising number of sex crimes, the lack of sexual satisfaction in many monogamous relationships, and the high levels of physical and mental problems related to sex. In a country like the Netherlands, gays and lesbians may have equal rights, but they are only accepted under the condition that they behave "normally"—which, in reality, means being heterosexual, both in terms of gender and sexuality.

TOWARD THE TWENTY-FIRST CENTURY

During the eighteenth-century Enlightenment, a discourse developed that saw sexual practices as being natural instead of cultural, more male than female, private rather than public affairs, and based in loving couple relations as opposed to pleasures that are separate from love. Sex was seen to be driven by a personal identity that distances the other from the self as opposed to being based on a curiosity that reaches out to the other. Since the sexual revolution, a norm of equal sexual relations has been added to this list. The 1960s did not break down this heterosexual, restrictive view on sexual relations and gender identities, but rather ingrained it deeper in social life. This ideology impeded the public cultivation of multigender polymorphous sexualities stimulated by curiosity and making sex food for thought or an inspiration for the arts. The dichotomy of male and female remains generally unchallenged, as does the sexual dichotomy of homo and hetero. Straight women at least reached closer to equality than did gay men and lesbians—sexual norms apparently being stricter than gender norms.[26]

Much has changed in the twentieth century, in particular the change from an ideology of inequality to the opposite one that demands equality. Women may have made great leaps forward but are still regarded more as objects than subjects of sex. The same is true for gays and lesbians, whose emancipation has not disrupted the concept of heterosexuality as the norm. Newspapers repeatedly report about biological research that tells how different males and females are, or that homosexuality is innate—always privileging the natural over the cultural despite the fact that gender and sexuality have no meaning without public, cultural expressions. Pornography is much more widely available in printed form and on the Internet but remains controversial in many jurisdictions. Even the American Civil Liberties Union (ACLU) and Amnesty International only defend sexual practices as long as they are private affairs, neglecting the fact that many people have no access to private space and that public pleasures of sexuality are not monstrous acts, as many people seem to believe, but mostly innocent. The sexual norm has become monogamous (preferably heterosexual) sex in private.[27] Regardless of how much may have changed in a century, by and large, the heterosexual norm goes unchallenged and is often even unperceived. Sexual and gender diversity remains a utopian ideal.

CHAPTER TWO

Heterosexuality

FRANCIS RONSIN

Trans. Corr. by Joanna Oseman

Up until the end of the eighteenth century, sexuality had been not only a natural source of pleasure and sin, and of artistic and poetic inspiration, but also the fuel of fierce sermons. Christian churches, dominant and powerful in the West, took great pains to meticulously draw the line between licit behavior and acts of abomination, and reprehensible sexual practice was often confused with religious heresy. An example of this is seen in the Old French *bougre,* which can be defined both as a passive homosexual and a heretic. Many people, however, defied clerical orders, at the risk of severe punishment both on earth and in hell, and unsurprisingly, libertine justifications of hedonism went hand in hand with vehement attacks on religion.

The nineteenth century saw the rise of rationalism and science, which began to compete with religion to determine the causes and significations of physical and human phenomena. From Lamarck's classification of invertebrate animals (1801) to Darwin's *On the Origin of Species by Means of Natural Selection* (1859) and through to Mendeleyev and his periodic table of elements (1869), scholars worked to define and classify in order to understand. Sexuality could not possibly remain the exception to this rule, and it was not long before the Hungarian journalist and writer Károly Mária Kertbeny—in a letter to Karl Heinrich Ulrichs in May 1868 and through anonymous pamphlets published in 1869—made the first clear distinction between *Homosexualität* and other neologisms of his invention, such as *Monosexualität* (masturbation) and *Hetero-* or *Normalsexualität* (heterosexuality).[1] These protests opposed the introduction of the article against unnatural intercourse of Prussia in the law of the newly unified German State.[2] This notion of heterosexuality had several competing meanings ranging from bisexuality to fetishism that would remain in the field of scientific literature for several decades to come. The majority of men and women were, during this time, ignorant of the existence of these words or, if they came across them, demonstrated only curiosity or surprise at the practices described.

BIRTH OF A SCIENTIFIC OBJECT

While they are of great historical interest, Kertbeny's linguistic inventions hold a primarily anecdotal significance, as it was not until the end of the century that the term "heterosexuality" spread to scientific fields around the world. This came about after the great success of Richard Krafft-Ebing's work *Psychopathia Sexualis* (1886),[3] translated and edited in England in 1889, in the United States in 1893, and in France in 1895. The first American to employ the term "heterosexuality" was the doctor James G. Kiernan,[4] and the first Frenchman to follow suit was Marc-André Raffalovich.[5]

Krafft-Ebing was a psychiatrist and a forensic expert, fields from which he drew the majority of his case studies, and the title of his work itself explicitly suggests that the issue at hand is pathology. Kiernan was also a psychiatrist and a teacher of forensic medicine, and Raffalovich, a writer and friend of Oscar Wilde, though not a doctor himself, was a regular contributor to the *Archives d'anthropologie criminelle*, whose founder and director, Alexandre Lacassagne, held a chair in forensic medicine at the University of Lyon.

Heterosexuality, in its original sense, was primarily the concern of alienists and criminologists. A new profession was born: that of forensic psychiatrist, a court expert in the field of psychiatry. His role was to differentiate between delinquents deserving of a prison sentence and those suffering from illness and thus requiring hospital treatment. Even before the publication of the famous *Psychopathia Sexualis,* the number of books and journals dedicated to the excessive behavioral patterns of the latter, to the causes of their conditions, and to the necessary treatments, was considerable. In other works, more modest in their claims but just as widely produced and sold, doctors or pseudo-doctors went so far as to describe legitimate sexual practices.

Sigmund Freud (1856–1939) subscribed to the teachings and concerns of the most renowned psychiatrists of his time before going on to combine the

theoretical foundations and therapeutic techniques of psychoanalysis in order
to construct an understanding of the origins of his patients' afflictions. He soon
began to measure the determining role played by the libido—or sexual drive—in
the psychological foundations of the individual. He became convinced that the
repression of this libido was the primary cause of neuroses. While it is true that
Freud came as a shock to dominant Victorian morality, he was nonetheless
as attached as his psychiatric peers to the most traditional of sexual practices
and sexist concepts. He was well known, for instance, for his active denunciation of the dangers of masturbation, and coitus remained, in his opinion, the
natural purpose of sexuality. He frequently described women as subordinate
to men, dominated by their "penis envy" and "castration complex."[6] As for
homosexuality, it is not uncommon, according to Freud, for it to be the unfor-
tunate result of the difficulties of heterosexual relations.

Parallel to this, feminist activism of the second half of the nineteenth century
and the beginning of the twentieth century was doing a great deal to push to
the public forefront a particular image of relations that we qualify today as heterosexual. Feminists of the period defined and denounced the double standard
of sexual morality through which women were portrayed as pure and flawless,
victims of male depravation that was tolerated only because it was considered

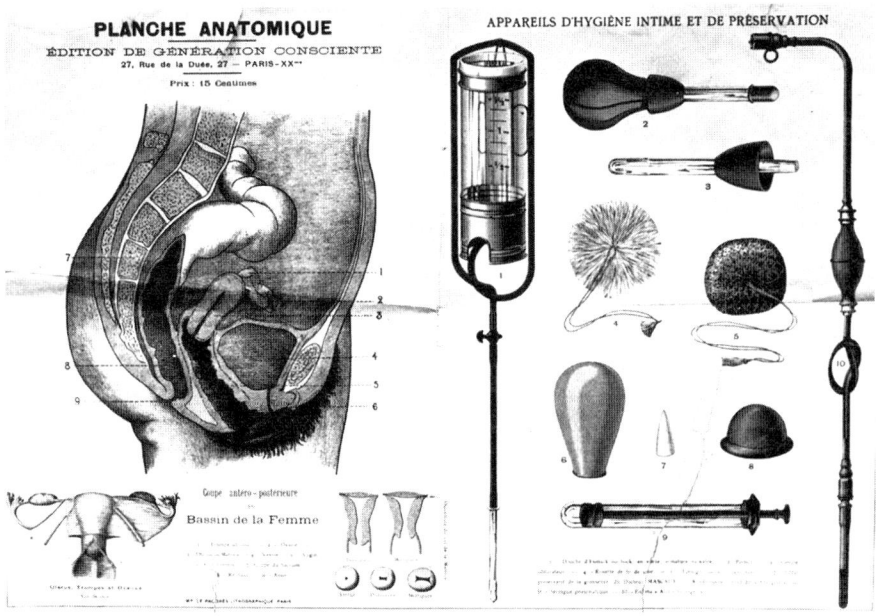

FIGURE 2.1: Anatomic print and catalogue of hygienic and contraceptive devices for women.
Poster from the French Neo-Malthusian journal *Génération consciente* (ca. 1910).

a natural tendency. Often associated with puritan Protestant movements, they did not stop at protesting the tolerance of prostitution, pornography, and the consumption of alcohol (a masculine vice), nor at demanding female equality in both the political and family arena, and an equally moral sexual education for boys and girls. Instead, they went on to condemn justifications and supposed facilitators of sexual liberation (seen as a male trap), such as the increased availability of contraception and abortion.[7] These issues had, until this point, been the concern of so-called neo-Malthusian organizations, active in many different countries, which combined demographic arguments—a fear of overpopulation—and more revolutionary, and often anarchist, ideas in an effort to persuade men, and particularly women, to take control of their own fecundity.

German doctor Albert Moll (1862–1939) and English doctor Henry Havelock Ellis (1859–1939) became the first academics to openly embark on a scientific study of sexuality, in all its forms, with relation to pleasure. Moll published in 1897 a monograph on homosexuality; also in 1897 *Untersuchungen über die Libido sexualis* (Researches on the sexual libido), which separated

FIGURE 2.2: *L'affranchie. Mon ventre! … c'est à moi … seule!* (The liberated woman. My belly! … it belongs to me … alone!) Illustration by A. F. Mac (pseudonym of Felix Delmarle, 1889–1952) published in the Neo-Malthusian journal *Génération consciente* ca. 1910.

sex from reproduction; a 1909 book on the sexual life of children; and edited after Krafft-Ebing's death his *Psychopathia Sexualis*. After breaking with Christianity and dabbling in diverse forms of literary work, Havelock Ellis published his first study on sexuality, *Man and Woman: A Study of Secondary and Tertiary Sexual Characteristics*, in 1894. *Sexual Inversion*, the first volume of his *Studies in the Psychology of Sex* (vols. 1–7, 1897–1928), was published in 1897. The book had first appeared the year before in German as *Das Konträre Geschlechtsgefühl*. His studies were translated into many languages, but distribution was blocked in England and the United States. A few lines from his short layman's book *Little Essays of Love and Virtue* (1922) suffice in illustrating the boldness of his thinking in a persistently puritan England. In Chapter 5, "The Love-Rights of Women," he states that "The social claims of women, their economic claims, their political claims, have long been before the world. Women themselves have actively asserted them, and they are all in process of realisation. The erotic claims of women, which are at least as fundamental, are not publicly voiced, and women themselves would be the last to assert them."[8]

CONFLICTS OF THE INTERWAR ERA

Before World War II, the fight against the corruption of morals had achieved notable success in countries under the influence of Protestantism, particularly in the Anglo-Saxon world and northern Europe. As peace returned, however, initiatives advocating public and private moral standards benefited greatly as patriotic and nationalist movements, strengthened by the war, gained power. As a result, the 1920s was set to see confrontations of which the results have been highly contradictory.

On the one side, the Roaring Twenties saw many women—flappers in the United States, *garçonnes* in France—claiming rights thus far reserved for men. In an atmosphere of celebration and economic prosperity, and to a background of jazz music, they cut their hair, threw out their corsets, riled conformists with their public drinking and smoking, and wore their skirts above the knee in the name of sexual liberation.

On the other side, in 1920, the same year that the Nineteenth Amendment to the U.S. Constitution gave voting rights to all American women, the sale of alcohol was prohibited in the United States, and a French law revoked any rights to advice for women on how to control their own fecundity or access to necessary products. At the same time, some major literary works—*Lady Chatterley's Lover*, a novel by D. H. Lawrence (1928), *Tropic of Cancer*, a novel

FIGURE 2.3: Josephine Baker. In Magnus Hirschfeld, *Geschlechtskunde* IV. *Bilderteil*. Stuttgart, Germany: Püttmann, 1930.

by Henry Miller (1934), and even *Memoirs of a Woman of Pleasure*, a novel written in 1748 by John Cleland—were deemed pornographic and banned from sale in the Anglo-Saxon world. Margaret Sanger's American Birth Control League, along with several English organizations such as Marie Stopes's Society for Constructive Birth Control, and the Workers' Birth Control Group run by Stella Browne and Dora Russell, among others, had some success in developing campaigns in favor of birth control. In France, however, where Henry Miller had freely published his first novel, activists who tried to follow suit were frequently prosecuted and imprisoned. In fact, under the influence of Margaret Sanger, the birth control agenda—without any revolutionary or demographic objective—progressively succeeded prewar neo-Malthusian theory. This greatly reduced much opposition and brought a great deal of support. France was not to see such a change until after World War II, and neo-Malthusians continued to be denounced as anarchist agitators and accused of sabotaging national demographic vitality. In the period between World War I and II, the issue of birth control dominated the discussion of heterosexuality, and those intellectuals engaged in the fight for sexual reform, along with a new wave of feminists and activists from a number of left and far left groups, stepped up to participate in the debate.

As for the work of sexologists, Havelock Ellis was not alone for long. The beginning of the twentieth century saw the creation of national, and later international, organizations that united scholars, freethinkers, social activists (Havelock Ellis was a member of the Fabian Society, which later lay the foundations of the Labour Party), Marxists, anarchists, and feminists in the fight for sexual liberty and free access to divorce, sterilization, contraception, and abortion.[9] The British Society for the Study of Sex Psychology, created in 1913 by George Cecil Ives, Edward Carpenter, and Laurence Housman with the membership and collaboration of Havelock Ellis, Magnus Hirschfeld, Marie Stopes, Norman Haire, and Stella Browne, is but one such example.

The German doctor Magnus Hirschfeld (1868–1935) is most well known for his active support of persecuted homosexuals. His *Zeitschrift für Sexualwissenschaft* (1908, Journal for Sexual Science), the first journal to be exclusively concerned with sexuality; Arztliche Gesellschaft für Sexualwissenschaft und Eugenik (Medical Society for Sexology and Eugenics), which he created in 1913 with the collaboration of Ivan Bloch, among others; and Institut für Sexualwissenschaft (Institute for Sexual Science—1919) were concerned with sexuality in the general sense and the fight against venereal diseases, and they advocated sex education, contraception, and women's rights. In 1921, he organized the First Congress for Sexual Reform in Berlin, and went on to cofound the World League for Sexual Reform with Swiss doctor Auguste Forel and Havelock Ellis. Assemblies were held in Copenhagen (1928), London (1929), Vienna (1930), and Brno (1932), and local divisions began to appear in several countries, headed by well-known figures: Dora Russell and Norman Haire in England, Fernand Mascaux in Belgium, Johannes Rutgers in Holland, Dr. Robinson and Margaret Sanger in the United States, Eugène Humbert in France and Alexandra Kollontai (a close ally of Lenin) in Russia. Hirschfeld was hailed "the Einstein of sex" by American journalists, but in 1933, the Nazis—who had harassed him on previous occasions—had barely been in power before they confiscated the contents of the institute and burned his library.

When, parallel to the creation of Hirschfeld's society, Albert Moll founded a rival association, the Internationale Gesellschaft für Sexualforschung (International Society for Sex Research), Berlin's status as the world capital of sexology was confirmed, and it was to remain as such until 1933. A disciple of Krafft-Ebing, Albert Moll was politically conservative, and in 1926, he organized his first International Congress for Sex Research, to which leftist Hirschfeld was not even granted an invitation. He presented it as the first congress on sexology of a truly scientific nature, implying that the 1921 conference had, in his opinion, been nothing more than a display of propaganda. Moll's scholarship, however, was exceptional and his studies were of tremendous value, despite his work being marred by his permanent hostility toward Hirschfeld and Freud who, unsurprisingly, did not hold him in very high esteem.

For a long time, the overwhelming majority of psychoanalysts continued to hold to the belief that heterosexual coitus was the most natural and preferable way to satisfy sexual desire. The theory of sexual economy, developed by Wilhelm Reich (1897–1957), went against the Freudian principle that reproduction was the main function of the sexual organs and instead began to consider the importance of the pursuit of pleasure. However, his main works were centered on heterosexuality and the couple. In 1923, the Frankfurt School united philosophers and social science specialists around collective projects based on the dialectics of Marxism, and those of its members who were the most concerned with sexuality—Erich Fromm, and particularly Herbert Marcuse—also concentrated their efforts on heterosexuality.[10] This did not, however, prevent Reich and Marcuse, grouped with others under the term "Freudo-Marxism," from being rightfully recognized as prominent figures in the fight for sexual liberation and understanding in the period of intellectual and political unrest of the 1960s and early 1970s.[11]

The Surrealist group, almost as soon as the movement was founded, began playing around with ideas of revolution and psychoanalysis, and questionnaires such as *Pourquoi écrivez-vous?* ("Why Do You Write?") and *Le suicide est-il une solution?* ("Is Suicide a Solution?") began to appear in its magazines. Between January 1928 and August 1932, they held twelve conferences on the research into sexuality,[12] in which the core contributors included André Breton, Louis Aragon, Antonin Artaud, Paul Eluard, Raymond Queneau, and Max Ernst. Though not devoid of provocative intent, their accounts did a great deal to broaden the field of sexuality. It came to light at these meetings that Breton—himself a psychiatrist who had met with Freud—was a proud fetishist. Raymond Queneau, when asked by Breton, "Which sexual positions do you most enjoy?" replied: "sodomy, what is known as 'doggy-fashion', sixty-nine," and Benjamin Péret responded, "the so-called 'lazy position', the woman sitting upright with the man lying on his back, sodomy, sixty-nine."[13] Madame Léna, one of the only women to take part in the study, stated daringly, "When I masturbate I enjoy it right to the end, thinking of a woman I loved very much—my sister."[14] After twelve sessions and tens of

FIGURE 2.4: "Sexologie problème vital" (Sexology, vital problem). Special issue of the popular French journal *VU*, June 29, 1932.

pages of this type of declaration, the poets, once again, showed themselves to be more informed on the subject than the scholars. Although participants in these investigations were few and had been selected in an unconventional manner, and despite the fact that the audience was limited to subscribers of their papers, it could be said that the Surrealist studies foreshadowed the larger-scale surveys that were to become, in the second half of the twentieth century, the main method in the investigation of sexual practices. And so in the 1920s and 1930s, sexuality went on to become the center of intense intellectual and militant activity in Europe.

However, as dictatorial regimes spread across a large chunk of the continent, the cause was shaken to its core as many scholars, thinkers, and activists were forced to flee their countries in an effort to save their freedom and even their lives. The United States in particular benefited from the intellectual unrest of Germany and Austria, and it was also the United States that saw the birth of large-scale, statistical investigations into sexual behavior, which were about to take quite a turn. Clelia Mosher (1863–1940) carried out the first statistical survey of sexuality to focus on the female experience.[15] The feminist Katherine Bement Davis (1860–1935) published *Factors in the Sex Life of Twenty-Two Hundred Women,*[16] in which female homosexuality was addressed for the first time in a neutral and objective manner. Robert Latou Dickinson (1860–1935), comrade of Margaret Sanger and member of the World League for Sexual Reform, brought out *A Thousand Marriages: A Medical Study of Sex Adjustment* in 1931 and, in 1934, *The Single Woman: A Medical Study in Sex Education,* with a preface by Havelock Ellis.[17]

In those European countries that now fell under the control of nationalist dictatorships, the issue of sexuality was pulled strictly in line with the political philosophies of the regimes in power. In the Mediterranean countries of Italy and Spain, the policy was straightforward: a return to strictly following the rules of traditional morality, influenced by Catholicism and favoring male dominance.

FIGURE 2.5: "La femme coquette, sans enfants … n'a pas de place dans la Cité, c'est une inutile" (The coquette, without children … has no place in the city, she is useless). Pronatalist propaganda in occupied France during World War II. Collection of Francis Ronsin.

This change was welcomed by a large portion of the population and particularly by women.[18] The Nazis' apprehensive attitude toward sexuality, however, was much more complex. Wilhelm Reich took on the task of explaining that the reason why the criminal theories of the regime held such immense appeal for many Germans had its roots in the sexual frustrations they must have experienced in childhood.[19] Subsequent studies showed that the Nazis' dual sexual morality, based on the opposition of races—pure/impure and master/slave—was far from being uniformly repressive and used the fantasies of one group to justify the subjection and degrading of the other.[20]

FROM WORLD WAR II TO THE SEXUAL REVOLUTION

The issue of sexuality, having previously been dominated by an essentially pathological approach and centered around supposedly normal heterosexual relations and the right to motherhood, only began to really move away from these preconceived notions in the wake of World War II. These reflections and researches arose from societies now more concerned with finding contentment in economic prosperity, social progress, consumer growth, and technological advancements than with addressing issues that could stand in the way of their newfound tranquility. Many women who had been called up to support the war effort now returned to their homes, and marriages and births were plentiful: the baby boom had begun. The contradictions of this conformism remained the preoccupation of an elite, but the calm was misleading; the next generation—baby boomers and the children of prosperity—were to rebel against them with great force.

In 1949, French philosopher Simone de Beauvoir published the remarkable *Le Deuxième Sexe*,[21] in which she demonstrated that the modern concept of femininity has its origins in historical male dominance and that women generally identify themselves through their relationships with the superior sex : as mistress, wife, or mother. She famously stated "one is not born a woman : one becomes one," underlining her belief that the image of the woman is not the result of the laws of nature, but rather one that is crafted by social and cultural conditioning.[22] She strongly criticized previous studies of sexuality done by psychoanalysts, sexologists, and activists who based their works on the accepted, traditional notion of the sexes and their relationships, placing great importance on motherhood. Met with much opposition when it first appeared in France, *Le Deuxième Sexe* was hailed as an essential piece of work when a new wave of feminism, based on principles similar to Beauvoir's, began to develop in the 1960s. Simone de Beauvoir is considered to have been instrumental in raising the question of *gender*, a term used in this sense for the first time by John Money in 1955.[23]

A further demonstration of the desire to break down conformist barriers was seen in 1938, when a body of students from the University of Indiana demanded that female students who were, or desired to be, married be offered classes on the topic of sexuality. Although some such classes were already in place in the United States, the fear of transmission of venereal disease meant that high schools tended toward the promotion of abstinence. In higher education, however, home economics classes could easily incorporate a study of the sexual organs and their functions.[24]

The task was handed over to Alfred C. Kinsey, professor of zoology. His character aside, the fact that Kinsey was a zoologist was to be of considerable importance. The notion of sin finds no place in zoology, which holds to the fact that animals do not have souls. Not being a doctor, Kinsey's reasoning was not presented in pathological terms, and his lack of involvement in the legal sphere meant that any notions of guilt or misdemeanor were alien to him. He did not judge but rather observed, and what he observed was an alarming insufficiency in the statistical studies of male and female sexual desires and behaviors. He set out to remedy the situation.

From 1938 to 1963, Kinsey and his colleagues interviewed in person 5,300 men and 5,940 women, asking each an average of 300 questions so direct as to surprise, and even shock, a good number of the participants. With the aim of collecting statistics on the methods employed in the quest for sexual satisfaction, an unrepresentative sample of volunteers of both sexes, single and married, was questioned on masturbation; homosexual relations; anal, oral, and coital penetration; and on their experiences with prostitutes and animals.

The study was so thorough that it provided enough material for two books: *Sexual Behavior in the Human Male* (1948) and *Sexual Behavior in the Human Female* (1953), exposing its human readership to broad and unexpected horizons concerning the expression of desire. Ninety percent of men and almost two-thirds of women admitted to masturbating, and half of the men and a quarter of the women interviewed confessed to having extramarital sexual relations,[25] a considerable number of them with same-sex partners. The studies were an enormous media success, had many editions and translations, and made Kinsey famous in some circles, and infamous in others.

With the financial support of Margaret Sanger of Planned Parenthood Federation of America (PPFA) and of her wealthy friend Katherine Dexter McCormick, Dr. Gregory Pincus (1903–1967) created the first contraceptive pill in 1956. The pill was first authorized in the United States as a treatment for irregular menstrual cycles, but in 1960 was marketed as a method of contraception. Quickly adopted by a large number of American women—used by more than one million women two years after its commercialization and by five million five years later—and later in many other countries, the pill played an important role in what was to become known as the sexual revolution of the 1960s. The dissociation of sexuality from procreation, a relatively easy and viable choice for women themselves to make, was a revolution in itself.

These diverse manifestations of women's desire for recognition and independence were quickly assessed and exploited by merchandisers, who used the social evolution for the advancements of their commercial products. One example: 1959 saw the creation of the Barbie doll, which has since been sold in hundreds of millions of models around the world (not counting imitation products) and is the perfect demonstration of the development of mass consumerism and of the way in which generations of young girls have been pushed to imagine their future. The phenomenon has leant itself to an abundance of studies,[26] of which only a few aspects are to be considered here. Barbie is not to be pushed around in a baby carriage. She no longer represents the child that generations of young girls were encouraged to desire. Rather, she is a young adult, a representation of a new ideal to aspire to. Further, Barbie, as well as being an astounding consumer of cosmetics, jewelry, and furniture, and aside from her immense capability for the most prestigious of professions and the most athletic sports, has a body intended to reflect the dreams of women and the desires of men. Her long blond hair, her svelte figure, and her breasts and hips certainly played an important role in the seduction of her boyfriend, Ken, who came into her life in 1961.[27] Barbie, however, has retained her freedom, never taking a husband and never bearing children.

THE SEXUAL REVOLUTION AND ITS CONSEQUENCES

Having distinguished between the sexual revolution as part of the consumer culture on the one hand and as part of a revolution for life on the other, we can take up once more the question of its relation to psychoanalysis.[28]

Betty Friedan (1921–2006) is often considered to have been the leading pioneer of the second wave of American feminism. After the remarkable success, in 1963, of her first book, *The Feminine Mystique*,[29] she was instrumental in the founding of the National Organization for Women (NOW) in 1966, and became its first president. *The Feminine Mystique* was awarded the honor of seventh place in the list of the "Ten Most Harmful Books of the Nineteenth and Twentieth Centuries," published by the weekly conservative magazine *Human*

Events. She was ranked lower than Kinsey's report (fourth) and just behind Karl Marx's *Capital* (sixth). Her account of the sacrifices made by suburban housewives was as terrifying as it was convincing, and she succeeded in inspiring a considerable number of women to fight for their rights and freedoms. However, her refusal to tackle questions of a sexual nature and to link lesbianism to feminism meant that she remained a relatively moderate reformist in the context of the youth rebellion, whose main objective was the radical destruction of any law or practice that stood in the way of sexual liberation, in all its forms. The names of other antipatriarchy activists, such as Kate Millett, Shulamith Firestone, Germaine Greer, and Gloria Steinem, erupted from campuses, while classics dealing with sexual liberation were being rediscovered, and Charles

FIGURE 2.6: *The Meeting Place,* by Paul Day, inside the St. Pancras Station, London. The statue aims to reflect the romantic nature of train travel. The couple is modeled on the sculptor and his French wife. Day first intended to show a kissing couple, but the city and the railways company found that too risqué. Photo: Francis Ronsin.

Fourier's *Nouveau monde amoureux,* hidden for over a century and a half by his disciples, was published for the first time in France in 1967.[30]

During the 1960s and 1970s, aspirations of sexual liberation, coupled with a condemnation of economic oppression, seemed to inspire a revival of the human sciences around the world. Freud had previously defined sublimation (*Sublimierung*) as the "capacity to exchange [an] originally sexual aim for another one, which is no longer sexual but which is psychically related to the first aim."[31] The rebirth of Freudo-Marxism brought with it this redefinition: that sublimation is the enslavement of sexual energy in order to benefit capitalist society. Freudo-Marxist theses are often complemented by those of so-called antipsychiatry.

Heavily influenced by the groundbreaking works of Michel Foucault and Thomas Szasz,[32] anti-psychiatry developed across the Western world, particularly in the United Kingdom (Cooper and Laing) and Italy (Basaglia). What traditional psychiatry considers as normality was now seen as a sign of submission to social conditioning, ideology, and the powers that be. A further affront to Freud and Freudians alike came in 1972, when Gilles Deleuze and Félix Guattari published their *Anti-Oedipus,* in which they state, in relation to the famous complex: "everybody knows what psychoanalysis means by *resolving* Oedipus: internalizing it so as to better rediscover it on the outside, in social authority."[33] In *The Will to Knowledge,* the first volume of his *The History of Sexuality* (1976), Michel Foucault too underlined the significance of ideological conditioning. For him, the social making of sexuality comes first and includes forms of repression and disciplining. It is also worth remembering that Kinsey, analyzing the results of his investigations in conjunction with other sociological factors, stated that many people would be shocked to learn that the civilization they allowed to influence their language and clothing was equally responsible for their sexual conduct.

It would be out of the question to give here a comprehensive list of all the scientific surveys that followed the publication of Kinsey's work, on an increasingly international scale, but we may nevertheless cite a few of the more noteworthy before going on to consider current trends in this type of research.

In 1954, the gynecologist William H. Masters embarked on a study of methods of erotic stimulation, in which he was joined in 1959 by psychologist Virginia Johnson, who was later to become his wife. Together, they measured physiological responses observed in the individual and the couple during sexual activity, and in 1966, the thousands of accumulated items of data were compiled in a book: *Human Sexual Response.* Contrary to Freudian tradition, they underlined the importance of the clitoris in the arousal of the normal adult female.[34] They also advocated the development of sexual behavior therapy as an alternative to psychoanalysis in the treatment of sexual dysfunction, and in so doing created a new profession: the sex therapist.

Shere Hite was a disciple of Kinsey and also of Masters and Johnson, whose work she often criticized. Following radical feminist Anne Koedt (*The Myth of the Female Orgasm*, 1970), she wrote a remarkable report, in which she compiled thousands of female testimonies collected over a four-year period. The result, *A Nationwide Study of Female Sexuality* (1976), which was translated into nineteen languages and sold over thirty-five million copies, contested the idea that women suffered a genetic dysfunction that presented difficulties in reaching orgasm. The cause of these difficulties, according to her, is cultural in origin and the consequence of much ignorance surrounding the body and the mechanisms of female pleasure. While the majority of women may state that they are unable to reach orgasm during intercourse, the majority of those same women declare that they experience no such trouble when indulging in the clitoral stimulation of masturbation. Shere Hite was the author of a number of other important studies and investigations. In 1989, she was forced to leave the United States after she became the victim of violent attacks. In 1995 she renounced her American citizenship and took on German nationality.

Two bells sounded to mark the end of the period of wild romanticism, built up after 1968, during which it seemed that the outdated world of capitalism, patriarchy, and puritanism had come to an end. In 1980, the American majority took a firm stand against supposed decadence and anarchy by electing Ronald Reagan, champion of the neo-conservative revolution, to office. In 1981, the scientific field began to worry about the appearance of a new deadly syndrome, which a year later became known as AIDS, and whose virus was to finally be identified in 1983. Freedom had run into a barricade of caution and wariness.

The new government quickly introduced a neo-conservative program that was to demonstrate that abstaining from premarital sexual relations and from infidelity to one's spouse were the only ways to tackle the problem of unwanted teenage pregnancy and venereal disease. The Adolescent Family Life Act, passed in 1981, established a system of support to schools and organizations that promoted the practice of abstinence. Reagan's presidential successors went on to maintain or even enlarge this effort, which was receiving further subsidies from a number of states. Between 1996 and 2004, one billion dollars was devoted to a system of sex education that disregarded desire and pleasure and denounced the efficiency of the condom. This money allowed the creation of an astounding number of organizations such as Not Me, Not Now, True Love

Waits, Friends First, and The Silver Ring Thing Movement, where 2.5 million young Americans were swearing to remain virgins until they married.[35] Similar associations appeared in a number of other countries, but none were to see the success of their American counterparts.[36] In Poland, the high school campaign for sex education and the prevention of HIV by the gay rights group Lambda Krakow was banned by the city's mayor in December 2005.

This desire to bring the younger generation back to the most traditional of sexual moralities was also, strangely enough, responsible for the creation of a small sector of the punk music movement. Appearing on the scene in the 1980s, straight-edge groups used a triple-X sign to symbolize their rejection of alcohol, drugs, and casual sexual relations.

The efforts of the Moral Majority, however, came up against such powerful economic hurdles that their minimal success is easily explained. The pornography industry has been responsible for the making of many a fortune in Hollywood. Barbie is but one particularly eloquent example of the explosion of the body within the sphere of commerce. The exhibition of the bare, predominantly female, form has become omnipresent in advertisements. The body is exploited as both the greatest selling tool and the easiest target of commercial companies. The body care market mobilizes enormous sums of money in order to generate even more enormous profits. The desire for a product is magnified by its association with the desire for bodily perfection. And the body in these cases is synonymous with sexuality—a sexuality that requires up-keep and care in both its physical and psychical sense. The obligation to have sexual attributes that conform to a physical appearance dictated by accepted social ideals in order to be granted access to libidinal pleasures (themselves standardized by society but presented as indispensable in the search for self-fulfillment) has helped make the fortune of many experts, including a certain number of scholars, some honest practitioners, and an overwhelming majority of opportunists.

Plastic surgery, in particular the remodeling of the figure, offers the opportunity to correct the injustices of nature. People are now strongly encouraged to regularly consult doctors who specialize in the care of the sexual, gynecological, and urological organs. When it comes to the expression of sexual desire and pleasure, any insufficiency or deviance from the norm can lead to the treatment of a psychologist, psychoanalyst, psychiatrist, or sex-therapist.[37] Internet users are constantly bombarded with invitations to improve their ability to satisfy the female libido, something that apparently demands the use of pharmaceuticals that work to increase penis size and ensure a longer-lasting erection, as with Viagra.

Sex education within the school system continues to be hindered by concerns for morality. Although banished from the classroom, where it could have been addressed in a rational manner, initiation into the world of sexual pleasure is far from hard to come by. The boastful revelations of friends and classmates certainly still have their place, but they now fade into the background against the increasing flow of uncontrollable pornography, gossip columns, sexual confessions, and pop-psychology analyses and continue to dominate a large section of the specialized and general media. The virtues and modesty of previous generations now seem outdated, as exhibitionism—although still punishable in the public arena—has become a common, and often obtrusive, media practice.

Drawn as always to sensationalism, the media have given seemingly disproportionate attention to the supposed increase of individuals, single and married, seeking recognition for their asexuality, to the point of referring to it as a new sexual revolution. There has been a birth of movements aiming to unify and represent these nonsexual people. In the United States, the Asexual Visibility and Education Network (AVEN), created in 2001 by David Jay, offers a comprehensive catalogue of diverse objects bearing the slogan, "No sex, please." In the Netherlands, The Official Nonlibidoist Society, strongly influenced by Indian mysticism, presents its Internet site—http://www.theofficialasexualsociety.com—as "THE website for gay and bisexual nonlibidoist women."

Even more overtly reactionary is the profusion of Websites aimed at heterosexuals that call on remaining so-called real men to resist the conspiracy of feminists and homosexuals. A large number of these groups are relatively moderate and principally campaign for more equal custody rights after marital separation. Others, however, express themselves with a violence directly inspired by the most virulent of nationalist and racist publications, which is hardly surprising when you consider that they are often associated with the extreme right. The National Coalition of Free Men, The Australian Men's Party, the Everyman Web site, Straight Pride,[38] and even feminine organizations such as The Independent Women's Forum,[39] resort willingly to the most warlike of language in their attack against so-called feminazis—also referred to as communists—or the radical gay agenda.

The feminist movement, however, receives quite the opposite criticism from elsewhere. Having won many a victory over repression in the twentieth century, the movement is now accused of reverting to nineteenth century moral causes, no longer concentrating its efforts on criticizing the social system, but rather focusing on the faults of the male sex. This female cause is now principally associated with the denunciation of male violence: physical and verbal abuse, rape, sexual harassment, misogynous and homophobic remarks, and responsibility for the pornography industry and prostitution. As for the evolution of previously discussed investigations into sexuality, the most striking aspect is their tendency to deal predominantly with these same themes.

In 1995, at the World Conference on Women, held in Peking, each participating country committed to conducting a survey on violence toward women. In France, L'Enquête nationale sur les violences faites aux Femmes conducted telephone interviews with a representative sample of 6,970 women, aged between twenty and fifty-nine. At the time of the study, one in ten women claimed that they suffered from domestic violence. The number of women raped each year was estimated at 50,000. The results of these surveys were compiled in the impressive *World Report on Violence and Health,* published by the World Health Organization in 2002. The feminist role was clearly reiterated in the report: "Women's organizations around the world have long drawn attention to violence against women, and to intimate partner violence in particular. Through their efforts, violence against women has now become an issue of international concern." The guilty role of the male was also underlined: "Intimate partner violence occurs in all countries, irrespective of social, economic, religious or cultural group. Although women can be violent in relationships with men, and violence is also sometimes found in same-sex partnerships, the overwhelming burden of partner violence is born by women at the hand of men."[40]

Nevertheless, along with other ideas that fall into the category of postfeminism, some women do believe that, having now obtained substantially important legislative reforms, a more harmonious and mutually affectionate coexistence with men, as they are, is possible. These same women believe that feminism has gone seriously off track, with the number of indictments against men multiplying to such an extent.[41]

It is through the medium of demographic statistics that the failure of the Moral Majority becomes undeniably apparent. The silent majority has broken through and has drastically altered its relationship to sexuality. The majority of heterosexuals who lived through the period considered in this volume were brought up with the almost unanimously accepted rule of sexuality = love = marriage. Even at the beginning of the twenty-first century, the number of people aged sixty and over who had never married represented only ten percent of the population in Sweden, and five percent in the United States. Considering that marriage implies more or less regular sexual relations, frequently limited to a single partner, the increase in divorce rates—and as a consequence, the freedom to develop new relationships—can be seen to have played a primary and positive role in heterosexual development over the twentieth century.

Fierce opposition from influential and intolerant groups—particularly Catholic organizations—meant that the right to divorce was not granted in some countries until very recently: 1981 in Spain, 1997 in Ireland, and 2004 in Chili. In countries where that right was already in place, a drastic increase in its frequency did a great deal to vastly reduce the stigma of the divorcé and, more importantly, the divorcée. The majority of developed countries have seen their annual divorce rate at least triple over the last thirty years. In 2000, 55 of every 100 marriages in the United States ended in divorce, compared to 51.2 in Finland, 44.5 in Denmark, 42.6 in the United Kingdom, 39.4 in Germany, and 38.3 in France.

As divorce became more accepted and widespread, people began to realize that heterosexual love did not necessarily have to be everlasting, and that the possibility of men and women having several, at least successive, sexual partners was relatively large. In the same way, marriage slowly began to lose appeal, and was seen as an option that no longer had so much meaning and that often ended in prolonged, expensive, and bitter battles in the courtroom. The following statistics clearly demonstrate this tendency away from marriage as an institution.[42]

This shift in thinking is even more striking given the fact that unmarried women are now more inclined to consider having children. This would previously have created an unshakeable stigma for both the mother and the so-called bastard child, and, as a consequence, has been responsible for many a rushed marriage and abortion. This family situation, though, has become quite accepted and is even the majority in Sweden,[43] which is outdone further still by countries such as Estonia (56.2 percent out-of-wedlock birth rate in 2001), and Iceland (63.3 percent).

Considering that, for the majority, the legalization of contraception and abortion makes it possible to avoid pregnancy without giving up an active

Table 2.1:   Marriage Rate Per 1,000 People.

	1950	1960	1970	1980	1990	2001
United States	11.0	8.5	10.6	10.5	9.8	8.2
Russia	11.6	12.5	10.1	10.6	8.9	6.9
Spain	7.5	7.8	7.3	5.9	5.7	5.1
France	7.9	7.0	7.8	6.2	5.1	4.9
UK	8.1	7.5	8.5	7.4	6.5	4.8
Sweden	7.7	6.7	5.4	4.5	4.7	4.0

Table 2.2:   Extramarital Birth Rate Per 100 Live Births.

	1950	1960	1970	1980	1990	2001
United States	3.9	5.3	10.7	18.4	28.0	33.5
Russia		13.1	10.6	10.8	14.6	28.8
Spain	5.2	2.3	1.3	3.9	9.6	19.7
France	7.0	6.0	6.8	11.4	30.1	43.7
UK	5.0	5.2	8.0	11.5	27.9	39.5
Sweden	9.8	11.3	18.4	39.7	47.0	55.5

sexual life, it is even more remarkable that such large numbers of women are willing, or even choose, to have children outside the confines of marriage.

Adding to these previous observations the fact that, in developed countries, the clear majority of young people today consider masturbation and homosexual relations to be acceptable ways of seeking pleasure, it is true to say that the perception of sexuality—although it may not have taken as insurrectional a form as some would have hoped—has undergone such an evolution over the last century that it would be quite legitimate to qualify it as a revolution. Because of its associations with political history, the term "revolution" implies a fundamental and violent overthrow of the dominant structure, and nothing quite this extreme occurred in the case of sexuality. The scholars and militants who struggled to free humanity from preconceived notions and taboos could have easily despaired as they continued to come up against the resistance of irrational conformism. Nevertheless, for historians, who readily employ the term "revolution" for multigenerational movements such as the industrial revolution, it is evident that the large majority of young people at the start of the twenty-first century see sexuality—as a whole, but particularly their own sexuality—in a way that now holds almost nothing in common with the thinking of their great-grandparents.

CHAPTER THREE

Homosexuality

FLORENCE TAMAGNE

Not all cultures have a concept for homosexuality (as opposed to heterosexuality), nor do they distinguish a category of homosexual persons. Whereas ancient Greece promoted pederasty, sodomy became, in the Christian Middle Ages, a crime against nature subject to capital punishment. The sodomite, however, should not be confused with the homosexual, since the crime of sodomy could refer to same-sex sexual practices but also heterosexual ones, as well as to crimes against God and the state, such as treason, heresy, or witchcraft. Same-sex relations between women were rarely, if ever, mentioned. Most of the time same-sex relations were not clearly distinguished from bisexuality or transgenderism, notably transvestism.[1]

In the eighteenth century, a specific concept of homosexuality emerged, with the creation, in some European capital cities, such as Paris or London, of so-called sodomites' assemblies or molly houses, which gathered men, often from the lower classes, united by a common culture of codes and rituals. The term "homosexuality" was coined later, in 1869, by the Hungarian writer Karoly Maria Kertbeny in a letter he wrote to the Prussian minister of justice asking for the suppression of the laws condemning sexual acts against nature. Other medical terms of the same period continued to be used at least until the middle of the twentieth century ("invert," "unisexual"), while others were created by homosexuals in order to identify themselves ("uranian," "homophile"). The word "lesbian," even if ancient, was not commonly used before the end of the nineteenth century. Most terms, however, remained slang words with insulting overtones ("queer," "fairy," "dyke").

In competition with the judiciary, the medical discourse tried to stand out as the authority on homosexuality. However, doctors, psychiatrists, and psycho-analysts disagreed on its origins and potential treatment. For those who held it as a sign of degeneracy,[2] homosexuality, whether innate or acquired, remained a perversion that could sometimes be cured, either by hypnosis, hormonal injections, or simply physical and moral hygiene. On the other hand, K. H. Ulrichs and the sexologist and homosexual militant Magnus Hirschfeld popu-larized the theory of the "Third Sex,"[3] according to which the invert had "a woman's soul trapped in a man's body,"[4] and needed no cure. Freud refuted both theories, but whereas he refused to consider homosexuality as a disease and upheld the hypothesis of the primary bisexuality of the human being, his definition of homosexuality as "an arrest of sexual development" could hardly be held as positive and liberating.[5]

Within the middle and upper classes, the identity-building process of homosexual men and women owed more to classical culture (pederasty and sapphism), Christian tradition (spiritual fellowship, monastic friendship), the quest for homoerotic undertones in art and literature (from Michelangelo to Walt Whitman), and the writings of the pioneers of homosexuality (Edward Carpenter, K. H. Ulrichs, John Addington Symonds) than to medical theories, even if those were often carefully analyzed and sometimes adopted. In fact, for a long time, the homosexual was not so much defined by his or her sexual practices than as by his or her gender (feminine/masculine) and gender roles (active/passive). For example, until the 1950s and 1960s, the male homosexual subculture was not homogenous: first, there were effeminate queens who used female nicknames and did not try to hide their sexual preferences, at the risk of being mocked and looked down on; second, there were men known as trade, prostitutes, soldiers, sailors, working-class men who did not regard themselves as homosexuals but justified their practices by sexual frustration or the lure of money; and, finally, there were self-identified homosexuals known as "queers," who were often looking for masculine and supposedly straight partners.[6]

Although used since the beginning of the twentieth century, the word "gay" did not take precedence as a synonym of "homosexual" in the United States before Pearl Harbor, and in Europe before the 1970s. With its positive con-notations, the word "gay" broke with former stereotypes and managed to convey the desire for recognition of many homosexual men and women. It was also ambiguous enough to maintain the secrecy of the subculture at a time when prejudices were still deep rooted, even though the sexual liberation of the 1960s would rapidly contribute to major social changes. At first used for both men and women, "gay" soon referred only to homosexual men, with women often choosing to identify as lesbians as a way to fight invisibility. In the 1990s, the reclaiming of the insult "queer" expressed the rejection of a normalizing gay subculture, which seemed monopolized by a white male elite, and the acknowledgment of groups that had been marginalized within the homosexual community, such as bisexuals, transvestites, transsexuals, and transgender people. Today the acronym LGBT is commonly used to refer to lesbian, gay, bisexual, and transgender people, but some versions add, for example, queer and intersex.

1920–1939: ROARING TWENTIES, GLOOMY THIRTIES?

Repression and Social Control

In the first half of the twentieth century, Europe presented an uneven situation in regard to the legislation on homosexuality. Latin and Catholic countries, such as France, Italy, Spain, or Portugal, under the influence of the Napoleonic penal code, did not criminalize same-sex sexual relations, even though they could prosecute any affront to public decency as well as indecent exposure. Germanic, Anglo-Saxon, and Slav countries, mainly under Protestant or Orthodox influences, adopted, generally between the end of the nineteenth and the beginning of the twentieth century, specific laws that criminalized sexual relations between men. In the same way, former British colonies, such as the United States, Canada, Australia, or New Zealand set up very repressive laws. Even if such laws were no longer enforced, sodomy remained subject to the death penalty until 1796 in Pennsylvania, 1861 in England, 1876 in South Australia, and 1883 in New South Wales. The road to decriminalization was sometimes full of pitfalls. In the Netherlands, homosexuality had been decriminalized in 1811, a decision confirmed in the penal code of 1886. In 1911, nonetheless, the age of consent was raised to 21, instead of 16, in the case of same-sex sexual relations between men or between women (section 248bis of the penal code). In Sweden, homosexuality was decriminalized in 1944, but the age of consent for homosexual relations was raised and the control of deviant sexualities reinforced.[7]

In Eastern Europe, the situation varied according to the country. Poland, under French influence, decriminalized same-sex sexual relations between consenting adults in 1932, a decision that was not questioned when the country later became a people's democracy. In Romania, however, homosexuality was not criminalized before 1936. From then and until the fall of Ceausescu's regime, homosexual men and women were actively hounded. During the same period, Hungary, East Germany, and Czechoslovakia became progressively laxer. The Russian situation was also quite remarkable. In 1917, sodomy laws had been abolished, and the Bolshevik regime gained a reputation of sexual tolerance, but same-sex practices were not seen in the same way in all parts of the empire. Furthermore, from 1934, homosexuality could bring a sentence of up to five years' hard labor. Repression, which existed before this date, increased. Homosexual men ran the risk of being imprisoned or sent to the gulag, where they often suffered cruelty from other prisoners. Lesbians were generally committed to a psychiatric hospital, in order to be cured.[8]

Few countries indeed, apart from Austria (1852), Sweden (1864), Finland (1889), and some Swiss cantons, criminalized lesbianism. Even when they did, few women were in fact prosecuted. Attempts at criminalizing lesbianism in Germany (1909) and in England (1921) failed. It seemed that social control either from the family or the church was enough to regulate women's sexuality. Above all, it was feared that a new law would inform ignorant women of the existence of such practices. Anyhow, a majority of doctors held lesbianism for a very rare perversion, which they described as a transitory phase specific to adolescence or as the product of seduction. Depending on the time and country, lesbianism would be considered with fascination (for example in France, where lesbian eroticism was a favorite topic of decadent literature) or indignation (in 1928, Radclyffe Hall's novel *The Well of Loneliness* was the target of a violent lesbophobic campaign in Britain) but never taken seriously.[9]

Repression varied according to police and justice actions. In most countries, even those that, like France, had decriminalized same-sex sexual relations, the vice squad watched homosexual cruising grounds, such as public parks, bathing houses, and male urinals. All homosexuals were not equally at risk. The most vulnerable were those who, by necessity or by inclination, were drawn to high-risk behaviors like cruising urinals or whose very appearance was interpreted by the police as a sign of inversion. Working-class and lower middle-class men who, for lack of time and private lodgings, favored public locations, were over-represented in the criminal statistics, whereas some upper-class homosexual men could hope not to be bothered. However, the threat of public scandal and social discredit still hovered over them, combined with the fear of blackmail.[10]

The First Homosexual Movements

As a direct response to these threats, homosexual activism was on the rise in the 1920s, especially in Germany. In 1897, the first homosexual movement, the WhK (Wissenschaftlich-humanitäres Komitee, Scientific-Humanitarian

Committee) had been founded by Magnus Hirschfeld. It notably circulated a petition demanding the repeal of Paragraph 175 of the German Penal Code, according to which "acts against nature" between men, or between men and animals, were punishable by a prison sentence and the loss of civic rights. Such luminaries as Thomas Mann, Albert Einstein, Emile Zola, and Leo Tolstoy signed it. In 1919, Hirschfeld founded the Institute for Sexual Sciences in Berlin, which rapidly attracted numerous foreign visitors eager to consult his unique documentation on homosexuality and transgenderism. In 1921, he took part in the organization of the First Congress for Sexual Reform, which later led to the formation of The World League for Sexual Reform. Hirschfeld, however, failed to win unanimous support. For example, Adolf Brand, the founder, in 1903, of the Gemeinschaft der Eigenen (Community of the Special), which championed an idea of virile companionship derived from Greek pederasty, blamed him for his medicalized vision of homosexuality and his strategy of social assimilation. Brand's desire to recreate a premodern masculine society, devoted to the cult of friendship and adolescent beauty, influenced both nationalist and youth movements. The Weimar Republic saw the creation of numerous other homosexual movements, which often welcomed both men and women. They concentrated on community life and the publishing of periodicals, such as *Die Freundschaft* (Friendship) or *Die Freundin* (Girlfriend). Though they offered thousands of homosexuals a way out of isolation, they did not obtain the abolition of Paragraph 175, their main purpose, despite the backing, in the 1920s, of the democratic (DDP) and left-wing parties (SPD, KPD). From the 1930s, as Germany sank into chaos, the struggle for homosexual rights was no longer a priority.[11]

Outside Germany, this activist model found some resonance in the Netherlands, where the NWHK (Nederlandsch Wetenschappelijk Humanitair Komitee, or Dutch Scientific Humanitarian Committee), a by-product of the German WhK, was founded in 1912, and in Switzerland, where *Der Kreis/Le Cercle*, a highbrow bilingual monthly—and also the name, given only in 1943, of a homosexual organization—was published starting in 1932.[12] In France, where homosexuality was not prosecuted, and where identity movements came up against the Republican universalist model, the rights of homosexuals were defended by intellectuals, such as André Gide, the author of *Corydon* (1924), who conducted a mostly one-man campaign against prejudices. The only attempt at a homosexual journal, *Inversions,* launched in 1924, did not receive support from the intelligentsia and was rapidly censored.[13] In England, in 1914, Magnus Hirschfeld encouraged the creation of the BSSSP (British Society for the Study of Sex Psychology) presided over by Edward Carpenter and

Laurence Housman.[14] The decriminalization of homosexuality was, however, only one of its goals, and its influence remained, once more, limited to intellectual circles. Homoerotic tendencies were noticeable in the British upper class, thanks to homosocial institutions such as the public schools, universities (Oxbridge), and clubs. The "cult of homosexuality" (a term coined by Noel Annan) celebrated by The Apostles in Cambridge, the Bloomsbury Group, or Oxford Aesthetes, who saw love between men as the highest form of love, was, however, not devoid of contradictions, deeply misogynous, and never publicly admitted.

Homosexual Identities and Cultures

As famous as these intellectual circles could have been, they were just one facet of the homosexual subcultures that developed at the time, especially in European and American metropolises where population intermingling made casual encounters easier. At the end of the nineteenth century, a series of scandals, especially Oscar Wilde's trials in 1895 in England and the Eulenburg affair in 1907 in Germany revealed to the general public the existence of homosexual prostitution rings and established the stereotype of the decadent dandy. In order to escape repression, some homosexual men and women chose to migrate to what they thought would be more friendly territories. Belle epoque Paris had welcomed expatriate Amazons, such as the American poetess Natalie Barney, who revived the cult of Sappho in her salon. Capri became, for a time, the rallying point of intellectuals, artists, and socialites at odds with their motherland, whereas for numerous homosexual adventurers, servicemen, and civil servants, colonies offered an easy way to fulfill their desires in the anonymity of a homosocial environment.

After World War I, the homosexual subculture became more visible. Writers (Christopher Isherwood, Klaus Mann), painters (Otto Dix, Tamara de Lempicka), and photographers (Brassaï, Berenice Abbott) bore witness to these flaming years. In Berlin, Paris, or London, at masked balls, raving queens nicknamed after ancien régime countesses or famous American actresses triumphed and attracted hundreds of onlookers and sympathizers, while in cabarets, same-sex couples danced together.[15] In New York, Bowery clubs had welcomed so-called fairies since the 1890s. From the 1920s, sissies and bulldaggers met in Harlem, which became, together with Greenwich Village, the main center of homosexual sociability. Speakeasies, illegal bars that mostly catered for a heterosexual clientele, were also quite popular with queer men and women, irrespective of their race. This punctual alliance between the African-American community and homosexual men and women could be understood as the confluence of two stigmatized minorities, in revolt against the moral order of Prohibition.[16]

The geography of homosexual meeting places often matched up with the one of underworld of crime, drugs, and prostitution. In Paris, Montmartre, Pigalle, and Montparnasse gathered most of the gay and lesbian bars, whereas in London, young hustlers haunted Piccadilly. Professional and amateur prostitutes rubbed shoulders: next to young men forced on the game because of the economic crisis, provincial working-class boys who saved money to start a family would be found, as well as guardsmen or sailors, who used their attractive uniform to beef up their meager pay. Some did not hesitate to fleece their clients, or to blackmail them. Many homosexual men from the middle and upper classes, like the English writers Joe Ackerley, W. H. Auden, Christopher Isherwood, or Stephen Spender, did not hide their attraction to working-class boys whose strength and assumed lack of inhibition contrasted with their own intellectual and puritan upbringing. The wish for an ideal friend, as expressed in E. M. Forster's novel *Maurice* began to supplant the cult of adolescent boys, although still popular.[17]

Public parks, street urinals, sports clubs (where gentlemen and working-class men could mix), swimming pools, YMCA changing rooms, and saunas all offered numerous opportunities for sentimental and sexual encounters. These apparently informal meetings were in fact strictly organized: body language, double entendre, and the use of symbolic colors like lilac or mauve had to be carefully interpreted if one wanted to be safe. An exaggeration of the flapper fashion, the Eton crop, men's suit, cigar, and monocle became the codes of the masculine lesbian, whereas her partner often kept a more feminine appearance, as could be seen in the couple formed by the English writer Radclyffe Hall and her lover Una Troubridge. Surely upper-class socialites as well as intellectuals could dare to challenge conventions. In her novel *Orlando* (1928), Virginia Woolf declared, in veiled terms, her love for Vita Sackville-West. For most women however, parental and social control made such revealing impossible.[18]

In the nineteenth century, romantic friendships between women from the middle and upper classes had not been uncommon. Some single and financially independent women, notably professors, had lived together as couples, forming what had sometimes been called "Boston marriages." Some transvestite women (also called "passing women"), especially among the working-class, had succeeded in pursuing a career and marrying as men. However, the spreading of the model of the congenital invert, developed by British sexologist Havelock Ellis

FIGURE 3.1: "Männliche Frauentypen aus einem Berliner Lokal für gleichgeschlechtlich gerichtete Frauen" [One of the many lesbian clubs of inter-war Berlin, where women could wear masculine clothes]. In Magnus Hirschfeld, *Geschlechtskunde* IV. *Bilderteil* (Stuttgart, Germany: Püttmann, 1930, 590).

from 1897, as well as the publicity given to famous lesbian or bisexual women such as Colette, Greta Garbo, or Marlene Dietrich, made women couples more and more suspect. Lesbian desire, when not associated with already stigmatized and marginalized social groups, such as prostitutes, prisoners, or actresses, should be kept silent. Because they were uninformed, many young women could not put a name to their desires. For those who, thanks to their upbringing, had access to books, literature could nevertheless provide a fair number of positive references.[19]

Although the expression remains polemical, the existence, at the time, of a homosexual culture based on common references and shared images is well documented. The ideal homosexual library gathered classics (Plato's *Symposium*, Shakespeare's *Sonnets*) and contemporary works (Proust's *Cities of the Plain*), avant-garde novels (*Nightwood* by Djuna Barnes) and popular ones (*Der Skorpion* by A. E. Weirauch). For those who knew the codes, chanson (Damia, Susy Solidor), blues (Bessie Smith), theatre (Noel Coward), and dance

FIGURE 3.2: "Colette sur son balcon" (anonymous). The French novelist Colette, whose
series *Claudine* featured a love affair between
two women, was a figure of scandal in belle
époque Paris. Musée Carnavalet, Ph 2265.

(Russian ballet) offered numerous allusions to same-sex love. In 1926, Edouard
Bourdet's play *La Prisonnière*, which dealt openly with lesbianism, enjoyed a
huge success, first in France, then in Europe and the United States.[20] In 1919, the
first homosexual film, *Anders als die Andern* (Different from the Others), directed
by Richard Oswald, was released. Conradt Veidt played the part of a homosexual musician who commits suicide after being blackmailed. At the end, a plea
for the abolition of Paragraph 175 was delivered by Magnus Hirschfeld, who
co-wrote and acted in the film. In 1931, *Mädchen in Uniform* (Girls in Uniform)
by Leontine Sagan, adapted from Christa Winsloe's novel, related the history
of a young girl in love with her professor in a German boarding school. From
1930, however, Hollywood implemented a strict censorship (known as the Hays
Code), with the result that lesbian and gay characters faded from the screens.[21]

As a matter of fact, the new visibility of homosexual topics in popular culture should not make us doubt the reality of homophobic prejudices. Because

they often broke age, class, and race barriers, same-sex relationships were perceived as a threat to the established order. Because queer men and women had to keep their inclinations secret, they were accused of forming a vice freemasonry, whose undercover influence was particularly strong in strategic circles such as the media, diplomacy, and foreign affairs. During World War I, the homosexual had already been pointed out as the enemy from within, an unreliable coward prone to betray his country. During the 1920s, the possible collusion between lesbianism and feminism came under scrutiny, even though women's rights movements tried to evade the lesbian question. The new woman was accused of endangering familial structure and to bring about depopulation.[22] In the critical context of the 1930s, these accusations would receive a new response.

Nazism and Homosexuality

Shortly after Hitler came to power, the Berlin homosexual subculture was forced to go underground. On May 6, 1933, Magnus Hirschfeld's institute was sacked. In June 1933, the WhK broke up. Most homosexual movements chose to wind themselves down. Journals were forbidden; meeting places were closed. A few bars, however, remained open thanks to support from the SA (Sturm Abteilung, or Storm Battalion), and, in some cities, repression was delayed. Homosexual men and women responded with different strategies: some chose to emigrate, while others contracted marriages of convenience. Most lived a double life, under the threat of police raids and anonymous denunciations. Some homosexual artists, such as the actor Gustaf Gründgens, who had friends in high places, were not bothered.[23]

Nazi discourse on homosexuality was never fully consistent, which entertained confusion. For example, from 1934, communist propaganda identified homosexuality as a fascist perversion. Certainly, the Nazi party counted some notorious homosexuals, such as Ernst Röhm, the leader of the SA; strong homoerotic undercurrents were also perceptible in the art favored by the regime, in particular sculpture (Arno Breker, Joseph Thorak) and cinema. It is, however, essential to distinguish between what was mainly a manipulation, through the myth of the Männerbund (the Manly State), of masculine friendship to political ends and Nazi views on homosexuality. In a context of demographic fear and struggle for lebensraum, the homosexual man, if he refused to meet national requirements—to become a husband and a father—had no social value. In his speech to SS (Schutzstuffel, or Protective Squadron) Generals on February 18, 1937, Himmler described homosexuality as a foreign import, and homosexual men as potential traitors. However, since he thought that a majority of these men had been seduced and could therefore be cured, he encouraged medical experiments (hormonal or psychological treatments, castration), which he hoped would allow homosexual men to go to the front, without fear of contagion.[24]

The "night of the long knives" (June 29 to 30, 1934) was a turning point. Röhm's elimination, although motivated by political reasons, was presented by Hitler as a crusade against immorality. Afterward, the accusation of homosexuality was commonly used to discredit political opponents, for instance within youth movements, the army, or the Catholic Church. On September 1, 1935, the new Paragraph 175, which aimed at all kinds of homosexual desire, went into force. Lesbianism, however, was not criminalized. Repression increased: the number of persons to be tried increased ten-fold between 1934 and 1938; sentences were also heavier. The number of convictions decreased with the beginning of the war, probably because fighting homosexuality was no longer a priority.[25]

All convicts did not suffer the same destiny. Some of them, like the so-called corruptors of youth, prostitutes, and repeat offenders, could be sent to concentration camps before they had been judged, and sometimes without ever being judged. Others were sent there after their prison sentence had been served, in order to be re-educated through labor. Some were exceptionally released, for example in 1939, for Hitler's birthday, or because they were pronounced cured. Inside concentration camps, the destiny of homosexual prisoners varied according to where and when they were sent. Even though they could be found in Dachau or Oranienenburg from 1933, homosexuals—who were, from 1937, progressively identified by a pink triangle, which they were forced to wear on their jacket—represented less than 1 percent of the camp prisoners, which deprived them of any decisive influence. Like other prisoners, they were subjected to awful detention conditions, but it seems they were particularly at risk. They were more often sent to disciplinary units and had to perform exhausting tasks, for example in Sachsenhausen clay pits. Isolation was also a problem. Nazis often imposed solitary confinement as a way to prevent what they saw as potential contagion. Furthermore, fellow prisoners did not trust them. Sexuality was used by some SS guards and *Kapos* as a means to control prisoners. They often chose young prisoners as so-called minions, a fact that increased confusion between sexual practices that were nothing short of rape and abuse of power, on the one side, and a survival strategy, on the other side. Even though, as a group, lesbians escaped such persecutions, some of them were arrested under provisions of the Austrian law that criminalized feminine homosexuality, or for some minor offence, and were deported as asocial or communists. Some

FIGURE 3.3: The Homomonument in Amsterdam (1987) that consists of three pink triangles
on street level commemorates the gay men
and women who died during World War II,
but also all men and women who have been,
or still are, persecuted because of their sexual
orientation. Photo: Marian Bakker, Arnhem.

were put in the camp whorehouse, and systematically raped, which was seen
as a way to reaffirm gender hierarchy in a patriarchal order. In total, more
than 100,000 homosexuals were put on file by the regime; between 5,000
and 15,000 homosexuals were sent to concentration camps, where most died
under dramatic conditions. It was only in 1985 that West Germany publicly
recognized homosexual persecution under the Nazi regime, but the question of
compensation still lingers on today.[26] Amsterdam was the first city to build, in
1987, a memorial dedicated to the pink triangles in the city center.

1939–1969: IN THE CLOSET?

World War II

Paragraph 175 only applied to the inhabitants of the Reich—that is, Germany
and its annexed territories. The risk of degeneration supposedly raised by

homosexuality was of little importance among people already considered as inferior. Therefore, the destiny of homosexual men and women in countries allied with or occupied by Germany could noticeably vary. In Italy, Mussolini enacted antihomosexual decrees under Nazi pressure. Homosexuals were jailed or sent into exile in the islands; those who were members of the fascist party were forced to resign. In the Netherlands, homosexuals were not systematically prosecuted. In France, Paragraph 175 only applied to the departments of Alsace and Moselle, which were annexed to the Reich. The homosexual subculture flourished, however, in occupied Paris. On the other side, the Vichy Regime, as a response to concerns regarding demoralization in the navy and youth corruption, passed the law of August 6, 1942 (confirmed at the Liberation), which raised the age of consent from 13 (15 in 1945) to 21 in the case of same-sex relations.[27]

World War II, as World War I had before, played a decisive part in the construction of modern gay and lesbian identities, in Europe and in the United States. During the war, the surveillance of homosexual practices was no longer a priority. Passionate relations between men or between women could sometimes flourish. Gender norms were challenged, even within the military. Army theater is one of the most original examples of those disruptions. Already during World War I, for example, in German or Austrian prisoner of war camps in Russia, *Plennytheater* had been set up, with young officers playing female parts in drag and attracting a lot of male attention. Canadian troops also saw the creation of theater companies, such as the Dumbells in 1917, or the Tin Hats in 1942. Although homosexuality was subject to court martial, these very popular drag acts were supposed to keep troops' spirits up and did not arouse suspicion. In the late years of World War II, when women were more numerous in the army, men who kept on impersonating women were more and more criticized and some were discharged on psychological grounds.

The U.S. Army generalized this discharge system. For the first time, during World War II, special measures were set up aimed at keeping homosexuals out of the military. So-called experts, notably army medical officers, were supposed to determine, through a superficial examination and interview, the sexual orientation of the men (and women from 1944) who came to enlist.[28] Only the very naïve, or the most effeminate (one of the supposedly telling signs), ran the risk of being discovered. Some, however, realized their true feelings thanks to this simple questioning. Camp intimacy brought men closer, and it was common for men to dance together at parties or to share the same bed. The transfer to Europe sometimes coincided with the discovery of the homosexual subculture. London, in particular, experienced a gay golden age.[29]

The war also offered lesbians opportunities for acknowledgment. Already in 1928, Radclyffe Hall, in *The Well of Loneliness*, had referred to enlisting in ambulance units as a founding experience for women during World War I. Even though the press worried about possible unnatural relations, it also emphasized the supposedly masculine qualities of women who took an active part in defending the country. This phenomenon was even more common during World War II, when many women went to enlist with short hair and men's clothes, endowed with the aura of Rosie the Riveter. In the American army, the WAAC (Women's Army Auxiliary Corps, later WAC), created in 1942, counted about 150,000 women, all volunteers, who chose to enlist because of patriotism, but also to assert their independence, and, for some of them, to enjoy a women-only environment. The authorities put up with lesbian friendships, as long as they remained discreet, for they helped to strengthen solidarity. At the end of the war, however, many gay men and women received an infamous blue discharge for homosexual offences. Landed from the so-called queer ships in American harbors, many chose to stay where they were and joined the growing homosexual subculture of cities like New York, Boston, Los Angeles, and San Francisco.[30]

The Lavender Scare

After the war, a movement back to normalcy implied the reaffirmation of traditional values and the denunciation of deviancies. In the cold war context, the old fear of the homosexual traitor reappeared in America. The Lavender Scare, directed against homosexuals, who were deemed as dangerous a menace to national security as communists, was the often ignored counterpart to the famous Red Scare orchestrated by U.S. Senator Joseph McCarthy. What seemed at first a political manipulation aimed at embarrassing the Truman administration turned into a long-term strategy. U.S. Senator Kenneth Wherry, among others, insinuated that sex perverts had infiltrated the State Department, and that the Soviet Union held a list of high-ranking homosexual employees in government, originally compiled by Hitler for spying purposes. In total, more than 5,000 civil servants were dismissed under the pretext that their homosexuality, interpreted as a form of instability, represented a security risk. In Washington, the gay and lesbian subculture—which had blossomed since the Great Depression because of the influx of young single men and women eager to benefit from the employment opportunities offered by the federal government as part of the New Deal, but also to escape the morally oppressive climate of their native region—was harshly struck. For many men and women, to hide one's sexual orientation became a necessity.[31]

The Lavender Scare had consequences beyond the United States. Most international organizations connected with the United States, such as the United Nations Educational, Scientific and Cultural Organization (UNESCO), the World Bank, or the International Monetary Fund (IMF), as well as many of their allies within the North Atlantic Treaty Organization (NATO), took measures in order to exclude homosexual civil servants from their administrations. At a time when Britain was facing mounting protests in its empire as well as losing ground on the international stage, homosexuals proved convenient scapegoats, especially after the Cambridge spies affair of 1951, when double agents Guy Burgess and Donald Maclean, who were both homosexual, defected to the Soviet Union.[32] In many European countries, the 1950s were a time of difficulties for gay men and women. In Germany, the tragedy of the pink triangles was not acknowledged after the war. West Germany retained the 1935 version of Paragraph 175, whereas East Germany reverted to the former version of the law. In West Germany, more than 45,000 homosexuals were convicted under Paragraph 175 between 1950 and 1965. It was four times more than during the Weimar Republic. Under the influence of the Christian Democrats, familial values were reaffirmed. France experienced the same evolution. In 1960, the Mirguet amendment, which defined homosexuality as a social scourge, resulted in the aggravation of sentences for indecent exposure, in the case of same-sex relations between men or between women.[33]

From 1952 to 1973, homosexuality was classified by the American Psychiatric Association as a mental disorder. Whereas Freud had refused to analyze homosexuality as a disease, some of his followers, such as Sandor Rado or Charles Socarides, claimed that there was only one sexual orientation, heterosexuality, and that psychoanalysis could cure homosexuals. In addition to the psychotherapeutic treatments already in use, a new range of therapies aimed at curing homosexuality was proposed, from aversion therapy to lobotomy, depending on the countries. The Kinsey reports on human sexual behavior, published in 1948 and 1953, had shown that 37 percent of the male subjects as well as 13 percent of the female ones had at least one homosexual experience, which contradicted the idea that homosexuality was a rare pathology. Kinsey proposed to rank sexual behavior on a scale that went from 0 to 6, from exclusive heterosexuality to exclusive homosexuality, with an additional seventh grade for asexuals. A heated argument ensued. For some observers, the reports confirmed their fear that homosexuality was on the rise and that homosexuals were all the more dangerous because they could not be easily identified. Others took the opposite view, and considered that the reports brought new arguments in favor of the recognition of equal rights for homosexuals.[34]

Homophile Movements

Confronted with the rise of homophobia, gays and lesbians tried to react and unite. In 1951, *The Homosexual in America* by Donald Webster Cory (pen name of Edward Sagarin) was published. The book, which was aimed at the general public, offered a unique description of the homosexual subculture from the inside and denounced the way homosexual men and women were daily discriminated against. The same year, Harry Hay founded the Mattachine Society following the example of civil rights movements. Organized like a secret society, divided into cells, the Mattachine Society had gathered more than 2,000 people by 1953. After the resignation of its founding members, whose communist sympathies had been revealed, the new leaders rejected the minority group model and gave up activism in favor of information and education work. They thought that changing mentalities was a long-term process, to be brought about only from above, thanks to the help of various experts, sociologists, psychologists, or doctors.[35] The same was true with the first American lesbian rights organization, the Daughters of Bilitis, founded in 1955 in San Francisco by Del Martin and Phyllis Lyon. Motivated by a desire for recognition and social climbing, as the title of their journal *The Ladder* attested, the Daughters of Bilitis were dedicated to helping their members adjust to society and fight isolation and invisibility.[36] Under observation by the police and the FBI, these organizations lived in fear. From 1961 onward, however, some states, such as Illinois or Connecticut, began to decriminalize same-sex relations between consenting adults. Within the Mattachine Society, the official line was being more and more contested, notably by Frank Kameny and Jack Nichols, the founders of the Washington section, who advocated activism on the model of black liberation movements. Denying experts any legitimacy to talk about homosexuality, they encouraged homosexuals to speak for themselves, claiming that "Gay is good." From 1965 onward, demonstrators picketed the White House and other public institutions to protest against federal government antigay policies while at the same time alerting the media, therefore calling more and more attention to the homosexual cause.[37]

Homophile movements were also created in Europe. Following the example of the Danish *Forbundet af 1948*, they often referred to the Universal Declaration of Human Rights from 1948, which promoted equal rights and condemned any form of discrimination. In West Germany, homophile magazines, inspired by the homosexual press of the 1920s, were rapidly censored. In France, however, the homophile journal *Arcadie*, created in 1954 by André Baudry, a former seminarist and philosophy teacher, survived for almost 28 years. Concerned about respectability, in a period of moral

FIGURE 3.4: Pamphlet *The Homosexual Citizen*, August, 1966. The Mattachine Society of Washington, DC, published leaflets in order to inform gay people of their rights. Washington, Kameny Papers Project.

conformity, *Arcadie* condemned provocative behavior, such as that of the flamboyant queens and hustlers from Saint Germain des Prés, as well as the promiscuity and the bar culture. Highly criticized in the 1970s for its reformist and assimilationist stance, *Arcadie* nonetheless urged its members to be open about their sexuality and played an essential role in educating the public.[38] Besides, members of Club Arcadie benefited from numerous services. In the Netherlands, the NWHK was succeeded by the COC (Culture and Recreation Centre) in 1946. In 1951, it organized an international conference, which resulted in the creation of the International Committee of Sexual Equality (ICSE), with the mission of coordinating the activities of the different homophile movements across the world.[39]

The situation was somehow different in Britain. Most of the founders of the Homosexual Law Reform Society, created in 1958, were not homosexuals. Leading personalities, writers, MPs, and archbishops became involved in the fight for the decriminalization of same-sex relations. In 1954, a sensational trial, involving Lord Montagu, his cousin Michael Pitt-Rivers, and the *Daily Mail* journalist Peter Wildeblood, brought out into the open the police abuses of power in the dealings with homosexuals. As a result, a Committee on Homosexual Offences and Prostitution was established under the presidency of Sir John Wolfenden. Published in 1957, the Wolfenden Report recommended that "homosexual behaviour between consenting adults in private should no longer be a criminal offence,"[40] but advocated harsher sentences in the cases of public indecency and sexual relations with minors.[41]

Cities of the Night

In this gloomy context, many homosexual men and women led a double life and took care to hide their sexual preferences from anyone but trustworthy persons. If the closet remained, for some, a cause for shame, fear, and isolation, others got a thrill out of anonymous cruising. Gay life was organized as a secret world, with its own rites, norms, and values, even its own slang (known as *polari*, or *parlare*). Clandestine meetings that took place, for example, in tearooms (public toilets) were regulated by complex codes that protected the users from the police and potential gay bashers, but also organized the sex market according to age, gender, and sexual roles. The urinals were frequented by regulars (known as tearooms queens) but also casual visitors whose assumed heterosexuality seemed all the more attractive. Gay bars such as Cedar Tavern in New York, which attracted artists, critics, and writers; The Black Cat Cafe in San Francisco, where the transvestite José Sarria performed; but also bikers' bars, especially in California, played an essential part in the organization of a gay and lesbian subculture.[42] A specific lesbian subculture, organized according to strict gender codes, emerged in some working-class bars. *Butches*, who sported short hair and a masculine garb, affected a virile behavior, whereas the more feminine *femmes* used make up and followed fashion and were generally subjected to less constraints. Because of its visibility, the butch/femme scene was often the target of homophobic aggressions, with women being insulted or attacked in the streets or around the bars. On the other hand, many women who did not fit stereotypes (*Kikis*) felt out of place in a subculture that was rigidly defined by role models. Many lesbians, especially from the middle class, were reluctant to spend time in places they often found squalid and depressing, and where their reputation was at risk. They preferred to organize private parties at home and rejected the butch/femme model, which they saw as a parody of the straight couple. Butches were their main target, since they were accused of reproducing male chauvinism in their relationships. However, many isolated women had no contact at all with the lesbian subculture. Social pressure forced many to contract a marriage, either to please their family, keep their group of friends, protect their professional career, or, simply, to start a family, have a child, and live a supposedly normal life.[43]

The lack of positive reference to homosexuality, in pop culture as well as in daily life, contributed to the sense of isolation. Except when it was treated in a burlesque way (*Some Like It Hot*, by Billy Wilder, 1959), male homosexuality was represented in the movies as a menace, especially in film noir (*The Maltese Falcon*, by John Huston, 1941; *Rope* by Alfred Hitchcock, 1948) and always doomed to death (*Victim*, by Basil Dearden, 1961; *The Servant*, by Joseph Losey, 1963). Lesbian characters were generally reduced to stereotypes: teachers and students (*Olivia*, by Jacqueline Audry, 1950), prisoners (*Women's Prison*, by Maurice Cloche, 1958), mad or criminal women (*Rome, Open City*, by Roberto Rossellini, 1945; *Rebecca*, by Hitchcock, 1940). Therefore, lesbian and gay audiences often preferred to make their own stories, either by identifying with straight characters (Marlon Brando in *A Streetcar Named Desire*, by Elia Kazan, 1951, came to embody male eroticism, in the same way as other male actors, this time gay, but in the closet, such as James Dean or Montgomery Clift) or by building their own myths (Judy Garland).[44]

Literature offered more opportunities, with a new generation of homosexual writers, like Gore Vidal, Truman Capote, James Baldwin, or Tennessee Williams. Countercultural writers, especially those from the Beat generation, such as Jack Kerouac, Allen Ginsberg, or William Burroughs, shared close links with the gay subculture and paved the way for the sexual revolution. In 1963, *City of the Night* by John Rechy bluntly revealed the nightlife of American big cities as seen through the eyes of a male hustler, while underground filmmaker Kenneth Anger staged fetishist gay bikers from Brooklyn in *Scorpio Rising*. Painters (David Hockney, Andy Warhol), movie directors (Paul Morrissey), musicians (Lou Reed, David Bowie) made gay topics a staple of pop culture. In fact, if for some gay artists, such as Jean Genet, Francis Bacon, Pier Paolo Pasolini, or Rainer Maria Fassbinder, homosexuality was the last refuge of nonconformism, gay desire was also being reclaimed by a more commercial subculture. Pulps, cheap novels with sensational back stories made a specialty of lesbian passions. Even though they targeted a male audience, they soon gained an iconic status among lesbians. Physique magazines filled a niche in the homoerotic market, associating sexy photographs of muscular semi-naked male bodies with suggestive artworks by artists such as

Tom of Finland, whose drawings of cowboys, policemen, or bikers borrowed from sadomasochistic aestheticism and would soon become the symbols of the gay liberation.

FROM 1969 TILL TODAY: LIBERATION UNDER WAY?

The Lesbian and Gay Liberation Movements

During the night from June 27 to 28, 1969, the Stonewall Inn, a gay bar of Greenwich Village in New York was raided by the police. The regulars, among them many African American and Puerto Rican transvestites and prostitutes, instead of heading back home, chose to face the police, armed with bricks and bottles. Riots went on the following days, with crowds shouting "Gay power" and singing "We are the Stonewall Girls." A powerful symbol of the fight against shame and oppression, the Stonewall riots are today regarded as the start of the modern lesbian and gay liberation movement, even though some earlier but less known events can be found (for example, Vanguard, an association of gay young prostitutes had been founded in San Francisco in 1966).[45] In July 1969, in the immediate aftermath of Stonewall, the Gay Liberation Front (GLF) was born. Its leaders did not come from the former homophile organizations but from the ranks of the New Left. This new generation of activists aligned themselves with feminist, black, and antiwar movements and elaborated a more radical discourse than their forebears, rejecting capitalism and middle-class conformism, especially the nuclear family, marriage, and monogamy. Political activism took precedence over the gay bar culture, which was accused of creating a ghettoized culture by keeping sexuality outside the public eye. "The personal is political," the feminists had claimed. "To come out of the closet" became the slogan of the gay liberation. Whereas in the 1950s the phrase used to refer to one's entrance into the gay world after one had become aware of one's homosexuality, it soon became a moral imperative. To come out became a way to fight internalized homophobia as well as to commit oneself to the gay and lesbian movement. On June 28, 1970, the anniversary day of Stonewall, the first Gay Pride Parade, which gathered between 5,000 and 20,000 people, marched through the streets of New York. In Europe, Canada, and Australia, the liberation movement was also getting started. Between the end of 1970 and the beginning of 1971, the Gay Liberation Front in England, Fuori! in Italy, the Homosexuelle Aktionsgruppen in West Germany and the FHAR (Front homosexuel d'action révolutionnaire, or Revolutionary Homosexual Action Front) in France were created. In a break with the strategy of integration favored by homophile movements, the lesbian and gay liberation groups stimulated public provocations. In France, whereas Guy Hocquenghem, a former Maoist militant analyzed, in *The Homosexual Desire* (1972), "the privatization of the anus," the FHAR affirmed "our arsehole is revolutionary," and the Gazolines, a group of radical queens, chanted during far-left demonstrations: "Make-up is what truly matters."[46]

Very soon, tensions appeared within the movement. In the United States, lesbians, who felt they had been made invisible by the GLF, tried to get closer to the feminist movement, which, however, seemed rather reluctant to embrace what some of them saw as the lavender menace. By stating that lesbianism was a choice every "Woman-Identified Woman" could make, lesbian feminists marked a turning point.[47] In 1971, NOW (the National Organization for Women) passed a resolution that supported lesbian rights. However, the doctrinal rigidity of lesbian feminists, who accused bisexual women of treason and heterosexual women of collaborating with the enemy (men), fostered tensions within the movement. Lesbians from ethnic minorities, in particular, suffered from lesbian separatism, which compelled them to break off with their communities.[48] In the same way, in France, the MLF (Mouvement de Libération des Femmes, or Women Liberation Movement) was divided between the followers of Simone de Beauvoir, who had dedicated a—controversial—chapter to lesbians in her seminal book *The Second Sex* (1949), and the followers of Antoinette Fouque (the *psychépo* tendency), hostile to lesbian visibility within the movement. Lesbians, although they had been at the origin of the FHAR, decided to leave it because of the reigning male chauvinism. They created informal groups, such as the Gouines Rouges (Red Dykes) or joined the MLF, where they played an essential part in the fight for the right to abortion, the criminalization of rape, or the denunciation of pornography. In 1980, Monique Wittig stood in favor of lesbian separatism ("lesbians are not women"),[49] which led to a new schism. This attempt at radical lesbianism did not gain much support in France, but the author of *The Lesbian Body* (1973) found a positive reception in the United States, where her writings inspired materialistic feminists as well as queer theorists.

The lesbian and gay liberation movements were short-lived. Revolutionary movements were on the decline, whereas the refusal of any hierarchy as well as the multiplication of schisms put an end to radical groups and paved the way for a more reformist approach. In the United States, movements such as the GAA (Gay Activists Alliance), founded in New York in 1969, focused on the fight for equality, using political lobbying and direct action (such as zaps, later used by ACT UP) in order to increase lesbian and gay visibility and promote a positive image of homosexuality in the media. In France, one of the GLHs

(Groupe de libération homosexuelle, or Homosexual Liberation Group) from provincial France had a candidate in the local elections; in 1978 gay candidates ran in general elections. Everywhere, identity groups, whether based on a social, cultural, professional, or religious basis multiplied, from gay doctors to leather dykes. Whereas there were about 10 of these organizations in San Francisco in 1971, there were more than 300 in 1987.[50]

The Emergence of a Gay and Lesbian Community

The 1970s and 1980s saw the flourishing of the gay and lesbian subculture. In the United States, San Francisco attracted thousands of homosexual men and women, who fled the conformism of provincial America to settle in the

FIGURE 3.5: "Le rendez-vous hebdomadaire des gays" [The weekly meeting of gays], *Le Palace Magazine*, n°12, Paris 1982. In the 1980s, Le Palace, a Parisian discotheque, became famous for its gay parties. Clones used to wear color-coded handkerchiefs in their back pocket to indicate their sexual preferences. Lyon, Bibliothèque Municipale: Chomarat P 2190.

Castro neighborhood. Canada (Toronto and Montreal), Australia (Sydney), and Europe (Amsterdam and Copenhagen) saw the quick expansion of gay areas, organized around bars, shops, and clubs. In Spain, however, it was only after the death of Franco, in 1975, that the homosexual subculture could assert itself, in step with the *movida*. At the beginning of the 1970s, Saint-Anne Street in Paris, symbolized the culture of the ghetto, with its private clubs whose entrances were strictly guarded, the culture of the ghetto, where one merely wandered at night. From the 1980s, the Marais Quarter offered the opportunity to live one's sexuality in the open. Although bars were no longer reserved to an elite, they now mostly applied a gay-only policy and were more and more specialized in order to cater to all members of the community (transvestites, sadomasochists, etc.). The gay scene was all about youth and body cult. Cruising became an art in itself. The so-called Clones, who frequented the gyms, saunas, and backrooms, usually sported a moustache or a beard, kept their hair short and their body toned, and wore the same kind of outfit: tight pants and tight t-shirt, sometimes a plaid flannel outer shirt and black combat boots. In clubs like the Palace in Paris, gay men danced to the sound of disco hits from Village People, Gloria Gaynor, or Donna Summer. Numerous ways of living one's sexuality were experienced, from monogamy to polyamory, from anonymous sex to orgy—everything seemed possible.[51]

In contrast with the gay subculture, part of the lesbian cultural renaissance took place in small towns and rural areas. Lesbian women developed their own meeting places, such as feminist bookshops, women centers, tearooms, sports clubs (softball, handball, etc.), and film or music festivals. The 1970s and 1980s were also marked by the debates on femininity, language, women's cultures (matriarchy, witchcraft, etc.) as well as on lesbian identity, lesbian desire (from vanilla sex to sadomasochism) and sexual roles (butch/femme). The Lesbian Nation utopia was not without its dogmatism: political correctness triumphed.[52] Everywhere, new media, such as the radio (*Fréquence gaie* was launched in France in September 1981) were taken over by gays and lesbians, and the gay press was booming: *Gay News*, then *Gay Times* in London, *The Advocate* in the United States, and *Gai-Pied* and *Lesbia* in France echoed the debates that took place within the gay and lesbian community. Publishers like Gay Press in New York, Rosa Winkel in Berlin, and Gay Men's Press in London were founded, retailed by bookshops such as Prinz Eisenherz in Berlin, Vrolijk in Amsterdam, or Les Mots à la Bouche in Paris. Thanks to the relaxing of the Hays Code, homosexuality could be more openly treated in Hollywood movies (*Midnight Cowboy*, directed by John Schlesinger, 1969, won Oscars for Best Director and Best Picture), although stereotypes remained very much alive (*Cruising*, by William Friedkin, 1980, had Al Pacino as a cop who went undercover in the New York sadomasochism gay subculture in order to catch a serial killer). In Europe, next to political movies such as *It Is Not the Homosexual Who Is Perverse, but the Society in Which He Lives*, by Rosa von Praunheim (1971), the late 1960s and early 1970s saw the release of many critically acclaimed movies that dealt with homosexual topics, notably those directed by Pier Paolo Pasolini (*Theorem*, 1968), Federico Fellini (*Satyricon*, 1969), Luchino Visconti (*Death in Venice*, 1971), or Rainer Maria Fassbinder (*The Bitter Tears of Petra von Kant*, 1972). The 1980s, however, offered a series of independent movies whose scenarios provided, for the first time, an alternative to the drama and guiltiness that had for so long haunted the representations of homosexuality on the screen (*My Beautiful Laundrette*, by Stephen Frears, 1985).[53] Best-sellers, such as *A Boy's Own Story*, by Edmund White (1982), or *Oranges Are Not the Only Fruit*, by Jeannette Winterson (1985) played a role in the normalization of homosexual themes in literature, while in the art field, gay and lesbian images became more visible. In 1982, the New Museum of New York displayed for the first time an exhibition dedicated to gay and lesbian artists. The idea of a possible gay art, dealing with homosexual themes and produced by gay and lesbian artists for the benefit of a gay public, remains, however, deeply contested. British artists Gilbert and George, for example, defend the notion of an "Art for All."[54]

AIDS

A new era for lesbian and gay militancy began in the 1980s, when the homosexual community was struck by the AIDS epidemic. The first cases of what was called, at first, gay cancer then, AIDS (acquired immunodeficiency syndrome), were first identified in 1981, on the West Coast of the United States. AIDS was described in 1982 as a viral infection, but it was only in 1983 that the Pasteur Institute in Paris isolated the human immunodeficiency virus (HIV). The first HIV test was launched in 1985. HAART (highly active antiretroviral therapy), introduced in 1996, can slow the course of the disease, but there is still no vaccine or cure.

At first skeptical of what they saw as a new example of moral panic, the leaders of gay associations in Europe and the United States did not take immediate precautionary measures. Bathhouses, symbols of the sexual revolution, were closed only in 1984 in the United States, after huge controversy within the Gay Men's Health Crisis, created in 1982 in New York. In some countries, like Sweden or Britain, homosexual associations were quicker to understand the full extent of the danger. Nevertheless, from the beginning, some LGBT groups took action. Bringing together patients and health professionals, voluntary AIDS organizations, such as the San Francisco AIDS Foundation (1982) or Aides in France (1984) focused on public education and service provision for people living with HIV/AIDS and tried to mobilize public opinion in order to gather subsidies from reluctant governments. The creation of ACT UP (AIDS Coalition to Unleash Power) by Larry Kramer in New York in 1987 marked the radicalization of the movement, which refocused its action on political lobbying, demanding greater access to experimental drugs and more money for medical research. In the same way as American and British organizations Queer Nation and OutRage founded in 1990, ACT UP gives priority to media visibility, favors direct action (die-ins, etc.), and does not hesitate to use more controversial methods such as the outing of gay public figures still in the closet.[55]

The AIDS epidemic has deeply shattered the LGBT community, if only because it led to the death of thousands of people, among them many young men,

FIGURE 3.6: "Be Good in Bed": The use of condoms promoted as a way to prevent the spread of the AIDS epidemic. Advertisement by the Terrence Higgins Trust. Color lithograph, ca. 1995. Wellcome Library, London.

and scarred a whole generation. Because of the tragedy, many homosexual men and women who had never been militant before decided to act and joined AIDS organizations. Sexual practices also changed. In order to prevent the spreading of HIV, the use of condoms and regular testing were promoted. Safer sexual practices were also given wide publicity, with the success of jack-off parties and new interest in nonpenetrative sex such as masturbation, voyeurism, exhibitionism, or sadomasochism. Since the 1990s, however, barebacking (unprotected intercourse) has been on the rise for various reasons: weariness, negligence, lack of information, transformation of AIDS into a chronic disease, and revolt against normative injunctions. A small and highly controversial minority actively pursues HIV infection (bug chasers).

The AIDS epidemic brought back all kinds of stigma, from ostracism to rejection and discrimination. In the United States, the 1970s had already seen the rise of homophobia, exemplified by the antihomosexual campaign of the singer Anita Bryant and the attempt in California by Senator Briggs to prevent gay and lesbian people and those who supported gay rights from working in public schools. Tensions reached a peak on November 27, 1978, when San Francisco gay City Supervisor Harvey Milk and Mayor George Moscone were murdered.[56] Under the Reagan presidency, religious conservatives, such as Pat Buchanan, saw in AIDS a curse from God. At the same period, Pope John Paul II took a tougher stance on homosexuality and rejected condoms as a counter to AIDS. In 1987, the Jesse Helms amendment banned people affected with AIDS from traveling or immigrating to the United States. In 1988 in Britain, the Thatcher cabinet passed Section 28 of the Local Government Act, which stated that local authorities should not "promote or publish material with the intention of promoting homosexuality." In other countries, such as the Netherlands, there was no such backlash against gay and lesbian people.

Despite the homophobic rhetoric, the AIDS epidemic in fact made homosexuality more commonplace thanks to popular media campaigns such as those organized by the Elizabeth Taylor AIDS Foundation in the United States, or the Sidaction in France. By making public their disease, figures such as the actor Rock Hudson (who died in 1985) also contributed to awareness. The Names Project, a huge quilt dedicated to AIDS victims, and launched in 1985 in the United States, attracted a lot of attention and united the community in grief and compassion. More generally, the courage, solidarity, and dignity shown by gay and lesbian people made a lasting impression on the public.[57] On a different level, ACT UP played an essential part in the fight against invisibility and indifference, thanks to the use of shocking images and powerful slogan such as SILENCE = DEATH, written on an inverted pink triangle that recalls the death of thousands of homosexuals in Nazi camps. Confronted by censorship, some homosexual artists, such as Keith Haring and Derek Jarman, made AIDS a central feature of their work. After the success of the film *Philadelphia* by Jonathan Demme (1993), AIDS ceased to be a taboo subject on the screen.

The AIDS crisis also called into question the gay movement, which appeared less and less representative of the LGBT community as a whole. On a theoretical level, the 1990s saw the emergence of queer theory, a new field of gender studies that contested the traditional identity politics of recognition of the gay and lesbian liberation movement, by claiming that identities are not fixed and should not be reduced to normative categories of gender and sexuality. Inspired notably by Michel Foucault, and derived from both gay and lesbian studies and feminist studies, queer theory is exemplified by the work, among others, of Judith Butler, Teresa de Lauretis, Eve Kosofsky Sedgwick, David Halperin, and Michael Warner.[58] Outside the University, the queer resistance to heteronormativity found numerous applications, from gender performance (drag queens, drag kings) to pop culture, especially on the Internet (slash fan fiction, for example, rewrites popular books or TV shows in order to reveal homosexual subtexts).

The Fight for LGBT Rights

On a legal level, the fight for equality and LGBT rights focused at first on the abolition of anti-homosexual legislations. The end of the 1960s saw the decriminalization of same-sex relations between consenting adults in England and Wales (1967), Bulgaria (1968), West and East Germany (1968–1969), Canada (1969), Finland and Austria (1971), Norway (1972), and Malta (1973). In Australia, the decriminalization of homosexuality took place at different rates depending on the states (1972 for South Australia, 1997 for Tasmania). Discriminations based on the age of consent often took longer to be removed (1971 for the Netherlands, 1982 for France, 2000 for Britain, for example). If intergenerational sex was, for a long time, part of the homosexual imagination, and if one still saw in the 1970s, the creation of pedophile groups in the following of the gay movement, sex relations with minors are today explicitly condemned by LGBT associations. Homosexual relations that were for a long time based on difference in power and structured according to age, class, or gender, tend more and more toward sexual equality.

All discriminations did not immediately disappear. In East Germany, gay publications were banned until 1988. In Britain, the Sexual Offences Act did not apply to the army and the navy. Initially limited to England and Wales, the

Act was implemented in 1980 in Scotland and in 1982 in Ulster. The British Army opened to gays and lesbians only in 2000. The U.S. Military authorizes gays and lesbians to serve in the army but only if they submit to the "don't ask, don't tell" policy enacted in 1993. In the case of Eastern and Central European countries, whereas Slovenia and Croatia decriminalized same-sex relations in 1977, one had to wait until 1991 in Ukraine, 1992 in Estonia and Latvia, 1993 in Russia and Lithuania, 1995 in Albania and Moldavia, and 1996 in Romania. The European Union was the driving force behind these changes, as it made the abolition of discriminations based on sexual orientation one of the conditions for admission. The ILGA (International Lesbian and Gay Association), created in 1978, tries to federate LGBT associations across the world. In some countries, however, such as Poland, Romania, or Russia, they face strong opposition. Verbal and physical abuses against gay and lesbian people are commonplace. LGBT pride parades have been the scene of violent fights between demonstrators, the police, and far-right provocateurs.

FIGURE 3.7: Maastricht Gay Parade, 1995. Pride parades are both festive and political events, where the diversity of the gay and lesbian subculture is celebrated. Photo: Marian Bakker, Arnhem.

Since the 1990s, new demands have emerged, especially regarding the rights to marriage and adoption for same-sex couples. Throughout the twentieth century, homosexual and bisexual men and women have contracted heterosexual marriages, either marriages for love or marriages of convenience. In the 1970s, however, marriage was denounced both by gay liberation groups and feminists as a symbol of bourgeois conformism and male domination. With the AIDS epidemic, the demand for the recognition of same-sex unions became vocal, when numerous gay couples, struck down by the disease, were confronted by inextricable legal, fiscal, and administrative problems: they were refused access to the hospital when they wanted to visit their partner, found it impossible to ask for a leave in order to take care of him, or were evicted from the apartment they used to share. Following the example of Denmark in 1989, numerous European countries have now adopted laws or statutes that in some way recognized same-sex unions (Norway in 1993, Sweden in 1994, Iceland in 1996, The Netherlands in 1997, Belgium and Catalonia in 1998, Aragon and France in 1999, Germany in 2001, Britain in 2005, for example). Not so frequent are the countries that recognized same-sex marriage (The Netherlands, Belgium, Spain, and, outside Europe, Canada as well as five American states in 2009), or adoption by same-sex couples (The Netherlands, Sweden, Belgium, Iceland, Britain, Spain, Canada, and some American states). Numerous gay and lesbian couples already have children, for example from a former heterosexual relationship or donor insemination. Lesbian and gay men claim their rights to be recognized as parents, in a society where family (single-parent families, blended families, etc.) as well as procreation (in vitro fertilization, surrogacy, etc.) have changed a lot. Opponents of LGBT parenting, when they do not link homosexuality to child abuse, put forward anthropological (a child should be raised by both a father and a mother), psychoanalytical (risk of gender confusion), and religious arguments. The Anglican Church and Protestant churches are divided on these questions, but the Catholic and Orthodox hierarchies have never ceased to denounce homosexuality as a sin, and both remain strongly opposed to the recognition of same-sex couples. In the same way, Islam condemns homosexual practices, which some fundamentalist groups see as a consequence of Western decadency.

CONCLUSION

In Western countries, the LGBT world is in constant evolution. On the one hand, it is more and more homogeneous, thanks to the standardization and globalization of lifestyles, at least for the middle class. Some places, such as Mykonos in Greece, Ibiza in Spain, and Key West or Fire Island in the United

States have become favorite gay resorts. With the Internet, meeting people with the same interests is much easier than in the past. On the other hand, the lesbian and gay subculture appears more and more diversified—one could even say fragmented—along gender, class, age, ethnic, religious, or cultural criteria: gay bears, lipstick lesbians, uniform fetishists, and piercing addicts all have their own social networks and dating sites on the Web.[59]

Homosexuality has gained visibility in the media. Since the 1990s, with the introduction of gay and lesbian characters in successful shows like *Friends* or *Buffy The Vampire Slayer,* series have been entirely centered around gay (*Queer as Folk*) or lesbian (*The L World*) characters. In 2005, the movie *Brokeback Mountain* by Ang Lee, enjoyed a worldwide success. The popularity of house, techno, and electronic music, for which gay and lesbians clubs and DJs played a pioneering role, have attracted a lot of attention to the LGBT subculture from young partygoers. The same could be said about fashion, with the visibility of gay fashion designers (Gianni Versace, Karl Lagerfeld, Calvin Klein, Tom Ford), photographers (Herb Ritts, Bruce Weber), and the display of a more androgynous appearance by young urban metrosexuals. Apparent progress can also be a matter of sheer opportunism: business companies and advertisers are eager to target what they see as sophisticated consumers with high purchasing power (pink marketing); producers take care to avoid controversy and entertain an image of political correctness by including a gay or lesbian person in their TV show; and movie and music video directors are all too aware of the titillating quality of girls making out on screen.

The change is real, even for traditional institutions. Universities offer courses and degrees in gay and lesbian studies, gender studies, or queer studies. Some Protestant churches now ordain lesbian and gay clergy and perform same-sex marriage ceremonies. In 2001, the mayoral elections of Klaus Wowereit in Berlin and Bertrand Delanoë in Paris proved that it was possible to come out as a gay man without inevitably endangering one's political carrier. Homophobia, however, has not disappeared. At school, at the workplace, in the streets, or even within the family, women and men are regularly verbally or physically assaulted, even murdered, because of their sexual orientation. Everywhere, hetero-sexism is institutionalized by laws, language, and social structures. The fight for full equality and recognition goes on.

CHAPTER FOUR

Sexual Variations

GERT HEKMA

By the time of the Great War, most perversions had received names and been described in the medical literature of the fin de siècle. In various editions of Richard von Krafft-Ebing's *Psychopathia sexualis* (there were seventeen German editions between 1886 and 1924), more and more so-called perverts got the chance to tell their sexual stories. After the author's death in 1902, later editions were published by Alfred Fuchs and Albert Moll, both well-known specialists in the nascent discipline of sexology. Other doctors followed suit in their discussions on sexual variation, most notably in Germany, Austria, and France. Henry Havelock Ellis wrote the standard English study on sexuality, which included delineating sexual perversions.[1] The main variations discussed in this literature were homosexuals, uranians, or sexual inverts and sadists, masochists, and fetishists, while the exhibitionists, voyeurs, necrophiles (corpse lovers), coprophiles (scat lovers), zoophiles (animal lovers), and many other erotic specialties received less attention. In the beginning, the term "sexual inversion" included homosexuals, lesbians, and transvestites, with the latter given their own separate place in the work of Magnus Hirschfeld, *Die Transvestiten* (1910), the topic indicated in the subtitle, the "Erotic Drive to Change Clothing." The book included cases of men who would today be called transgenders, since transsexuals only became namable after sex change operations started in the 1920s. The grouping of homosexuals included pedophiles and ephebophiles (men who love prepubescent and adolescent boys, respectively). According to Hirschfeld, 5 percent of homosexual men were pedophile,

FIGURE 4.1: Narcissism. Both infantilism and narcissism were attributed to the perversions. This image is of a classic narcissist from the 1920s. From the Berlin Institute of Sexual Sciences. In Magnus Hirschfeld, *Geschlechtskunde* IV. *Bilderteil* (Stuttgart, Germany: Püttmann, 1930).

45 percent ephebophile, 45 percent preferred men their own age, and 5 percent were gerontophile (lovers of the elderly). Such specializations, of course, also exist among heterosexuals and lesbians.

As the title of Krafft-Ebing's book indicates, all these perversions, including homosexuality, were framed as psychiatric disorders. Nowadays, homosexuality is no longer a perversion nor a paraphilia (pseudo-Greek meaning "next to love"), the new word from the 1960s for perversion that did *not* include homosexuality. All the paraphilias remain part of the psychiatric handbooks except for homosexuality, which was promoted to normalcy in the United States in 1973. Although many new names (cordophilia for bondage or asphyxiophilia for sexual strangling) have developed since World War II, notably by John Money and his students,[2] the main and best-known terms date from the period just before 1900. New and less academic terms have developed more recently like mud wrestling, watersports, pony-play, balloon fetish, or fat admiration.[3]

Although the *Psychopathia sexualis* paid attention to lack of sexual desire, as well as strong sexual desire (called nymphomania for women and satyriasis for men), these behaviors were never recorded as perversions that were defined as aberrations in the aim of desire—meaning the object was not simply coitus with the other sex. Because many perversions could also be a part of normal sexual practices such as love bites or a predilection for certain underwear, psychiatrists differentiated between perversity, where the special desire was an addition or a prelude to the sexual act, and perversion, where it was the central aim. The masturbator or onanist was rarely included among the perverts, although self-stimulation was generally seen as a vice and a cause or result of psychic aberrations. Oral and anal sex in heterosexual relations may have been frowned upon or seen as sinful from a religious perspective, but they did not attract much attention from doctors.

This chapter will examine pedophilia, bestiality, sadomasochism, fetishism, exhibitionism, and voyeurism. Homosexuality is discussed in another chapter of this volume, and although the word "transsexuality" suggests a sexual content, it is more about gender than about sexuality, so that will also be set aside except to say that the most interesting aspect of transsexuals and even more so of transgenders is the gender indeterminacy of the persons—this makes it difficult to put them and their lovers in straightforward categories of homo- or heterosexual. Transgenderism not only defies gender, but also sexual dichotomies. We do not even have terms for the lovers of transgenders, the men and women who are attracted to men who look like women or to women who look like men.

Twentieth-century studies of sexual perversions are quite rare, and mainly we have to rely on medical studies for the earlier period. Recently, more information has become available because those people committing acts regarded as sexually perverted have started to speak out for themselves; their cases are no longer accessible merely by way of psychiatrists or journalists who report on sex crimes. The development of their perversions was quite different for each one of them, dependent on contents and contexts.

My own view on these sexual variations is straightforward. No sexual relation is morally wrong as long as it is not abusive, which means that it does not go against the wishes of the partner. Regarding pedophilia this raises the question of the age at which youngsters can give consent and, regarding bestiality, whether or not animals can do so. On the first point it is essential that young people learn at an early age what it means to be sexual citizens in order to prepare them for their sexual life so that they can engage with these pleasurable exploits consciously. There is no specific age at which this happens, but it is usually experienced sometime at the beginning of puberty. In cases of bestiality, abuse should be forbidden and nonabusive forms allowed. Some people claim animals can express their consent through their behavior, but to discuss such consent seems overblown compared to the nonconsensual mass murder of animals for the meat industry (see further discussion later in this chapter).

LOVE OF CHILDREN AND ADOLESCENTS

Pedophilia is defined in academia as the preference for prepubescent children, while ephebophilia stands for the love of adolescents. Most often both are grouped together under pedophilia, especially in the media and by the general public. Although the definitions may seem clear-cut, the age limits of childhood, adolescence, and adulthood are much less clear. These ages change throughout time, so the age at which girls start to menstruate has gone down by about 20 months in the twentieth century, from around 13.5 to 12 years. Moreover there is a large individual variation in biological development from around 8 to 16 years. Sigmund Freud assumed all children start as polymorphous-perverse beings.[4] According to him, the question of the age at which children are socially ready for sex depends to a large degree on both their sexual education and their erotic development. Often, moralists defend the idea that children are, and should remain, innocent. However, considering the widespread availability of erotic material involving sex scenes and the human capacity to sexualize all kinds of objects and situations, the idea that children are kept innocent is unrealistic and counterproductive. Youths became excited by devices to prevent masturbation, or by being punished by flogging, or by seeing others being treated so. Because children will later have to operate as sexual citizens, they need to be prepared for that role by enhancing their sexual knowledge and addressing their intellectual curiosity, not by maintaining their innocence and forbidding them access to sexual knowledge. Sexual education is food for thought, as eighteenth-century libertines said, and thus ideally serves educational purposes; children's curiosity stimulates intellectual development and critical thinking about themselves and the world.

Prior to 1800 in the Western world, relationships between adults and children of both sexes were taboo. However, in many countries, sexual acts with children were not always made into a specific crime as in general the legal focus was on sodomy and on extramarital and noncoital sex. Since children were not married, sex with them would be legally prohibited under fornication and sodomy laws, since these acts were outside the bounds of licit marital sex.

Only in the nineteenth century were laws on the age of sexual consent properly developed. The French Penal Code of 1810 forbade rape, public indecency,
and bringing minors under the age of twenty-one into habitual debauchery,
which meant prostitution (although the jurisprudence sometimes included
plural or longer-standing adult-minor sex relations). In France, the age of
consent was set at eleven years of age in 1832 and at thirteen years of age in
1863. In the Netherlands, the age of consent was set at sixteen years in 1886
for both sexes. The Netherlands was the first country to create different ages
of consent for homo- and heterosexual relations, setting them respectively at
twenty-one and sixteen years in 1911. Such very different ages of consent tied
to legal provisions created different definitions for sexual autonomy of children and for pedosexual relations. These legal ages are of course elusive tools
that have little to do with the sexual realities of adolescents and create incoher-
ent age lines. They may permit sexual relations between two minors that are
criminal the moment one of them becomes adult. They inevitably produce an
unrealistic dichotomy between innocent children and knowing adults.[5]

The differentiation of sexual relations between minors and adults was not
a big issue in the early twentieth century. The work of Freud was criticized not
because he discussed desires or real sexual relations between young and old,
but because he made clear that young people are sexual beings from birth.
Oscar Wilde was considered the embodiment of evil as a sodomite, not because the street urchins he had sex with were male adolescents. André Gide
was demonized as a homosexual, not because of his pedophile interests. He
was still awarded the Nobel Prize for Literature in 1947; it is unlikely he would
have received it today. Men who were persecuted for public indecency faced
no stiffer penalties for having sex with youngsters—unless it fell under age of
consent laws. Rather, abomination was heaped on effeminate homosexuals, or
on young male prostitutes, who turned their bodies into a trade and who sometimes robbed or blackmailed their clients. The art work of Wilhelm von Gloeden
and his colleagues was printed in male love journals such as *Der Eigene* and
was pedophile in modern terms, but they faced rejection because the pictures
showed male nudity, not because they were of adolescents. Von Gloeden was
not demonized as a pornographer; his pictures were published in art magazines
and adulated by the rich and famous of the fin de siècle. Thus, we can see that
the interest of homosexual men in boys was not specifically differentiated from
their interest in men, and the men they were attracted to were also often heterosexual men. Queers were simply weird people to whom many sexual and social
ills could be attributed. They recruited boys to fill up their ranks, and they were

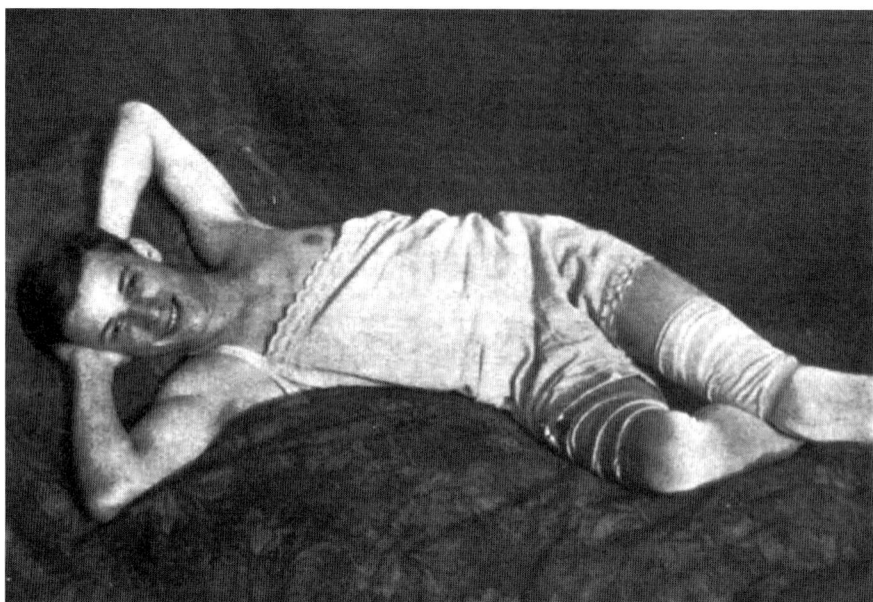

FIGURE 4.2: Picture illustrating both female underwear fetishism and love for adolescents. From Institut für Sexualforschung Wien (Hrsg), *Bilder-Lexikon der Erotik*, Bd III-1: *Sexualwissenschaft* (Vienna: Verlag für Kulturforschung, 1930).

accused of being weak, untrustworthy, effeminate degenerates and traitors of the nation. They endangered family life and reproduction because, notwithstanding the abjection homosexuals inspired, it was felt that their lifestyle was so attractive that straight people might easily fall into it.

Heterosexual pedophilia remained largely unmarked because it was seen as part of family problems that were the focus of social institutions, such as youth care and psychiatry. For a short period in the late nineteenth century, the authorities showed concern about incest but preferred to protect the nuclear family rather than its (incest) victims and saw sexual abuse of children as something done by perverted strangers. Nonetheless, incest of fathers with their daughters was very common and often seen as part of the cramped social conditions of the working classes.[6] When incest occurred in the upper classes, it met with a culture of silence or, at best, with recourse to psychiatric help for the abused, rarely for the abuser—as in Freud's Dora case.[7] Heterosexuals often had access to pedophile relations by way of the family in the form of incest; this was typically covered up to protect the honor of the family.

Another reason sex and love relations between adults and youngsters created less panic than they do today is because children were seen less as the precious angels they have become in recent years. Remarkable in relevant sexological literature is the idea that women were having sex with adolescents more often than men—according to Stekel, more boys were seduced by women, than girls by men.[8] He refers to Havelock Ellis's statistics that showed similar conclusions, but regrettably, these are without references. These woman-boy relations were part of a traditional sexual culture where older women—aunts, female teachers, prostitutes, spinsters—sexually initiated boys.[9]

Not all incest was heterosexual. Fathers, grandfathers, uncles, and brothers also sought sex with their younger male family members. Spanish author Juan Goytisolo describes in his autobiographical *Coto vedado* (1985) how his grandfather had sex with him in his youth. He speaks of these incidents in neutral terms, showing that not all incestuous relations had to have negative results. Such relations were portrayed in very positive terms by François-Paul Alibert in his *Le Fils de Loth* (1998, *The Son of Lot*, written in the 1930s) which opens: "Two young men romp on the beach. They are beautiful, they love each other. The one asks the other a question: 'Who has initiated you into love?' The answer comes uneasily: 'My father.'" This son was amorous of his father and particularly fond of his penis.[10]

Since World War II, there have been several periods of moral panics regarding child sexual abuse and lust murder in the Western world. The first major panic took place immediately after World War II as part of the moral reconstruction of Western societies. In the United States, it preceded the crusade against homosexuals and communists in the McCarthy era. The panic about child abuse and lust murder had not as yet become full-blown attacks directed against pedophiles specifically, but instead saw attacks against perverts in general. The sexual psychopath laws that many U.S. states subsequently enacted targeted, in addition to child abusers, gay cruising and other forms of sexual aberration. In fact, most victims of these laws were not child abusers or lust murderers (because their crimes were already covered in existing laws) but instead other innocent perverted acts that had not been criminalized before.[11]

The major novel on heterosexual pedophilia, and for some the best book of the twentieth century, was Vladimir Nabokov's *Lolita*, published in an English version in 1955 as one of the many scandalous books of Parisian Olympia Press. The book was forbidden in France and the United States for some years after its publication, but eventually its literary value was acknowledged, censorship laws were alleviated, and the book became available for the general public. Its main character, Humbert Humbert, seduces the nymphet Lolita, and marries her mother in order to stay near the girl. After the mother dies, he sets off with the girl on a tour of the United States and kills a rival for her affections while at the same time giving ironic comments on the United States.

During the 1950s, pedophiles became differentiated from homo- and heterosexuals in two ways. First, new European age of consent laws not only tended to distinguish between gay and straight sexual relations with minors, but created a category for pedophiles, who became the real sex criminals. Already in the 1930s and 1940s, Denmark, Switzerland, and Sweden had replaced general laws that criminalized all sodomitical acts, with age of consent legislation that decriminalized homosexual sex but criminalized pedophilic sex. Countries like the Netherlands, France, and Belgium had no general criminalization of homosexuality and produced specific homosexual age of consent laws in 1911, 1942, and 1965, respectively. These countries saw an ongoing differentiation between pedophiles and gay men, following arguments within the worlds of justice and psychiatry. Pedophilia, which had often been presented as a homosexual preference, became differentiated from it.

There were several reasons for mixing up pedophiles and homosexuals. In gay history many examples had been given of boy love, most famously seen in the form of ancient Greek pederasty. Establishing a higher age of consent for homosexual than for heterosexual sex simply had the effect of creating more gay pedophiles. Heterosexual pedophilia came in the form of incest, because it was so prevalent in families. Moreover, boys were taught to be sexually more curious than girls, and many homosexual men were available to offer them the opportunities for sexual exploration. Thus gay pedophilia is another example of how men created greater sexual opportunities among each other than they did with women in heterosexual spheres. Boys had more possibilities to learn how to be sexual beings, while girls were compelled to learn the opposite—how *not* to have sex, how *not* to become sluts. The reason for the new attitudes toward sex between youngsters and adults was a growing rejection of inequality in sexual relations from the 1950s on. It led to an increasing rejection, even demonization, of pedophilic sexual relations.

Second, from the late 1950s on, pedophiles began to organize and split off from homosexual organizations. Meanwhile, homosexual organizations became eager to get rid of pedophiles within their groups, as they wanted to be respectable and make clear they were not supporting child abusers. It was around this time that a revolution (see this volume's Introduction) took place in concepts and practices of sexual desire based on the idea of sexual inequality—sexual desire could only ignite between opposite poles—toward a new ideology that stressed the need for equality or sameness in sexual relations. The homosexual rights movement had always integrated men with interests in adolescents as well as straight men, such as sailors and soldiers, but now they stressed that modern homosexual men were not effeminate or pedophile and had no interest in normal or heterosexual men or in boys. Homosexual men developed into modern gays who adopted a masculine identity, were each other's equals, lived in couples, and had interchangeable sex. In the late 1950s, *Vriendschap*, the journal of the Dutch homophile movement COC (Cultuur en OntspanningsCentrum, Centre for Culture and Recreation), changed from a distinctly pedophile to a more masculine imagery. Homosexuals were the winners in this sexual revolution, but other sociosexual desires based on inequality fared much worse: pedophilia, prostitution, and bestiality all continued to be taboo acts, while traditional heterosexual marriage based on male privilege and female obedience came under critique.

In the Netherlands, two men began a campaign to defend the pedophile cause. Psychologist Frits Bernard (pseudonym Victor Servatius) founded the publishing house Enclave, which produced boy love novels and studies, while lawyer and later state senator for the Labor party Edward Brongersma (pseudonym O. Brunoz) became the intellectual champion of pedophilia. Both men contributed as editors of the COC journal, and became the main stimulus for pedophile emancipation, hoping they could follow in the steps of the successful example of gay emancipation. Brongersma also contributed as a successful political lobbyist. Both men were also active as producers of pedophile studies, and Bernard wrote two novels.

In the 1970s pedophile groups and journals started up all over the Western world: the North-American Man-Boy Love Association (NAMBLA), British Paedophile Information Exchange (PIE), and the Dutch Society for Sexual Reform hosted national and international conferences on the theme. These attracted mainly men interested in boys, while the other variations (lesbian and heterosexual) remained largely absent. In the Netherlands these pedophile groups met with some success. Social workers, a main psychiatric organization, and the chief of the Rotterdam vice squad all supported their claims for a lower age of consent and for acceptance of pedophiles whose relations with minors would often be innocent. These spokespersons attributed more damage to police inquiries into pedophilic relations than to these relations themselves. In 1977, the Dutch Center for Mental Health issued a report that supported these claims.

Apart from diverse, small, and dispersed groups of pedophiles, journalists, philosophers, film makers, and novelists also discussed the theme of child sexuality and adult-adolescent relations in various ways. The German anarchist Peter Schult and the French novelist Tony Duvert (the best gay writer according to Edmund White, brought to silence because of the demonization of pedophile love), who wrote *Quand mourut Jonathan* (1978) and several other novels and two books of essays, described and vigorously defended boy love, while his compatriot Gabriel Matzneff was more oriented toward girls. The angelic Hervé Guibert combined the themes of boys and cruelty and became famous because of his autobiographical writings on AIDS. The Deleuzian philosopher René Schérer (1974) endorsed the sexual rights of children and described, already before Foucault, the panoptical system, but in this case the school was the prison and the victims were the pupils. His apprentice, best friend, and close collaborator Guy Hocquenghem wrote the novel *Les petits garcons* (1983) on the first large pedophile scandal in France, in which both men were implicated, together with France's minister of culture, Jacques Lang, and many others. Several French academics and artists edited the book *Crazy of Childhood: Who Is Afraid of Pedophiles*, which would be totally impossible a decade later.[12] The U.S. writer Matthew Stadler continued to produce a

FIGURE 4.3: French book cover of *Crazy of Childhood: Who Is Afraid of Pedophiles* (1979). Collection of Gert Hekma.

steady stream of steamy novels that depicted boy-man relations, such as *Alan Stein* (1999).

In the 1980s, the climate changed completely. The rising demonization of unequal age relationships led to moral panics, first of abuse of girls by male family members, in particular fathers, and subsequently of abuse of both girls and boys by unrelated men who would come to be seen not only as sexual child molesters by the general public but also as potential lust murderers. In the United States, then also in western Europe and Australia, pedophile scandals became the regular fodder of the media. In many cases, such as satanic abuse accusations, no evidence was ever produced—the imagination of youngsters led to many false accusations, while police investigations sometimes ran out of hand because of community pressure, and as a result innocent men were accused of the most unimaginable sex crimes. Although some pedophiles are considered monsters, there is no reason to classify all older/younger sexual relationships as abusive. But the politicians followed the hue and cry from the media, especially after the scandal of the Belgian Dutroux case in 1996 in which a married heterosexual man (who allegedly had no special interest in girls and did not consider himself a pedophile) abducted both young women and girls because they were easy targets for him. The subsequent Stockholm World Congress against Commercial Sexual Exploitation of Children (August 27–31, 1996) put the issue high on the agenda—children being defined as under 18 years.[13] Pedophile priests and the hypocritical Catholic sexual morality were the next major issue to arise, particularly in the United States and Ireland.[14]

Many countries once more tightened up their laws on age of consent and child pornography, including virtual material depicting imagined children. Before the 1990s, the main objection to child pornography was that children were abused in its production and that child porn leads to child abuse. While before the 1990s, the possession of single samples of such material was not illegal, afterward any ownership of child porn was deemed a serious criminal offense. French scholars Marcela Iacub and Patrice Maniglier have pointed out that the percentage of prisoners for sexual crimes in the United States and France have more than quadrupled over the last thirty years, from about 5 percent to 20 percent.[15] In the United States nowadays, about two million persons are registered as sex criminals. There are more sex crimes, and, moreover, definitions of such crimes have been broadened and penalties have become stiffer. A large proportion of these men are prosecuted for crimes related to pedophile issues, they face the harshest penalties, and run high risks of being murdered in U.S. prisons (http://www.geocities.com/voicism/harm-master.html). Psychiatric programs targeting pedophiles in some countries make it impossible to ever get out of prisons and asylums if the perpetrators do not show regret for their sexual preferences. The pedophile has become the scapegoat of modern times, making reasonable discussion about pedophilia (or even discussions about the positive sides of the sexual life for youngsters) impossible. A Dutch pedophile group that started a political party of mutual love and liberty faced general and immediate demonization; some politicians even asked that the party be forbidden and that the founders be placed behind bars—thus denying even the cherished freedom of expression in liberal states.

LOVE FOR ANIMALS

Until the 1950s, bestiality remained a common sexual practice and was frequently prosecuted in court in the countries that criminalized it, such as Austria and Germany. Grassberger found some fifty prosecutions for sex with animals per year in Austria in the period between 1923 and 1965.[16] Most of those incriminated were male adolescents who received no punishment, as the courts considered it a minor crime. In the beginning of the twentieth century, about half of the about 500 annual prosecutions under the German paragraph 175 (counter-natural intercourse) were for bestiality, with the other half for homosexual practices.[17] Criminalization of sex with animals fell under antisodomy laws in countries with those provisions, including Austria, Germany, the United Kingdom, and Scandinavian countries.[18] In other countries, bestiality could be prosecuted as public indecency or cruelty against animals depending on the situation, but in fact prosecutions rarely happened in this period. Kinsey reported that 8 percent of the males and 3.5 percent of the females in the United States had had sex with animals once or more.[19] Most men ejaculated, while only 0.4 percent of all women experienced orgasm. Half of the farm boys had erotic experiences with animals, half of those to orgasm. Of course, none of these people created social movements at that time; in most cases it was a very individual experience in the countryside.

In nineteenth-century France, some bordellos and sex theaters had shows in which prostitutes had sex with animals such as dogs or donkeys. In Thailand a century later, sex between women and dogs was a specialty on offer. Anecdotal evidence in the recent past states that some Mexican bordellos organized competitions for prostitutes to see who could receive the biggest horse or donkey dick, but this may be urban myths—not uncommon with stories about extreme sex.[20] So what is the object of desire for the public: the prostitute, the animal's penis, or the humiliation? In recent years, some Danish farmers have made their farms into bordello's where clients can have sex with animals, and they seem to operate successfully.[21]

Although concrete data are rare, it seems likely that the prevalence of bestiality diminished after World War II. With the movement of people from the countryside to cities and towns, the strong diminution of people working in agriculture, and easier relations between young men and women, animals became less prominent in the sexual practices of Westerners. The trend seems to reflect that of homosexual emancipation: fewer men have gay sex, but the decreasing number that continues to practice it makes it into an identity, creating a lively sexual culture that sees more sexual activities among gay-identified people, more than they had before, when homosexual encounters were not exclusive to a homosexual minority. Prostitution seems to follow the same pattern. Similarly, people with a zoophile interest now see their predilection more as an identity and have started to organize themselves as animal lovers. They may not create a subculture, but they do have networks and Web sites that accommodate their preferences. One of them wrote a kind of bestial coming out book, *The Horseman* (1994), under the pseudonym Mark Matthews.

Notwithstanding the modernization of sexual cultures, some men and more boys continued to have sex with animals. The French-Algerian pederast poet Jean Sénac, who grew up in Oran in the 1940s, describes his early sexual experience with a chicken that did not survive his desires: "I penetrated. Warm! Good. A bit difficult. Warm. The shit. Fascinated. At the same time afraid, ashamed. I went in it, slowly, awkward. The point of my thing right into it. A rim of pleasure. Warm and like a skin that replies."[22] Marie-Christine Anest studied how male youngsters in Greece continued to have group sex with animals and with each other as forms of sexual initiation.[23] British Metro (November 16, 2006) reported the arrest of a man who had sex with a dead deer (bestiality plus necrophilia), and the question was whether the act fell under existing legal regulations.

The legal persecution of zoophile acts decreased, as such activities were taken less seriously. Most countries decriminalized bestiality—Sweden in 1944, West Germany in 1969, and Norway in 1972. Countries that followed the French Penal Code of 1810, including Spain, Italy, the Netherlands, and Belgium, had already abolished the crime in the nineteenth century. In all these cases, it coincided with the decriminalization of homosexuality, as both were punishable under the crime of sodomy, buggery, or counter-natural intercourse; homo-anal and bestial practices had always been criminalized together under such biblical laws, although hetero-anal sex most often received no

attention from police and the judicial system. In most cases the decriminalization of bestiality occurred without discussion. In Canada, Australia, the United
Kingdom, and half of the U.S. states, sex with animals has remained illegal
under different titles (http://www.lectlaw.com). With the growing movement
against sexual inequality, of which the pedophiles were the first main victims,
animal lovers now also face growing animosity toward their sexual pastimes.

New laws against sex with animals have recently been enacted or proposed.
France criminalized "maltreatment of a sexual nature" in 2004 and the
Netherlands made bestiality and bestial porn punishable in 2008, while
Sweden intends to do the same. Animal rights movements have been especially
strongly opposed to animal abuse and engage in coalitions with American Republicans, orthodox Christians, and Labour parties. The Dutch parliament
was in favor of such laws; the former minister of justice had opposed because
of their futility, but the present minister of justice was eager to follow the vox
populi—both being Christian-Democrats. Midas Dekkers stated: "As long as
neither partner suffers, there is in fact no possible form of sex that is sick, bad
or insane."[24] So far, there appears to be few reasons to criminalize bestiality,
since the data support the idea that some animals like such sex. When there is
harm or violence undertaken against animals, existing laws on animal abuse
can be used for criminal prosecution.

It was during the sexual revolution that bestiality received more attention,
and a few books on the topic were written, while pornography of sex between
animals and humans became more widely available. The leading Dutch porn
producer of those years, Wilhelmus, produced a book titled *Bestialiteit*[25] with
stories of zoophile love and mainly illustrations of sex between women and
various kinds of animals: mainly dogs but also a donkey, a cat, a bear, a gorilla,
and a cow.

That love for animals can be mutual has not only been shown by the
Horseman but also in real cases; one Australian woman was killed by her
pet camel when he jumped onto her for sexual congress.[26] A more common
example of dogs loving humans is evident all over when dogs mount the legs
of humans; they can also be taught to have sex with male and female humans, sometimes preferring it more than with their own species, particularly
when they have lived more closely with human beings than to their own kind
in their early years.[27] Voyeuristic zoophilia arises when people like to watch
animals having sex, a popular theme in nature documentaries and zoos. People
pretending to be animals, as in the cases of plushies and furries, is not considered real bestiality. The same is true for horse and pony play, erotic pastimes
that take various forms, of a master riding his human horse, or the human

ponies, alone or with others, being harnessed to a carriage. Often, the idea is about humiliation, which can be extended by means of breaking, feeding, or whipping them, putting them in a stable, having horse races, or selling them. Leather shops sell stirrups, pig masks, and dog collars, but the real material bought from specialized horse shops can be more exciting. Perversions are often mixtures of various fetishes, and these examples form a bridge between bestiality and sadomasochism.

SADISM AND MASOCHISM

In the first editions of his *Psychopathia sexualis*, Krafft-Ebing discussed lust murder, and in 1890 he coined the terms "sadism" and "masochism" after the names of author and philosopher Marquis Donatien A. F. de Sade (1740–1814) and his contemporary, Leopold von Sacher-Masoch (1836–1895). The latter had taught at the same university that Krafft-Ebing left in 1889 for Vienna. In fact, Sade was rather more of a masochist than a sadist, but because most people read his work as an exemplifier of sexual violence, he became marked as a sadist. Sadism became the preferential term for sexual pleasure derived from other people's pain, and masochism became the reverse. The pain can be mentally or physically inflicted. Krafft-Ebing realized that sexual violence was not always undertaken against the wishes of the victim but that there was also a substantial group of people who enjoyed sexualized violence, both as presumed victims and as perpetrators. The lust murderer became established as a different type of pervert than the sadomasochist, but it was the male masochist who became the figure of most medical discussion. According to the doctors, female nature was obedience and male nature dominance and no further explanation was necessary. The female sadist was thought to be more a figure of novels and erotic imagery, la belle dame sans merci.[28]

After the publication of Krafft-Ebing's work, there developed a lively medical literature on sadism and masochism, while the work of Sacher-Masoch inspired a parallel literature. This Austrian author created, with his *Venus in Fur* (1870, German original), a tradition of dominant women in fur who enslaved men, often using the contractual arrangements Sacher-Masoch loved as material proof of his submission. While Sade was a masochist and a passive sodomite, Sacher-Masoch also had his queer side by enjoying a severe beating by a male servant who had been requested to do so by his mistress.

Twentieth-century Germany, France, and England (and to a lesser extent in other European countries) developed a sadomasochistic subculture with its own bordellos, small networks, pseudo-serious studies, novels, and illustrative

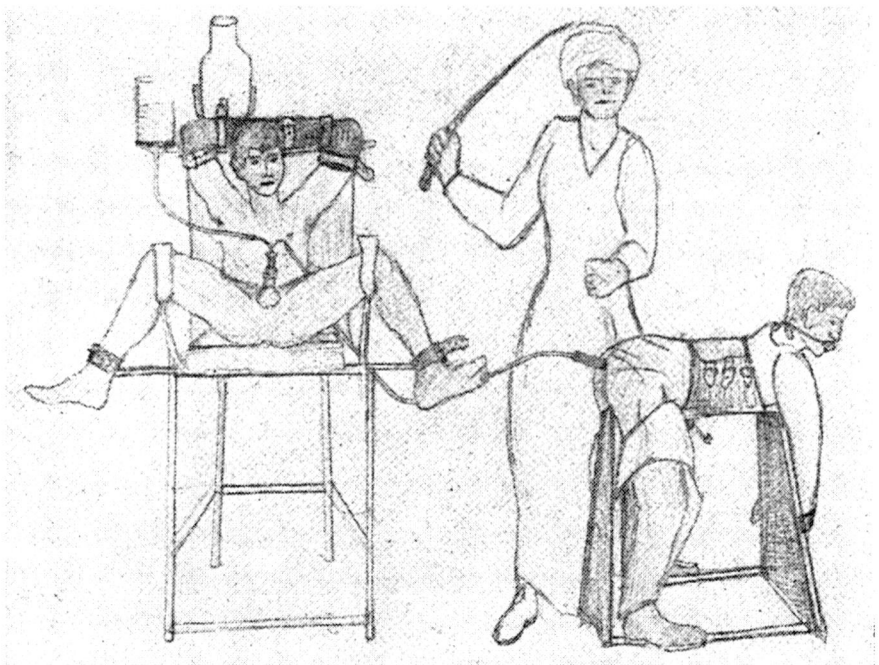

FIGURE 4.4: "Own composition." Self-made illustration by a masochist of bondage, piss sex, and flagellation, part of a series that accompanied his case study in Stekel's book on fetishism. In Wilhelm Stekel, *Der Fetischismus* (Berlin: Urban & Schwarzenberg, 1923).

material. Little is known about real-life experiences, because most of the books only depict imaginary situations and rarely the concrete lives of sadomasochists. Thanks to police reports, the existence of bordellos and specialized prostitutes are known, and some pictures show the abundance of sex toys in houses where sexual cruelty was being performed. In the life of Arabist and military man T. E. Lawrence being beaten up by a soldier was a very private practice, while Marcel Proust described gay sadomasochistic scenes in rather prudent terms. The German Ernst Schertel specialized before 1933 in the publication of kinky books that were abundantly illustrated with homemade porn and pictures of sexualized cruelty in times of war, or from the history of Roman games, slavery, corporal punishment, or police investigations.

The French, who had been leading in the field of kinky literature, continued to do so. After Sade, Rachilde, and Proust, authors and painters connected to the surrealists like George Bataille, Pierre Klossowski, and Pierre Molinier produced such material. Bataille's most famous work was on Sade and Gilles de Rais, in his novels, and also in *Eroticism* (1957, original in French) and *The*

FIGURE 4.5: Book cover *The Confession of a Whip Kid*. In Ernst Schertel, *Der Flagellantismus als literarisches Motiv* (Leipzig, Germany: Parthenon Verlag, 1930).

Tears of Eros (1961, original in French). Jean Genet described in his novels, plays, and movie *Un chant d'amour* (1950) scenes of cruelty and homosexual passion in a world of sailors and prisoners. Pauline Réage, pseudonym of Anne Desclos (1907–1998), scandalized the world with a novel of total female submission to men, *L'histoire d'O* (1954), which made people wonder whether a woman could write such books of sexual slavery. Twenty years later such books would become more general, while academic studies of sadomasochism have remained scarce until this day.[29] The punk and gothic scene copied many symbols, toys, and clothing styles from the kinky scene for their own presentations. Finally the fashion world took on symbols of leather and sadomasochism in the 1990s, with Jean-Paul Gauthier taking the lead.[30]

After World War II, the sadomasochist subculture saw some new developments. The major one was in the gay world, where a specialized sadomasochist scene started that included wearing leather of male icons such as motorcyclists, pilots, and police officers, all replacing the more feminine fur. This kinky scene started in tiny bars in the major gay capitals of the world like London, Amsterdam, Los Angeles, New York, Chicago, and San Francisco from the 1950s on. Specialized porn was being produced next to the bars, first in the more common male physique journals that sometimes added a slice of sadomasochism with whips and cages and later as a separate product. From the 1950s onward, Tom of Finland was the illustrator of this leather world, with his over-masculine soldiers, sailors, and police officers and their victims. In the 1960s, Larry Townsend emerged as the subculture's main author with porn novels, sadomasochist imagery, and *The Leatherman's Handbook* (1972). Leather shops became another addition to this kinky world after 1970. At the same time, the gay leather men started to join in motor clubs that organized events and parties where kinky sex could be practiced in couples and as groups. The leather bars of the 1970s attracted a public from all over the Western world—like the Argos in Amsterdam, the Anvil and Mineshaft in New York, the Gold Coast and Touche in Chicago, or the Keller in Paris. Some clubs became world famous for their specialized parties, such as the Catacombs in San Francisco, the Vagevuur in Eindhoven, Netherlands, the Boots in Antwerp, or the Laboratory in Berlin. The connection between leather and sadomasochism was strong, although not all leather men were into sadomasochism, and some aficionados rather liked military uniforms. Specializations started to develop, like mud games or fist-fucking. This world of promiscuous leather men was more severely hit by AIDS in the 1980s than were other gay subcultures, and sadomasochism was itself unjustly seen by some in the beginning of the epidemic as especially risky behavior. Many sadomasochist practices are in fact totally safe because they do not include penetration or exchange of sperm and blood. In the 1990s, the gay leather world started to bloom once more, and, apart from the leathery oldies, new groups made their appearance on the kinky scene: first skinheads, then men into rubber and later sport fetishists. Sometimes the dogmatism of an older generation devoted to black leather clashed with a younger generation that enjoyed a broader spectrum of colors, kinky fetishes, and sex games. Although sadomasochism remains the most visible subculture among gay specializations, this preference never made it to the ever-growing series of acronyms of the gay movement. In fact, all perversions are excluded from this short list of respectability, even among radical queers.

For some gay people the desire for violence and the symbols of gay-oppressive institutions (army, police, prison, sports) made them reject kinky practices, certainly when some men showed Nazi symbols on their outfits. Although some non-kinky people accused the leather world of being desirous of the enemies of the gay world, most kinky men know the problems and risks

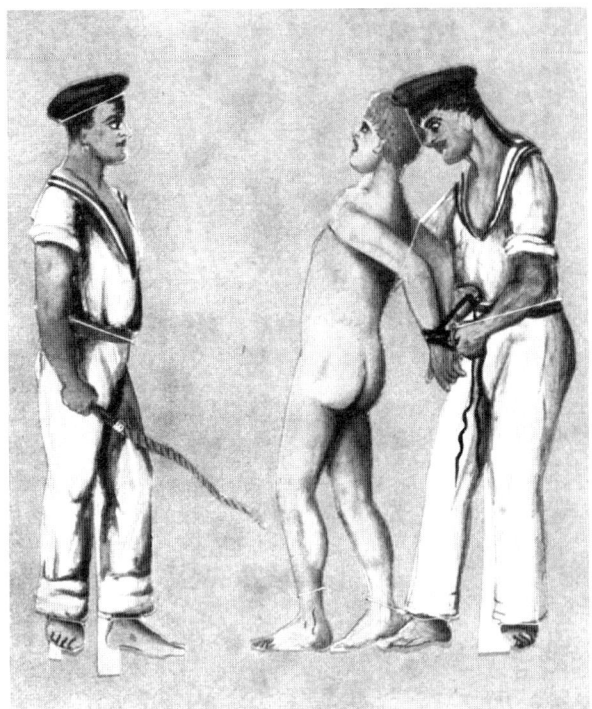

FIGURE 4.6: A masochist artist illustrating his desire to be beaten by sailors. He left his collection after his suicide to the Berlin Institute for Sexual Science. In Magnus Hirschfeld, *Geschlechtskunde* IV. *Bilderteil* (Stuttgart, Germany: Püttmann, 1930).

of sexualized violence so well that they would be the last to promote cruelty or right-wing macho attitudes.

The lesbian sadomasochist world is much smaller than its gay counterpart, but notwithstanding its size, it played a major part in the 1980s sex wars that feminists fought with each other. The issues were pornography, prostitution, and sadomasochism. Some radical or vanilla feminists (only interested in soft forms of sex) stood up against feminists who supported prostitution, pornography, and sadomasochism or who engaged in these practices. In the late 1970s, several lesbian women organized their own leather events, created journals such as *Off Our Backs,* and had their own group, Samois, which edited the collection *Coming to Power.*[31] This book became an object of controversy, and other feminists published *Against Sadomasochism.*[32] These cultural wars abated in the 1990s, but the opposed parties have not changed their minds. Leading feminists Patricia (now Patrick) Califia and Gayle Rubin, who defended sadomasochism, continue to write stories, novels, and studies on the topic. By now the kinky women have a rather steady place in the lesbian world.[33]

With the advent of the sexual revolution, heterosexual sadomasochists started to organize and created organizations such as the Eulenspiegel Society of New York.[34] Compared to the gay organizations, these groups were more timid and remained rather invisible. Also, because no parallel bar culture developed for straights, they resorted to general rather than specialized sex toy and clothing stores, or found their favorite toys on the Internet. The heterosexual organizations mainly catered to the sexual pleasures of their members, not unlike their gay and lesbian counterparts. A major difference between gay and straight sadomasochists relates to the circumstances of their coming out as lovers of sadomasochism. Gays, like transgenders, have already gone through a coming out as homosexuals; thus their engaging with sadomasochism is a kind of repetition of this first outing that takes less effort—an exertion straight people have to surmount for the first time. They often have in fact no desire to come out as sadomasochists because they restrain their pleasures to leisure time and private spaces and live respectable lives with their perversions in the closet.

The sadomasochist community nowadays prefers the acronyms BDSM, which means bondage and discipline, dominance and submission, and sadism and masochism (or slave and master). Some people reject the term "sadism" because they consider the Marquis de Sade a sex abuser. Older terms like algolagnia (pleasure in pain) have been forgotten.

The leather scene has been a target of police surveillance. On April 10, 1976, the Los Angeles police raided a slave sale in a gay bar, which was not even a serious sadomasochist occasion but rather a fundraiser.[35] The main scandal in Britain in 1990 came when police prosecuted fifteen gay men for running "a perverted sex ring" including public sex and so-called violent abuse of each other.[36] The police had accidentally found a videotape with the sex games these men played in various set-ups. Although all the sex had been consensual and no unwilling third party had been witness to these acts, the courts prosecuted them in the Spanner case for injury and public indecency, defined as cases where more than two persons participated (Spanner being the code word for the police operation). The court declared that in sports like football and boxing where the violence sometimes leads to serious damage, it is permissible, but ruled against it in cases of sex play.[37] Even the European Court for Human Rights decided that the United Kingdom had the right to prosecute these pastimes under the existing legislation, thus denying civil rights to sadomasochists. In reaction, Spanner committees were set up in Britain, France, and the Netherlands to defend the rights of kinky people. In general they quietly stopped functioning as no more large-scale cases were prosecuted, no other issues came forward in the media, and kinky symbols, toys, and clothing became fashionable. There is, however, no doubt that kinky fetish clothes as fashion statements say little about the social acceptance of kinky desires. Most people continue to find the combination of pain and pleasure a bit odd. The lack of acceptance of this sort of fetishism shows itself in the fact that most people hide their kinky fetish clothing in nonsexual formal occasions. Social prejudice is reflected in lack of tolerance as seen when a Belgian judge lost his job after the police discovered his wife was a practicing masochist, with him as a helping hand, despite the fact that they only did so only in private spaces. Sadomasochists irregularly face persecution in the United States because of their erotic interests, and most cases regard child custody battles after a divorce.[38] In 2008, there was a proposal in English parliament to criminalize extreme pornography, which would include sadomasochistic material.

The main problem sadomasochists now face is the rejection of the inequality of their relations and the question of consent. They do everything to explain their sexual relations as being consensual—the performance beforehand agreed upon and using a given code word agreed upon between them in order to stop the act. A better defense could have been discussing liberal and democratic ideals of consent and equality in the political and the sexual field. While they may apply in the first, they have different meanings in the second.

Notwithstanding continuing taboos regarding sadomasochism, there is a substantial group of people who enjoy and admit to kinky desires—according to sex surveys, about 10 percent of the adult population with more men than women. Because of the lack of visibility of sadomasochism, it is probable that many people do not even realize their desires in this direction, or repress them because of the taboos.

FETISHISM

Fetishism is diverse in its manifestations. The word stems from religious studies and is used by Karl Marx to describe the overvaluation of products under capitalism and by Alfred Binet for sexual theorizing.[39] It can refer to a special interest in body parts, sex acts (anal, oral, kissing, licking), clothing or clothing material (uniforms, underwear, silk, satin, fur, leather), personal characteristics (boyish, dominant, unmasculine), or situations (bedrooms, beaches, barracks, dark rooms). This definition is so broad that it includes all sexualities; for Binet it is indeed an alternative to the term "perversion." There were no criminal laws that persecuted such desires. The main reason why fetishists came into contact with the police was because they stole their beloved objects from shops, clothing stores, or other places. They rarely harassed people in order to fulfill their sexual desires. The most famous cases concern thefts of underwear, and the very specialist men who cut off the pigtails of women.[40] Because most fetishist desires are explored in private environments, often without partners, they rarely came to the attention of the police or subsequently of psychiatry. Fetishist desires often involve contemporary fashions, so their expressions easily fit into normal sex practices. In Paul Garnier's *Les Fétichistes* (1896), the author, who is a doctor, discusses mainly heterosexual men who go for female clothing (underwear, silk, various bonnets) and bottoms while the homosexual objects of desire, the topic of half of the study, are boots and genitals. In Wilhelm Stekel's *Der Fetischismus* (1923), the same fetishes are present with handkerchiefs, shoes, clothing and special materials, and (missing) body parts,

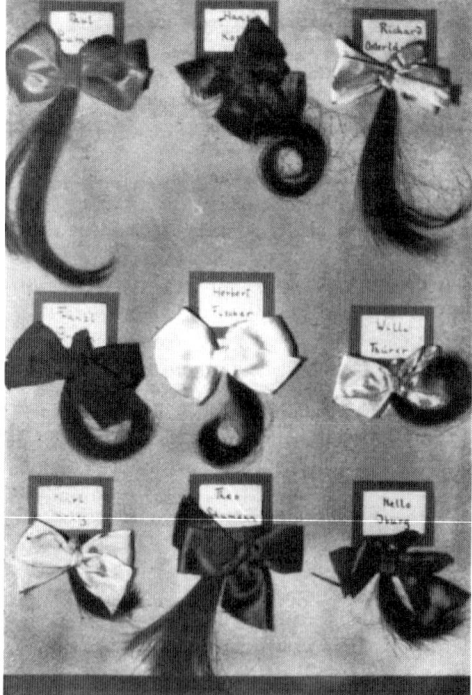

FIGURE 4.7: Collection of an apparently homosexual hair fetishist from a police archive. In Leo Schidrowitz, ed., *Sittengeschichte des Laster* (Vienna: Verlag für Kulturforschung, 1927).

while his cases are often mixed up with sadism, masochism, transvestism, or homosexuality and sometimes lead to theft. The close connections with fashion make these fetishes obvious indicators of hang-ups of particular periods. Very little historical study has been done on these topics. Why the preferred clothing in the sadomasochist subculture changed from fur to leather after World War II cannot be easily answered. The best suggestion lies in a change of fashion, where gay men developed an attraction to masculine bikers and pilots (often the type of soldiers who had fought in World War II) who were dressed in leather. Postwar film stars like James Dean or pop stars like Elvis Presley who wore leather became icons for the new subculture.

The sexual revolution of the 1960s brought a proliferation of sexual styles for men: from blue jeans and leather to more androgynous long hair, flowery shirts, and shiny material. This was a short-lived period of variety for men, as they quickly went back to jeans, boots, short hair, and white t-shirts. On the heterosexual side, there is a great variety of fetish styles, materials, and acts ranging from punk and gothic to soft and shiny female underwear to corsets and body parts. Europeans like big breasts while Brazilians show a greater interest in bigger bottoms. The gay leather scene went from leather to rubber and developed in the 1990s a wider range of fetishes.

Fetishism receives much attention in postmodern cultural studies because it connects sexual pleasure to the social world where the fetish is picked up, and breaks down the dichotomy of homo- and heterosexual and of subject and object. The fetish is an erotic internalization of an outside world and, when it refers to human objects, breaks them down into their constituent parts, such as breasts, penises, hair, or toes; characteristics, such as boyish, perverse, kinky, beautiful; or their covering, such as clothing and shoes. This specification makes general terms like male and female, homo and hetero, unnecessarily general because desires are about quite particular objects or fetishes—including acts like oral, anal, and kinky sex or situations like bedroom and beach that go beyond a certain person. According to McCallum the fetish challenges "the domination of the subject over the object" and eliminates the need for other subjects.[41] The fetish is not abstract but instrumental and stimulates agency and passion. It goes beyond the genders of sexual object choice. Different from love, sexual pleasures most often have a concrete and accidental aim that the concept of fetish captures nicely. Apter can thus say that "[f]eminist essentialism is resisted through fetishism's implicit challenge to a stable phallic referent."[42]

In this broad postmodern perspective all sex is fetishist. Queering sexuality could then break down the homo/hetero dichotomy and make everyone realize that sexual objects are more specific than male or female, and preferences more

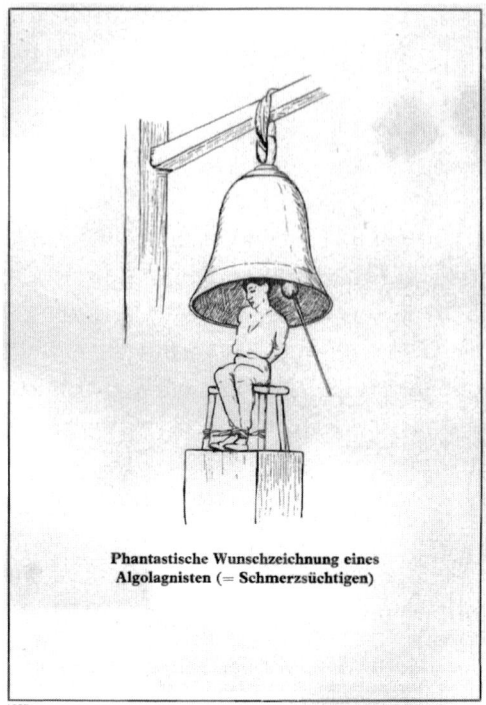

FIGURE 4.8: Subtitle reads "Fantasy Illustration
of his Wishes by an Algolagnist (pain desirer),"
here focusing on bondage and the sense
(hearing) with no phallic referent. "Algolagnia"
was used around 1900 as another term for
sadomasochism. Picture from the Berlin Institute
of Sexual Sciences. In Magnus Hirschfeld,
Geschlechtskunde IV. *Bilderteil* (Stuttgart,
Germany: Püttmann, 1930).

detailed than homo or hetero. Queer could better refer to concrete erotic spe-
cialization than to abstract generalization in terms of human or bisexual. Few
people realize the specialness of their preferences—indeed less than 10 percent
will admit to fetish interests. In a recent Dutch sex survey, 10 percent of the
men and 4 percent of the women did so.[43]

EXHIBITIONISM AND VOYEURISM

Exhibitionism is a much persecuted perversion but less demonized than pedophilia. Only in the late nineteenth century, when nude swimming and bathing

went out of fashion and nudity became totally excluded from public life, did exhibitionism come into existence as a sexual preference and rose to the forefront of police and psychiatric attention. Laws on public indecencies that had been used against sex in public places were now more often used against flashers.[44] Exhibitionism is a prime example of the social construction of social identities and mental disorders, as is its opposite agoraphobia (fear of public places). While some perversions, such as bestiality, fell into relative oblivion, and while others could expect a more humane attention in the early twentieth century, exhibitionism saw an increased pursuit by police and psychiatry. Yet the intensive interest of the authorities had little effect on prevention of such behavior, and exhibitionists were continually arrested, imprisoned, and hospitalized as repeat offenders. The continued attack on these offenders has been of no help for exhibitionists or their assumed victims, nor has it aided the prevention of escalating sex crimes of exhibitionists.

An interesting study of the exhibitionist groups that existed in the Netherlands since the 1970s shows that exhibitionism has many more guises than the typical figure of police and psychiatry reports.[45] These groups attracted women who were into nude dancing; a man who wanted to sit like a prostitute in his window in the Amsterdam Red Light District; a woman who, passing trucks in her car, shined a flashlight on her denuded genital region; and a transgender who lifted up her skirt while standing alongside a highway where no car could stop. The man in his window or the woman dancing in the nude were of course no nuisances to the public; rather, they were tourist attractions, which shows how contextual such a problem is. Exhibitionist groups were helpful in providing the troublesome exhibitionists with other outlets and showing them ways to avoid persecution by the authorities. Now nudism in some places has become more acceptable, the exhibitionists of the old days are losing their aura of abjection, and other perverts like pedophiles and zoophiles are taking their place.

The same has happened with the voyeurs of old days who had so little chance to enjoy seeing the nudity and sexuality of others. Peeping Toms, who peered into the windows of the homes of people expecting to see a live show, were generally disappointed. But with all the erotic material available nowadays, in the media, on the Internet, and in peepshows, the voyeur who pestered his neighbors has now become the client of the commercial sex industry or more quietly visits nudist beaches and camps.

Most sexual acts are a combination of exhibitionism and voyeurism, of showing and looking. As with fetishism, they are so general that it is hard to call them perversions. Both sexual variations of exhibitionism and voyeurism are main topics in postmodern studies, where the gaze has become a central theme, the ideal subject of communication and television studies. The media and the Internet have made all humans into voyeurs. We now look, sometimes in admiration, other times with abjection, to the many forms of eroticism that are available. People visit sex sites but still more look to erotic imagery on the news; from the stories of Clinton with his oral sex and sperm spots on skirts to the more sinister pictures from Abu Ghraib, the sexual fascination of the Western voyeur has never been restrained to the vanilla images of mainstream pornography. It has always included the more bloody material of Roman gladiators, Christian paintings of crucified and martyred saints (with Saint Sebastian becoming a sadomasochism icon), or the disaster paintings of Andy Warhol. Voyeurs may become the model type of sexual identity because of Western puritanism: looking at a screen, resisting their own desires, and rarely creating sociosexual pleasures.

CONCLUSION

There are many more perversions than those mentioned here. A general theme in all these sexual variations is that they address and often bridge major social dichotomies: of consenting adult and innocent child, of human and animal, of subject and object, of body and soul, of showing and seeing, of pain and pleasure, of consent and coercion, or even of life and death, as in necrophilia.[46] They have an interest beyond the concrete sexual practices that they refer to. They run from simple fantasies to murderous acts—not different from normal sexual preferences that neither offer protection against the violence nor conflicts of social life. It is better to acknowledge than to condemn or pathologize them as has been the tradition in religious, political, legal, and medical thinking. They are an intrinsic part of human culture.

CHAPTER FIVE

Sex, Religion, and the Law

DANIELA DANNA

In the past, the concepts of crime and sin were, to a large extent, concomitant, but since 1920, the concepts have been increasingly divergent. Now crimes can be committed that are not considered sins, and sins might take place that are not considered criminal acts. Overall, there has also been a definite and obvious reduction of the number of sexual behaviors that are considered deviant or forbidden. This shift has resulted from changes in society, most notably as a result of the promotion (in discourse and in practice) of differentiated forms of sex. This was mainly effected by the sexual liberation movements, which have acted with different degrees of success, worldwide. The exception to this overall change was the period between 1930s to the 1950s, when the general movement was regressive, reverting to past ideas. Another regressive trend has been the recent raising of the age of consent toward the late teen years in some countries. Furthermore, in many places since the new laws of the 1990s, prostitution has been increasingly restricted. Meanwhile, several countries have introduced stricter laws on pornography, especially child pornography (involving minors), now banned throughout the European Union.

Sexuality has entered the public sphere, and the debates have grown and become increasingly explicit, both in the mass media and in academic discourse. The following description of laws and religious prescriptions in the realms of sexuality dating from 1920 onward must start with a tribute to a short-lasting revolutionary change in the laws of the Soviet Union. In the 1920s, the most egalitarian and liberal legislation about sex and gender was the one put in place by the Bolsheviks, who created equal rights for men and women, the possibility of divorce and of abortion on demand, the cancellation of the crime of sodomy, and free circulation of birth control techniques. The traditionalist Orthodox Church was denied any influence in political life. This followed the ideas of those revolutionaries, who considered sexuality an area where the proletarians, and the people in general, should be liberated from religious, legal, and social constrictions. Other communist ideas deemed utopian by the external and internal politico-economical dynamics in the Soviet Union, together with the legislative framework inspired by the sexual liberation aspiration, did not survive the construction of a Stalinist totalitarian regime of the 1930s, and was reversed in the most repressive sexual-legal system, rivaling that of Nazi Germany.[1]

Apart from these two shifts, the period from 1920 onward has generally been characterized by waves of legal change that have progressively touched upon various countries, from the more to the less rich and industrialized, following citizens' mobilization to defend individual liberties from the core to the periphery of the West. Churches of every denomination took up the task of defending the traditional family and the repressive sexual order, allied with authorities of countries who wanted to limit the sexual options open to citizens to procreative sex only: the source of power lay in its numbers for the nation. As an exception, we can list the activities of the Protestant denominations in the German Democratic Republic (GDR), who were in favor of sexual minorities; they gave their approval of contraception, divorce, abortion, and homosexuality during the tenure of the GDR, as did Reform Judaism, Anglicanism, and some Catholic bishops.

In this period, there are two distinct clefts in the area of sexuality. The first is between Catholic/Orthodox and Protestant countries. Protestantism, in sharp contrast with its original Puritan aspiration, spearheaded legislative innovations in reducing the connection between crime and sin, while Catholic and Orthodox churches did not. The second cleft is between Eastern and Western blocs during the cold war period and its aftermath. The Eastern Bloc, with its expansion of the Soviet sphere of influence after World War II, applied the restrictive Stalinist code and strong political control over its citizens' movements, with a rhetoric on women's equality that did not endorse any social changes (except in waged labor). Nevertheless the change toward a more liberal stance in recognizing a private sphere, where sex (with birth control) could be practiced by consenting adults, had already started in the 1960s. Before its demise in 1989, though, the Eastern Bloc did not practice or openly discuss the changes of mores of the sexual revolution that had happened in the West in the 1960s. Nor did it take notice of the instances of feminism from the 1970s on, but maintained a traditional legislation on sexuality, especially on LGBT issues.

The objects of investigation in this chapter will be to discuss the laws regarding marriage and divorce, abortion, birth control, prostitution (these issues were hotly debated especially in the first part of the period under examination), sexual violence, age of consent, LGBT issues, and artificial procreation (all but the age of consent were more typical of the public debate that started around 1968). Religious prescriptions and changes will be dealt with in the final paragraphs, presenting the (not always) changing views of the different confessions on sexuality.

MARRIAGE AND DIVORCE

At the beginning of the modern age, in all countries throughout the world, adultery committed by a woman was legally considered more serious than adultery committed by a man, whose act could be sanctioned only if he maintained a concubine. So called honor crimes were condoned: indeed, the legal battle for equality between the spouses and for the abolition of honor crimes has lasted well into the twenty-first century. Another tradition which affected most societies was the prohibition of marriage between different social groups: followers (or those officially labeled as such) of different religions or persons belonging to a different race (also officially codified) could not marry. German Nazi and Italian Fascist discriminations against Jews and non-Aryans, and southern U.S. antimiscegenation laws are the most prominent examples. These marriage prohibitions signified class separations in a social hierarchy and were eventually prohibited by the United Nations' Universal Declaration of Human Rights (UDHR) in 1949. The UDHR inspired postwar constitutions, which included those of the defeated Axis powers, but U.S. marriage prohibitions in its Southern states lasted until 1967. Under the apartheid regime in South Africa, marriage between people registered as belonging to a different race was a crime from 1949 until 1985; between 1950 and 1985, even sexual relationships between different races were punished as crimes.

Another area of change around sexuality and the law is the admission of separation and divorce, now universally accepted in the West. The United States and other English-speaking European countries, including Australia, New Zealand, and Canada, based their law along the lines of the British and have allowed divorce since mid-1800, the Netherlands since 1811, France since 1884, Germany since 1900, and the Scandinavian countries from around 1920. No-fault divorce was introduced in Britain in 1969, in the United States from the late 1960s, and in France, Germany, and the Netherlands in the 1970s.[2] Portugal already had a divorce law allowing divorce by mutual consent in 1910, but this was overturned by the Salazar regime in 1940.[3] Republican Spain allowed divorce in 1932, but Franco overturned the law in 1939, and divorce was not reintroduced until after his death in 1981. Italy removed gender inequality in cases of adultery in 1968, introduced divorce in 1970, and established equal rights among spouses in 1975. The last Catholic country to introduce divorce was Ireland in 1996. Orthodox Greece introduced gender equality and no-fault divorce in 1983.

The Soviet Union introduced equality between spouses and divorce as a feature of socialism in all the Eastern Bloc that came to be governed by communist parties after World War II.[4] Gender equality is now promoted by the United Nations, in virtue of the Convention on the Elimination of All Forms of Discrimination against Women (1979) and the Beijing Platform for Action (1995), including equal rights to divorce, individual consent to marriage, rejection of the marital exception to rape crimes, and introduction of laws protecting wives from abuse by husbands, including injunctions against an abusive husband in order to prevent him coming near his wife's home or workplace. These legislative changes are being implemented worldwide.[5]

Up until the revolution in sexual mores of the 1960s and 1970s, the conservative objective of the protection of the family also meant discrimination of lone mothers and their children. The so-called Magdalenes in Ireland were forcibly interned in monasteries well into the postwar period: these were girls who had illegitimate children and who were then forcibly separated from their babies. The legal situation of illegitimate children (and the social situation of their mothers) slowly improved everywhere, reaching a nearly full equality with the legitimate children during the 1970s.

ABORTION

Abortion has become legal in the West in nearly all countries (if only to save the life of the pregnant woman, as in Ireland), except for Malta, which retains a total ban.[6] The legalization of abortion has been a long process, articulated in various phases, starting with the initial admission of therapeutic abortion—in other words, only in cases to save the life of a pregnant woman. Permission followed for abortion in cases of rape, then abortion in case of generic danger to the physical or mental health of the pregnant woman (but only with medical authorization), and, finally, abortion on request; the latter was allowed with the proviso of a time limit, before the embryo becomes too big for simple interventions, and before it can survive out of the womb. Now, with the advances of medical reanimation techniques, grounds have been found for a reopening of the discussion about time limits, mainly instigated by the Catholic Church.

The situation from 1920 on was of total prohibition, with laws targeting both the woman and the procurer, often with harsher penalties against the latter. After World War I, in many countries nationalism had strengthened prohibitions of both abortion and birth control, in order to replace the death toll of the war and in order to repopulate, and thus dominate, the colonies. The Soviet Union legalized abortion in 1920, but in 1936 criminalized it again. This was the same year in which the Spanish Republic legalized abortion on demand, together with birth control, but this position was overturned after a few years, when Franco defeated the Republic and restored Catholic Church

FIGURE 5.1: A Soviet poster warns of illegal abortions, indicating that illegal abortionists endanger women's lives, 1920s. In Institut für Sexualforschung Wien (Hrsg), *Bilder-Lexikon der Erotik*, Bd III-1: *Sexualwissenschaft* (Vienna: Verlag für Kulturforschung, 1930).

authority. Penalties were reintroduced, only to be removed with democratization after his death in 1975.

The Nazi regime introduced the death penalty for procurers in 1943 (the
Vichy regime had done the same the year before), but this was aimed at preventing abortion of Aryans, while abortion was rendered legal and even encouraged in the occupied areas in eastern Europe and even imposed on prisoners.
The anti-abortion legislation was extended to the states of the Soviet Bloc
after World War II until 1955: the Soviet Union started permitting abortion on
broad grounds, recognizing the self-determination of women and wishing to
avoid health risks of illegal abortions. It was followed by all the other countries
in the next couple of years except GDR (1961), Yugoslavia (already legal in
1952, in 1972 extended to woman's decision), and Albania (1991).[7] The fall
in birth rate that ensued made governments tighten up the requests to concede
permissions to abort—and give more provisions to families.

The 1960s also started a process of change in the West. In England, the
Abortion Act was approved in 1967, allowing abortion with a medical prescription, but abortion had been tolerated since 1938, when a legal case
against a procurer was decided in favor of acquittal (*Rex v. Bourne*, the performance of an abortion on psychiatric grounds). In West Germany, abortion
was allowed in 1974 but only in cases of danger to the life of the pregnant
woman (the restriction was due to a ruling by the Supreme Court the following
year). In the process of unification, Germany reached a curious compromise:
with a law approved in 1995, abortion is still legally forbidden, but the courts
don't condemn it any longer. In the United States, a Supreme Court judgment
in 1973 (*Roe v. Wade*) was decisive, defending the right of the woman to decide on abortion in the name of privacy and personal freedom. Abortion is
also legal on request in Canada, the Australian Capital Territory, the Scandinavian countries, the Netherlands, Austria, Greece, Spain, and nearly all the
Eastern European countries, while in Poland, it is legal only to save pregnant
women's lives, and in Hungary for social and economic reasons. Abortion is
also allowed for social and economic reasons in Italy, France, Belgium, the
UK, Iceland, Finland, and some Australian territories, while the rest have more
strict regulations, like the law in New Zealand, where abortion is legal only to
preserve the health of the woman or if the fetus is impaired.

The timing has been complex: in Sweden, France, and Austria, abortion on
request was made available in 1975 but only after a long process of progressive
expansion of medical qualifiers. Both in France and Germany, famous women
signed statements admitting to abortion as a part of the feminist legalization
campaign. In the 1980s, Spain and Portugal legalized abortion but only in

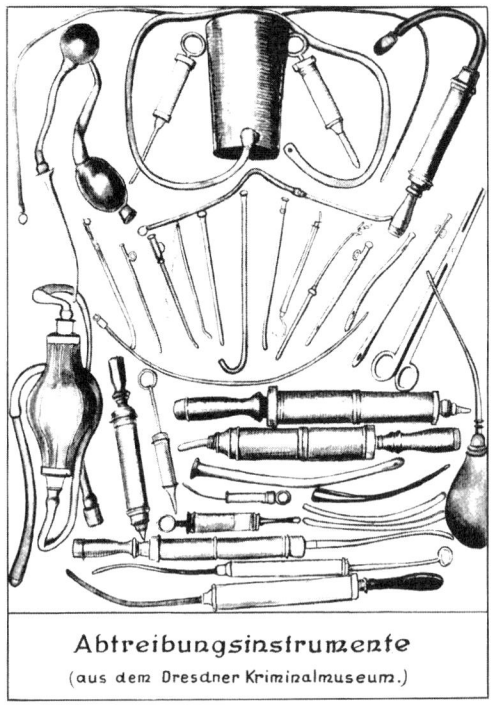

Abtreibungsinstrumente
(aus dem Dresdner Kriminalmuseum.)

FIGURE 5.2: Abortion instruments apparently seized by the German police, 1920s. In Magnus Hirschfeld, *Geschlechtskunde* IV. *Bilderteil* (Stuttgart, Germany: Püttmann, 1930).

cases of a risk to the health of the pregnant woman, of rape, and of fetal malformation. Belgium legalized abortion for social or economic reasons in 1990. In Switzerland since 2002 and in Portugal since 2007 it is now left up to the woman to decide. The most problematic countries are Ireland, where abortion is legal only in case of potential fatality of the pregnant woman, and Poland, where since 1993, abortion is permitted only for limited serious medical reasons and even then is sometimes denied by doctors.

In the 1990s, religious terrorist groups within the right to life movement started making attempts on the life of doctors carrying out abortion at clinics in the United States. Threats on women attending abortion clinics are also still being made in European countries such as Austria and Germany.

The invention in 1980 and the subsequent commercialization (first in 1989 in France) of an abortive pill, RU486, has stirred new controversy for the right to life movements, which tried to prevent countries from licensing the new drug. The process of approving the new drug has been completed in all countries except for Italy, Ireland, Portugal, Poland, and Canada (where its distribution was suspended in 2001 after one woman's death).[8]

BIRTH CONTROL

Birth control, together with divorce, was one of great controversies at the beginning of the twentieth century.[9] By the 1970s, the legal acceptance of its use was taken for granted. Birth control (and abortion) had been judged contrary to the military and economic interests of countries in the expansion of their population and had been effectively fought against right up until the years of the sexual liberation. France outlawed discussions of contraception and abortion in 1920, despite a very lively social movement in favor of birth control. As a part of the Stalinist backlash, divorce and birth control became less available in the Soviet Union in the 1930s.

In Protestant countries, the prohibition against contraceptives was cancelled in the period between World War I and II, when churches, too, changed their condemnation to acceptance. In 1938, Sweden withdrew the law forbidding contraception, which it had approved in 1910. The Italian Fascist penal code in 1930 prohibited propaganda that was in favor of birth control, though it left the condom industry alone since its products were indispensable for clients of prostitutes. In 1971, the Italian Republic Constitutional Court declared the prohibition unconstitutional. From 1935 to 1973, Ireland banned the sale of contraceptives and in 1944 banned Tampax, fearing that it would lead to the use of contraceptives; only in 1973 was the ban on contraceptives deemed unconstitutional by the Supreme Court. In France, contraception was permitted in 1967, and in Spain in 1978.

The commercialization of the contraceptive pill started in 1960 in the United States, making women's self-determination in matters of heterosexual sex and procreation a much easier accomplishment. In the course of the decade, the pill was introduced everywhere. In the Netherlands, birth control was a taboo subject before the mid-1960s but was then placed on the political agenda, with the result of admission of sale and publicity of its methods. At the end of 1960, in the UK, contraception was made available to unmarried women. Liberalization of contraceptives and abortion in the GDR dates from 1961, while Romania legalized birth control only in 1990.

Among the various methods used to prevent conception, voluntary sterilization was approved from the 1970s, beginning with northern Protestant countries (with the earlier exceptions of the United States and the Netherlands). It spread mainly in the United States, Canada, Australia, and Latin America. France approved it only in 2000, with a law that also mandated sexual education in all centers for the handicapped.

Eugenic programs (which had started at various times in different countries), had, by World War I, led to the mass sterilization of the mentally ill in the Scandinavian countries, Switzerland, Germany, and some U.S. states.

PROSTITUTION

During the late nineteenth century, regulations about prostitution discriminated heavily against the women involved. Social purity movements rose up to protest against the laws invoking their abolition. In the long run, the protests were successful: the first countries to abolish regulation of prostitution were those of northern Europe, starting with the United Kingdom in 1885, Norway in 1888, Denmark in 1901, the Netherlands in 1911, Sweden in 1919, and so on, with Catholic countries joining in only after World War II (France 1946, Belgium 1948, Spain 1956, Italy 1958) following the United Nations Convention for the Suppression of Trafficking in Women and the Exploitation of Prostitution in 1949. The legislation that took the place of regulation of brothels was called abolitionist and considered the exchange of sex for money *extra legem*: in other words, the law did not protect the contract, considering it invalid as contrary to public decency, but did not prohibit the act. What *was* prohibited were all forms of exploitation, which was loosely defined as taking part as third parties in earnings derived from prostitution: pimps were outlawed, as was providing any other kind of services to prostitutes, including renting a room or a house, living off the earnings of prostitution as lovers or adult sons, or providing lifts to working places. In some countries (UK, Denmark, Ireland) street soliciting was also forbidden. Only West Germany, Austria, Switzerland, and Greece retained the old regulations, while prostitution was prohibited in the Soviet Union, even in the absence of specific laws. Prostitution was considered a bourgeois vice with no reason to exist under communism.

The Nazis sent those prostitutes who did not want to be confined in brothels to concentration camps, a slow death sentence. After World War II, de facto prohibition was extended to the whole Soviet Bloc (Hungary already had prohibitionist laws). After 1989, the majority of Eastern European countries have adopted abolitionism, and toleration (with some exceptions, such as Latvia, which adopted regulation, and Lithuania, which adopted prohibitionism). The

United States never changed their prohibitions, with some exceptions at the local level, maintaining the spirit of the 1919 federal Standard Vice Repression Act, supported by local laws criminalizing every aspect of the sex trade (with the exception of Nevada). Portugal, too, had prohibited prostitution until 1963 and, until 1972, Canada maintained its laws prescribing the arrest of common prostitutes found on the streets, substituting them with a similarly repressive law against communication for the purpose of prostitution.[10]

Around 2000, a new model of regulation was introduced in the Netherlands and in Germany (and beforehand in 1984 in the Australian State of Victoria, later in other territories), which strived to consider prostitution as a trade in a nondiscriminatory way. These changes were applied only to citizens of these countries and of the European Union, but not to citizens of other countries. This, in effect, meant that this model made no change on the basic prohibition of exchanging sex for money by migrants, who were arriving in great numbers all over Western Europe after 1989. This meant that migrants were offered no protection; rather, their presence is contrasted by a more strict enforcement by the police of the general immigration rules, the laws protecting public decency, and the laws against people trafficking. Clients of prostitutes have been prosecuted in Sweden since 1999 and in Norway and Iceland since 2009, even if they do not infringe laws on the age of consent—generally set at eighteen for acts of prostitution in the abolitionist countries (where they have abolished regulations on prostitution) and regulationist countries (where they have retained laws against prostitution). The Finnish government is debating the possibility of introducing the same restrictive legislation.

SEXUAL VIOLENCE

The changes in laws and court practice on sexual violence took place during the 1970s, thanks to the activism of the women's movement. In many countries, the protection of the law was not accorded to the victim of sexual violence but was instead related to so-called public morals. The concept implied that sexual violence was to be repressed only in cases of public scandals. The idea that the rapist could escape judgment if he married the victim of his violence was replaced in law by the juridical concept of sexual violence as a crime against a person.

Court proceedings had previously been impeded by the scrutiny of the sexual morality of the victim; this discrediting practice was commonplace before the 1970s, based on the concept that a woman who had already lost her honor should not, and could not, be protected by law from sexual assaults (in some legislations, like that of West Germany, the supposed impossibility of raping a prostitute was explicitly written). These changes in law did not guarantee that court proceedings would restrain from attacks on the personal morality or sexual behavior of the accuser. In Britain, Italy, and Sweden, the persistence of this practice has been recently denounced.

International meetings sponsored by the United Nations from the 1970s onward expressed a common view, which is slowly entering legislations world-wide: laws must entail gender-neutral terminology, allow for recognition of sexual violence in acts other than penetration, and end the marital exemption from the crime of rape (based on the idea that marriage entails unconditional consent to sexual relations with one's spouse, known as conjugal duty). Recent laws also have attempted to outlaw honor crimes; introduce the specific crimes of partner battering, sexual harassment, and stalking; and introduce the possibility of protection orders by which a suspect is forbidden to come within a certain proximity of the victim. The 1993 United Nations Declaration on the Elimination of Violence against Women provided the basic reference document that ensures that these legislations are implemented, and is now monitored through reports form various countries and presented by a special rapporteur. The European Union is also pushing for recognition of the crime of sexual harassment in the workplace in all its member states, a process now on course.

AGE OF CONSENT

Statutory rape, too, is now the object of international pressure, seen in recent attempts to raise the age of consent. The Convention on the Rights of the Child (1989) states that the law must "protect the child from all forms of sexual exploitation and sexual abuse" and prohibits anyone from participating in "unlawful sexual practices." The convention agreed on eighteen as the appropriate age of consent (earlier for countries where the majority is attained earlier), though it says little else on the matter of sexuality. Nearly all countries worldwide have retained a lower age of consent, starting at twelve in the Vatican and thirteen in Spain, being the lowest in the West. In most European countries, the age of consent is between fourteen and sixteen, with few exceptions between sixteen and eighteen in the United States and Australia, and also eighteen in Malta. Some countries do not prosecute when there is less than 3–5 years difference of age between the partners.

There is a double trend evident: to raise the age of consent for heterosexual relationships, allegedly protecting even teenagers from pedophile relations;

while for homosexual relationships, where historically it was higher, to lower it in line with the corresponding heterosexual age, as a result of nondiscriminatory stances. Also, the legal majority has been subject to a lowering shift in all countries: generally from twenty-one to eighteen and exceptionally sixteen (Scotland, Western Australia) or seventeen (Queensland and Victoria). In many countries nowadays, there is no distinction in the age of consent between heterosexuality and homosexuality. In the period under examination, though, age of consent for same-sex relations was generally higher, coinciding with the legal majority at twenty-one or eighteen. In some countries (Germany, UK) after homosexual relations were decriminalized, the age of consent was set higher than the legal majority, at twenty-one. In France in 1942, a legal age of consent of twenty-one was introduced for both lesbian and gay relationships. Some countries did not prosecute homosexual relationships, nor discriminate regarding the age of consent.

In the Eastern Bloc, individual countries had different timings of the process. In the GDR, the age of consent was fourteen for heterosexuality, eighteen for homosexuality starting in 1968; Bulgaria also set different ages of consent decriminalizing homosexuality: fourteen for heterosexuality and twenty-one for homosexuality. Hungary lowered the age of consent for homosexuality from twenty (the age of consent that had been established with depenalization in 1961) to eighteen in 1978. Laws about prostitution usually set a higher age of consent in the case where a person had sexual relations in exchange for money than for unpaid encounters. This is also stated by the Palermo United Nations Convention against Transnational Organized Crime (2000).

LGBT (LESBIAN, GAY, BISEXUAL, TRANSGENDER/ TRANSSEXUAL) ISSUES

At the beginning of the modern age, same-sex love was generally forbidden by law only for males (Finland was an exception in including females in the law). This reflected an ancient custom of keeping regulation of women's behavior in the private sphere, through the authority of the pater familias (*famulus* in Latin means slave of the house and is the source of the word "family") with the right of the male protector to discipline his spouse, daughters, and servants, including by violent means if necessary. Only men were entitled to the public space, therefore the official prohibition regarded only sexual acts among men, with the law intended to preserve the family and to reinforce heterosexuality and reproduction in the interest of the state.

Also, transvestitism was forbidden and still is in many countries, at least in law; for example, in Italy the provision against transvestitism has recently been applied to transvestites working in street prostitution. Transsexuality, when it became surgically possible, was slowly allowed, with the first cases dating back to the 1930s. The protocols to reassign sex are rather rigid in many countries, but there is a movement to make it easier to register sex changes with the authorities, without having to go through any kind of surgery, and to consider sex identification a matter of privacy. Protocols exist, particularly in Anglo-Saxon countries, to surgically assign sex at birth to intersexed individuals, but these are also the subject of contestation by the intersexed movement.

Up until the 1960s, the majority of countries included an article in their penal code against same-sex relations, with the notable exception of countries where the Napoleonic Code was in situ, such as Italy. This was not an example of a policy of tolerance: the Italian authorities claimed that criminalization was unnecessary because of their insistence that same-sex relations simply did not take place, in spite of Italy's international fame as a gay paradise. Literary productions on same-sex love were condemned as obscene, as was the case in Britain with Radclyffe Hall's novel *The Well of Loneliness*, published in 1928. In revolutionary Russia, depenalization of homosexuality occurred with the abolition of the Czarist penal code, but by 1933 Stalin had recriminalized it. This persecution was matched by the Nazis, who that same year killed Nazi party leader Ernst Röhm, allegedly because of his homosexuality. Castration was performed in Denmark, the Netherlands, and many other countries as an experimental cure for sex crimes, with even worse atrocities committed in concentration camps. Gay victims of the Nazi regime received no compensation but were forced to continue serving time in prison in postwar Germany. The same happened in the Soviet Union, where homosexual men were sent to prison camps—about 1,500 each year in the 1960s—where they suffered greatly as a result of being at the bottom of prisoners' hierarchy. They were starved, forced to sleep outside the barracks, and raped and killed by the other prisoners, mainly to the indifference of the authorities. Lesbians were not mentioned in the Soviet code, and same-sex attraction in women was considered an illness to be confined and cured in psychiatric hospitals—or with sex reassignment surgery to become men. Lesbianism was not considered criminal, but it was seen as a disease—not as against the law, but as against nature.[11]

British courts condemned an average of 720 men yearly from 1920 to 1939. In Nazi Germany from 1920 to 1934, the average number was 700, but between 1935 (when the law against male homosexuality was extended to all sexual acts, not just sodomy) and 1939, there were more than 6,000 convicted each year. The Third Reich sentenced 50,000 men for homosexuality and sent between 5,000 and 15,000 to concentration camps, where they were often subject to medical experiments and other kind of tortures. The German occupation forces introduced an article in Dutch law forbidding all homo-sexual relations, while the Netherlands only saw the introduction of a higher age of consent in the penal code from 1911, from sixteen to twenty-one years. The extension of the law did not lead to more prosecutions.

In 1944, Sweden did just the opposite and cancelled its laws against male homosexuality. Other countries took some time to do the same: Hungary and Czechoslovakia (where lesbians had also been criminalized) in 1961, Britain in 1967, the GDR in 1968, and the Federal Republic of Germany (FRG) in 1969.[12] Against the trend, in 1960 France approved a law (the Mirguet amend-ment) defining homosexuality as a social scourge. The Statute of the Civil Ser-vants, the Labour Code, and the Renting Law, contained a morality (*bonne moralité* or *bonnes moeurs*) protection clause, implying that homosexuality should remain secret, in principle forbidding homosexuals to be public em-ployees. These discriminations were abolished in 1980. Albania criminalized homosexuality in 1959 and depenalized it in 1977, as did Yugoslavia—except that in some areas, it remained punishable. Poland was an exception in not adopting any statute against homosexuality and having the same age of con-sent for sexual relations of any kind—fifteen years of age. In the 1980s, in the West, only the Soviet Union and Romania continued to prosecute homosexual-ity (in Romania, this included the prohibition on both men and women from 1937) and only decriminalized it in the 1990s.[13]

LGBT issues have undergone a 180° change in the West.[14] Feminism in the 1970s influenced the rise of a gay and lesbian movement that obtained the protection of the law for one's sexual orientation from the 1980s on. The era of hostility against homosexuality has now ended in many countries, with the approval of laws actively prohibiting discrimination. Now the movement is fighting for equal rights, and a positive acknowledgment of homosexuality and homosexual relationships. LGBT movements in the 1980s have shifted from a negative battle against the penal codes to a positive battle to obtain anti-discrimination laws, now enacted in most countries (except for Eastern Euro-pean ones), along with the legal recognition of same-sex couples and families.[15]

Denmark opened the way towards the full equality of same-sex couples with hereerosexual ones, adopting in 1989 a law instituting registered partnerships. Other Nordic countries (the last was Finland in 2001) followed suit. This new institution is very similar to civil marriage (and growing closer), different in name but also because couples are still unable to get married in church (under discus-sion) to be jointly recognized as parents (now possible in Denmark and Sweden). Civil unions or legal recognition of same-sex cohabitations has been obtained in nearly all of Western Europe (Italy as an exception), as well as in some Eastern

European countries such as Hungary and the Czech Republic. After 2000, homosexual marriage has been made possible in some countries in the West, including the Netherlands, Belgium, Spain, Canada, Norway, Sweden, Portugal, some of the United States, the metropolitan area of Ciudad del Mexico, Argentina, and South Africa, where homosexuality is also specifically protected in the constitution.

Parental responsibility, a concept that derives from choice and cohabitation (different from parental authority, which is the legal institution that recognizes and limits the authority of the biological mother and father, and of the adopters) has been recognized for same-sex cohabiting partners who are parents— first in Iceland in 1996, and subsequently in the other Nordic countries, in the Netherlands, England, Germany, and Canada. The legal situation in the United States is a patchwork of advances and setbacks that change every day: Vermont and Connecticut have approved civil unions, same-sex marriage is allowed in Massachusetts and California, yet at the federal level, the Defense of Marriage Act (DOMA) in 1996 states that no same-sex marriages should be valid outside state jurisdictions. The U.S. president, Barack Obama, announced that he wants to get rid of DOMA. In 2008, a referendum blocked the Californian law on same-sex marriage. In some areas of the United States, adoption by foster parents or second-parent adoption is also allowed, as well as state recognition of same-sex marriage.

Among the least tolerant countries there have been positive changes, too: Russia decriminalized homosexuality in 1993, the same year as Ireland, preceded by the Ukraine (1991) and Latvia (1992).

ARTIFICIAL INSEMINATION

New medical techniques for artificial insemination, beginning in the 1950s, have been progressively placed under legal control, usually allowing only married couples to make use of them, as a way of promoting the traditional family. For example, in Austria only longstanding cohabiting or married couples can use artificial insemination techniques (1992); in the Czech Republic, this applies only to married couples (1992), in France, to cohabiting or married heterosexual couples (1994), and in Norway (1993) and Denmark (1997) to hetero couples and lesbian couples. Sweden approved a law in 1989 allowing only married or cohabiting couples to use artificial insemination techniques, and, in a unique case, the anonymity of the donors has been prohibited. Policies are usually left to the discretion of the individual clinics involved. Spain is the only country that wrote into its law that any woman, even if single, is entitled to have recourse to artificial insemination techniques. Some clinics in the Netherlands, in Belgium, in the UK, in Canada, and in some parts of Australia treat single women and lesbians in couples. Even before the new laws were introduced, tribunals attempted to repress the religiously contested practice of artificial insemination: an Italian court in 1959 condemned a woman for adultery, when she accepted artificial insemination by a donor's sperm.

SEX AND RELIGION

Traditionalism is a self-evident characteristic of all religions: the huge social changes in attitudes and practices around sex and sexuality in the twentieth century posed a big challenge to orthodox religions. With few exceptions, their response was to defend the "Ancient Regime." The most dramatic shift in thinking has been by some Protestant denominations, which have approved sex between nonmarried heterosexual couple as well as homosexual sex. This has been easier in Protestant denominations than in Catholic ones, as certain sections of the Protestant denominations are more democratic.

The belief in sexual sin is still prevalent among religious leaders, who generally take a moral stance in defense of the heterosexual family, and against what they consider sexual deviations.[16] Their aim, generally speaking, is to foster procreation and reinforce a hierarchical structure of family and society, with men at the top and women valued essentially as mothers. The Catholic and Orthodox churches still do not allow women to enter their ranks on an equal footing with men, and nuns remain at the bottom of the church internal hierarchy.

Catholicism

In 1917, the Catholic canonic law on abortion was codified with a prohibition on abortion declaring excommunication for all parties taking part in the act. The battle by the Catholic clergy in their so-called defense of life continues all over the world. The Catholic stance holds even in extreme cases, as seen in the cases of the nuns who had become pregnant after being raped in the Bosnian conflict in 1992, forbidden to request an abortion. In the encyclical *Casti connubii* (1930), Pius XI decreed birth control "shameful and intrinsically immoral" and a "criminal abuse." Paul VI reaffirmed the same opposition as to birth control and to techniques of artificial insemination and conception in his *Humanae vitae* (1968). Controversial bishops, such as Bekker of the Netherlands in 1963, have sometimes declared birth control a matter of conscience for the faithful; in this multireligious country, beginning in the 1960s, birth control, premarital sex, and homosexuality in steady relationships came to be widely tolerated by religious forces: Calvinists and Catholics agreed to constitute a private sphere of sexual morality for consenting individuals, while the state carried an obligation to protect people from violence and abuse of power and could take no moral stance.

In the United States in 1976, many bishops signed a letter supporting civil rights for gays and lesbians. In the Netherlands, a similar position was taken in 1979 by the Catholic Council for Church and Society. These positions were opposed by the Vatican, who also acted against the LGBT Catholic movement: in 1986 Dignity (a U.S. homosexual Catholic group founded in 1969) was refused access to any Catholic church following a pastoral letter on homosexuality signed by Cardinal Ratzinger, then head of the Congregation of Holy Faith. The pastoral letter refused recognition and use of premises to all groups who did not admit that homosexuality is immoral. An answer in defense of these groups came from individual U.S. bishops and all of the Dutch bishops, who authored a response to Ratzinger's document. In contrast with this rigidity in refusing homosexual behavior, transsexuality is accepted by the Catholic

FIGURE 5.3: Since gays and lesbians claimed rights, such rights have been controversial. Religious groups especially protested against sexual rights for women or LGBT people. Here is a demonstration of the Jewish Moral Committee at the Gay Pride Parade in New York, 1985. The posters declare that gays are perverts, homosexuality is an abomination, and refer to AIDS and sodomites. Photo: Gert Hekma.

Church, as it reinforces the rigidly polarized two-gender system. In the 1990s, there was a spate of sexual scandals on child sexual abuse committed by priests (the label includes post-pubescent teenagers), most notably in the United States and Ireland: it was later revealed that the church had merely moved the accused and the convicted priests to different parishes rather than expose them and allow their prosecution.

In contrast to Protestants, the Catholic popes have not yet given any approval of contraceptive practices (other than the rhythm method as Ogino-Knaus first described it in 1930). Nor have they approved of abortion in cases other than risk for the pregnant woman's life, of homosexual practice, of non-married sex, or of use of condoms to avoid transmission of illness. Sex is still viewed only as a means to procreation, with a slight addition from the Second Vatican Council (1962–1965) that allowed for sexual pleasure in marriage for the sake of the well-being of the couple. Divorce is not permitted, and Pope Benedict XVI has reaffirmed the refusal to give Holy Communion to divorcees. The Vatican Rota tribunal, however, can find ways to annul marriages, providing the couples can pay for it; or for royalty.

Pastoral practice by individual priests can be nevertheless very different from official doctrine. We Are Church, a democratization movement founded in Austria in 1995 and now diffused in eleven nations, is currently striving not only for the priesthood of women, but also for the recognition and blessing of same-sex unions, acceptance of sexual relations and marriage of clergy, and more democracy in the clergy.

Anglicanism

Divorce on grounds of impotence, frigidity, rape, desertion, adultery by the wife or adultery accompanied with cruelty of the husband had already been granted by 1920. Anglicanism accepted the use of birth control in 1930, when the Council of Lambeth presented both a favorable and a contrary opinion, leaving the choice to the conscience of the faithful. Family planning was agreed to by all Anglican bishops in 1958, starting a more open and accepting discussion on the matter the following year within the World Council of Churches, an assembly of Protestant confessions at Oxford. An Anglican priest who conducted the marriage of two lesbians in 1976 was admonished, but in 1979 the document "Homosexual Relationships" formulated an approval of particular conditions of same-sex sexual relationships, and in 1998 a statement was issued by the Lambeth Conference approving lay homosexuality while still refusing it to the clergy. The whole of the church did not agree: bishops from developing countries met at Kuala Lumpur and issued a different statement regarding promiscuity, denouncing all sex outside marriage, including homosexual acts and unchaste same-sex relationships. Controversy still rages: in 2008, two male priests celebrated their own civil union in the Church of St. Bartholomew the Great, one of the most famous English churches.

Protestantism

Nowadays most Protestants concur with civil legislation permitting abortion. The main exceptions are U.S. fundamentalists, who, since the beginning of 1980s, have turned to violence (including homicide) in order to stop the work of abortion clinics. The issue of homosexuality is generally accepted, depending on the presence and pressure from LGBT faith movements in the areas. The Evangelical-Lutheran Church in East Germany has approved of gay priests since 1983: its premises have been a harbor for homosexuals during the GDR regime. In the United States, there has been vast participation of LGBTs in congregations: more than 50 United Methodist congregations openly admit the LGBT faithful. Many LGBTs live among Quakers, where the religious community has consensually approved of their participation. There are also particular LGBT groups, like Integrity for Episcopalians, More Light for Presbyterians, as well LGBT denominations: for example, the Metropolitan Community Church was started in 1968 in Los Angeles and is now diffused in hundreds of English-speaking countries, as well as in Germany, France, Denmark, and Romania.

Lutheran and, in general, Protestant Dutch churches, approve and bless same-sex unions, while the Lutheran State Churches in Scandinavia are slowly approving homosexuality: first, by admitting openly gay and lesbian priests; second, by approving blessing of same-sex unions; and third, by discussing the possibility of opening up church marriage. In Sweden in 1996, a ritual of union has been invented for same-sex couples to be performed in church—no priest is forced to perform it if he or she disagrees with blessing homosexual couples. Norway State Church, the most traditionalist, does not allow homosexuality among its clergy yet, though in 2000 an openly gay priest was ordained, risking a splitting in the congregation. Some minorities are opposed to this: Indre mission, the fundamentalist branch of Danish Lutheran Church, and Seierkirke denomination in Oslo have both protested in public when the first same-sex unions were celebrated, as Methodists and Baptists did. A lesbian marriage was performed in an Evangelical-Lutheran church in Hamburg in 1984, a highly contested event at that time: in the course of the 1990s, synods in various part of Germany have approved the recognition of same-sex couples. Even in Italy, the Strasbourg Parliament resolution of February 1994 promoting equality of rights for same-sex couples has been supported by pastors of different denominations.

Orthodox Christianity

Orthodox Christians accept divorce and contraception as preferable to abortion, which they still consider a sin. Orthodox churches are supporting the antigay mobilizations in Eastern Europe (sit-ins or attacks against Moscow Gay Pride). The stance in Eastern Europe is most traditional, reflecting the fact that sexual liberation movements and feminism did not spread in the 1960s and 1970s as in Western European countries, mainly because of political repression in those countries.

In Russia, a coalition of Orthodox conservative groups, chauvinistic organizations, and the Communist Party started an anti-pornographic crusade in 1991, followed by attacks on women's reproductive rights and sex education in 1997. No legal changes ensued.

Judaism

Judaic law accepts divorce, objects to male homosexuality, and considers abortion a crime *en par* with homicide. Since the 1970s, in individual cases where interruption of pregnancy is medically advisable, rabbis can obtain permission for an abortion if there is a danger to the life of the pregnant woman. Reform Judaism permits same-sex union ceremonies and has many openly gay and lesbian faithful, especially in the United States.

Islam

Migration has brought to the West a variety of other creeds, among which Islam is the largest in numbers. Islam lacks a central authority, so moral stances can vary from one religious authority to the other. Family Koranic law allows many inequalities between the sexes. It accepts divorce, contraception, and abortion but only if the pregnant woman's life is at risk. Homosexuality is not permitted. A "Muslim Manifesto for Liberties," signed by intellectuals and compiled in France in 2005, has exhorted Muslim countries to introduce equality between the sexes and tolerance for homosexuality in the name of laicism, as other authors are doing in the name of Islamic feminism—while in the Netherlands, the imams remain clear in their statements against homosexuality.

INTO THE FUTURE

The period since 1920, as described in this chapter, shows an expansion of liberty in sexual expression, both in the civil and penal codes and in religious prescriptions. This development (with exceptions and variations) of course, shows that the general movement is clearly progressive. From 1920 to 2010, there has been a time of improvement in the living conditions in the West. But the present economic and ecologic crisis is a potential threat for the future, and might well reverse the balance of powers that has seen an expansion of sexual expression and freedom. The sociological school of the analysis of world systems foresees in the near future—with a social equivalent of the Prygogine's catastrophe theory in an upcoming turning point of the capitalist world system, which will reach a bifurcation point resulting in either a move toward greater freedom or a move toward a new state of oppression. And it will depend on the power of the different kinds of activism to see in which direction history will go.

CHAPTER SIX

Sex, Medicine, and Disease

ALAIN GIAMI

The permanent relationship between sexuality and medicine has been described as a process of *medicalization of sexuality* and theorized by authors such as Peter Conrad, Michel Foucault, George Lanteri Laura, and others. Even though doctors (as social actors) and medicine (as an institution and as a body of knowledge) have been concerned with sexual function and dysfunction from ancient Roman and Greek times to the medieval period[1] and on into eighteenth-century modernity,[2] a major shift occurred around 1830, when the word "sexuality" was invented in the French and English language, linking together notions such as nature, health, normality, and morality. The modern concept of sexuality was thus framed with different styles of reasoning, the medical and the psychiatric,[3] to manage the different aspects and dimensions of sexual conduct, subjectivities, and identities. The social construction of sexuality as the keystone to identity and subjectivity is part of the major enterprise of construction of the self that started in the beginning of the eighteenth century.[4] Beyond this social construction linking sexuality to subjectivity and identity, another dimension of sexuality, namely sex, has been the central locus of this process of medicalization. This process has included various attempts to control, in efficient ways, its normal functioning—first inside the realm of reproduction and then more recently from the perspective of sexual health.[5]

By the beginning of the twentieth century, the erotic and reproductive dimensions of sexuality started to be dissociated in the psychiatric and medical fields. The dissociation of these two dimensions of sexuality as belonging to different fields of knowledge and professional practice is part of the current process of the medicalization of sexuality. On the one hand, some professionals dealt with the non-reproductive aspects of sexuality and their physical, mental, and psychological dimensions and their consequences; on the other hand, other professionals dealt with the reproductive aspects and their correlates (contraception, abortion) and their consequences. The medicalization of sexuality is not only related to the development and the implication of the medical profession in the field of sexuality. Non-medical health professionals, particularly psychologists, contribute to the process of medicalization in their own way as part of a global framework of health interventions. All throughout the twentieth century, sexuality has become conceived more as a question of health and disease (and dysfunction) than of pleasure and sin.

This chapter explores these social transformations from various perspectives and is organized around the following topics: a discussion of the concept of medicalization of sexuality, a presentation of HIV/AIDS prevention understood as social response and dramatic change in sexual activity regulations, and finally a presentation of the evolution of conceptions of male impotence and medical treatment for this condition during the late twentieth century.

THE MEDICALIZATION OF SEXUALITY

The process of the medicalization of sexuality has been studied by several authors historians, sociologists, and anthropologists in France and in the United States. Among these, Michel Foucault, George Lanteri Laura, and Thomas Szasz developed different approaches to the beginnings of the medicalization of sexuality—either as an extension and transformation of religious responsibility for absolving sins and as part of the religious confession and judicial procedures concerning sexual offenders[6]; as a specific process of genuine medical appropriation of sexual conducts already considered as deviant by common morality[7]; or as an extension of the religious treatment of witchcraft.[8] From the eighteenth century on, some sexual conducts considered as sins, heresies, and crimes gradually came to be considered as diseases. We can think of masturbation and homosexuality as the major examples of the shift of meanings along the nineteenth and twentieth century. After the second part of the twentieth century, masturbation became the expression of, and way to, sexual health, particularly for women.[9] Homosexuality was excluded from the American Psychiatric Association classification of mental diseases in 1973, before it came back in the field of medicalization as a lifestyle related to the so-called gay cancer.[10] During the same period, sexual activities involving children (pedophilia) became gradually considered as a major sexual crime.[11]

The word "sexuality" appeared only recently in Western history, around 1830 in France and England, and was defined as a concept including sex difference, phenomena related to procreation, and behavior related to satisfaction. This definition appears in the French major dictionary *Petit Robert*.[12] Nineteenth-century medicine thus invented the social norm of the natural sexual instinct subordinated to the primacy of genital contact and reproduction. All non-procreative sexual activities were defined as sexual perversions or aberrations of the genital instinct.[13] By the end of the nineteenth century, sexologists elaborated listings of sexual perversions by considering them as forms of psychopathology.[14] The starting point of the medicalization of sexuality was characterized by the linkage between the erotic and the reproductive function of sexuality. This conception had strong consequences for the practice of sexology until the beginning of the 1960s, when medicine started to endorse the dissociation of the reproductive and the erotic through the development of hormonal contraception and the discovery of the psycho-physiological process of the so-called human sexual response cycle (HSRC) theorized by William Masters and Virginia Johnson.

Discussions about the medicalization of sexuality have been developed outside the arena of sexuality by sociologist Peter Conrad[15] and widely publicized by Leonore Tiefer.[16] Tiefer approaches the issue of medicalization first as a medical way of *knowing* sexuality based on mind-body dualism, the conception of the universal objective body, naturalism and biologism, the reduction of sexuality to its bodily aspects, individualism, and the construction of reified diseases and second as a medical way of *doing* sexology, including diagnostic practices, the use of technology, the objective of risk reduction, and the patient-doctor relationship. Tiefer observes that sexologists have exerted a strong influence on the process of medicalization of sexuality and raises the issue of the *overmedicalization* of sexuality that is happening currently. Her approach, however, is embedded in a defense of non-medical and feminist-oriented approaches to sexual disorders rather than a critique of the medicalization, which would also include a critique of the psychological approaches to sexual difficulties.[17] This point of view is based on a quite narrow conception of medicalization, which excludes the processes of psychologization and sexologization from the scope of the contemporary medical gaze of sexuality and can be considered as a rather corporatist point of view (defending the view of the psychologists against the physicians).[18]

FIGURE 6.1: A glamorous woman looking rue-
fully into her empty wine glass, representing a
warning against sexually transmitted diseases.
Sex, smoking, and drinking were often seen as
combined and unhealthy vices and important
objects for medical concern and intervention.
Ca. 1945. Color lithograph by Masters. Wellcome Library, London.

From this short review, one can observe that medicalization is a dynamic process that interacts with other forms of knowledge, practice, and power. Medicalization appears as a new way of conceptualizing sexual matters that is in some
cases independent of other approaches and in other cases based on a transformation of other approaches to so-called sexual problems. For example, in the
case of sex offenders, medical interventions are based on judicial codes, which
define the so-called disorder prior to its medicalization, while pharmacological
treatments are used along with cognitive behavioral approaches. This process
is identical to the one that was developed in the nineteenth century and described as the medical appropriation of sexual perversions.[19] Marital counseling brings together, in some cases, a religious approach to the couple as well as
a sexual health concern (including contraception and sexual pleasure).[20] Psychological approaches to sexual problems are part of a broader framework of

medicalization. Educational and preventive responses to HIV/AIDS are another of the many facets extended to the field of public health. In this view, medicalization is considered as part of a process of the moralization of society.[21]

This chapter is based on four assumptions. The first constitutes a critical perspective that is based on a conception of sexuality that includes its erotic as well as its reproductive functions. The dissociation of sexual pleasure and reproductive conducts is the product of the process of medicalization characterized by the autonomization and separation of sexual activity from reproduction. The second assumption considers medicalization as not only dealing with the

FIGURE 6.2: Cartoon figures of two women and two men look up at a sign announcing "Safer sex is a package." The poster encourages readers to be prepared, to communicate, to reduce the number of their sex partners, and to consider that there are more sexual practices than penetration, but is also says that one should always use condoms—a confusing message that mixes morality and medical care. Project for Education and Prevention of AIDS, 1990s. Wellcome Library, London.

enhancement of sexual function (such as the treatment of sexual dysfunction) but also with the repression of some aspects of sexual conduct considered as deviant. For example, one can consider the important development of the HIV/AIDS prevention enterprise as restricting sexual conduct and sexual pleasures for the sake of health. The third assumption considers non-medical approaches to sexual problems and forms of unsafe conduct as part of the process of medicalization that includes the use of non-medical psychotherapeutic techniques by nonmedical health professionals. Medical and non-medical approaches are both grounded on the idea of health and contribute in different ways to this common objective. Fourth, the enhancement of reduced sexual activity (impotence) and the limitations of some other aspects in the process of HIV prevention can be considered as two facets of the process of normalization of sexuality and sexual pleasures. On the one hand, medicalization develops the objective of enhancing some reduced aspects of sexual conduct, whereas on the other hand, the deviant or excessive dimensions of sexual conduct are to be reduced by educational or repressive approaches.

Historically, medical approaches to sexuality were generally based on the *reduction or inhibition* of the sexual activity and behavior of individuals who were considered to be deviant. This was true in particular for the repression of child and adolescent masturbation in the eighteenth century and further demonstrated by different forms of castration and involuntary sterilization of sexual offenders from the late nineteenth century to recent days in the United States and European countries.[22] Sterilization was supposed to reduce the libido and sexual drives and prevent the reproduction of deviance among individuals that were supposed to be degenerated.

Psychiatric definitions were applied to different forms of sexual deviations and homosexuality in the late nineteenth century. For example, heterosexuality was initially a concept that related to other non-procreative (erotic) relations such as homosexuality, masturbation, and zoophilia. Psychiatry, surgery, and pharmacology have played an important role in this process of the medicalization of sexuality as it applied to the reduction of nonprocreative sexuality.

In the mid-twentieth century, science and medicine started to dissociate eroticism and procreation and recognize the legitimacy and the normality of sexual acts performed to obtain pleasure independently of the objective of procreation. Erotically different gender sex (sexual intercourse) became the gold standard to measure and evaluate the so-called normal sexuality within the work of Kinsey and of Masters and Johnson.[23]

The process of dissociation between the erotic and the reproductive functions of sexuality was legitimated in the work of Masters and Johnson and with the invention of the contraceptive pill in the late 1950s. Non-procreative sexual activities inside mixed-gender couples with the objective of simultaneous orgasm and satisfaction became the norm of the new sexual democracy.[24] Modern sexology experienced a major change in perspective, becoming less interested in sexual deviations than in interventions aimed at the recovery of normal physiological and psychological sexual functioning. So the process of medicalization of sexology, including psychological approaches, began to be directed to the enhancement of a so-called normal sexuality. This process was extended to the normalization of homosexuality with its exclusion from the *Diagnostic and Statistical Manual of Mental Disorders (DSM)* in 1973.[25] The second part of the work of Masters and Johnson, which is much less famous than the first part, included nongenital practices and same-gender sex as normal ways of reaching orgasm. Homosexual individuals and same-gender couples started to be admitted to their clinic.[26] The World Health Organization (WHO) started to work on the concept of sexual health in 1975.[27] The following definition was elaborated:

> Sexual health is the integration of the somatic, emotional, intellectual, and social aspects of sexual being, in ways that are positively enriching and that enhance personality, communication, and love ... Thus the notion of sexual health implies a positive approach to human sexuality, and the purposes of sexual health care should be the enhancement of life and personal relationships and not merely counseling and care related to procreation or sexually transmitted diseases.[28]

The WHO definition of sexual health constitutes an attempt to extend the field of medical and health professionals far beyond the scope of disease. This definition represents an integration of well-being into the field of health, which is quite a modern conception seeking to replace the framework of religion. Health appears as a moral imperative[29] and health professionals as its secular priests.[30] This process has been called the *modernization of sex* by Paul Robinson, and it carries with it the idea of sexual optimism by considering that sex is no longer evil but instead a positive good for human development.[31] This new paradigm made possible some important scientific and medical changes.

The production of erection with the help of a substance was an old dream of humanity, as one is reminded of by all the herbal and liquid preparations that were used for such an objective throughout human history. Traces of such prescriptions were found in the late eighteenth century in the medical file of Elie de Beaumont (nicknamed Obese and Impotent), who was treated by famous

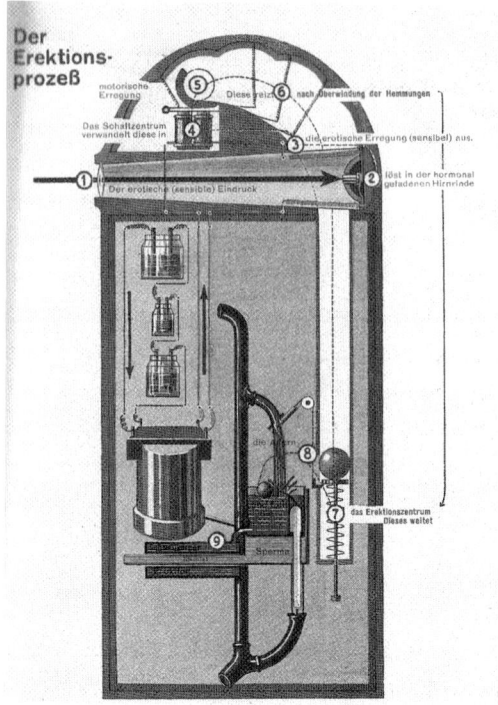

FIGURE 6.3: Magnus Hirschfeld worked together
with the chemical company Promonta to produce
Titus Pearls to enhance sexual potency. Illustration shows erection as if the genital system is
a machine. The pearls were based on the then
newly known hormones. In Magnus Hirschfeld
and Berhnhard Schapiro, Die Behandlung der
Impotenz in der ärztlichen Praxis, Hamburg:
Promota, 1930.

doctors such as Antoine Petit and Tissot.[32] During the nineteenth century, famous medical doctors working on male impotence and sterility already offered
to their clients the possibility to treat the reduction or absence of erection with
expensive substances that were prepared by the doctor himself.[33] This tradition
continued in the early twentieth century with various types of experimental
treatment for male rejuvenation, including chirurgical implantation of monkey
testicles in men by the French surgeon Voronoff.[34] Famous modern sexologists,
such as Magnus Hirschfeld, elaborated and proposed the Testifortan, a pill for
erection, which was more famous under the name of Titus Pearls.[35]

In the early 1980s, Ronald Virag, a French cardiologist, discovered the effects of Papaverine on erection.[36] This discovery can be considered as the magic
bullet for erection, since for the first time in human history men could use a

medical preparation to provoke an immediate and lasting erection. Medicine entered the field of the aphrodisiac: it was now possible to reach erection in a much more efficient way with the use of a medically controlled substance. In 1998, the Nobel Prize in Physiology or Medicine was granted to Robert F. Furchgott, Louis J. Ignarro, and Ferid Murad for their discoveries concerning nitric oxide, which opened the way to the investigation of the physiopathology and neurology of erection, giving birth to the first inhibitors of iPDE5, better known under the brand name of Viagra.[37]

This situation represents a radical change in the history of the relationships between medicine, medication, and sexuality to the extent that medicine started considering sexual activity and sexual health as positive values that should be treated in order to be stimulated. The process of dissociation between the erotic and reproductive aspects of sexuality is now quite advanced, and its reinforcement is part of the process of the medicalization of sexuality with, on the one hand, treatments of nonprocreative erotic sexual activity and, on the other, the treatment of infertility apart from erotic sexual activity.

The 1980s and the 1990s were thus characterized by a double perspective in the social function of medicine toward sex. On the clinical side, the medical treatment of sexual dysfunction can be considered as a way of improving and stimulating the sexual activity of some specific groups of the population (those living in a heterosexual, stable relationship). On the public health and education side, the reduction of the risk of HIV infection and limitations in sexual activity have been promoted for those who are supposedly exposed to sexual risks of infection.

Considered as a whole, medicalized approaches to sexuality can be used to stimulate or inhibit sexual activity, to facilitate or prevent procreation, to help people change their gender, to prevent or treat sexually transmitted infections, or to treat sexual offenders. A number of medical disciplines are involved, particularly: endocrinology, venereology, gynecology, andrology, surgery, psychiatry, urology, medical sexology, and public health. These medicalized interventions involve nonmedical disciplines (i.e., law, criminology, psychology, and social work), raising ethical issues in the societies in which they occur. The medicalization of sexuality is part of a more global process of the medicalization of society. Indeed, medical solutions are being found for more and more problems of daily life, such as excess weight, eating disorders, limitations on intellectual or physical performance, insomnia, and psychological well-being. General practitioners are on the front line of these treatments.

The medicalization of sexuality may be defined generally as:

- A body of basic knowledge and scientific concepts on sexuality, which evolves over time;

- A social organization of health professions founded on professional training and certification, professional practices, and interaction between members of health professions (doctors and psychologists in particular) and their patients;
- A form of social control and regulation of sexuality based on efficient technologies and on the ideology of health, which reinforce or counter other forms of control such as those previously exercised by religion;
- A subjective experience of individuals, which leads them to believe that problems related to sexuality or reproductive life are pathologies that can be treated medically.

The process of medicalization of sexuality is illustrated in this chapter with the analysis of the evolution of ideas about HIV infection and male impotence. I made the methodological choice of using the term "male impotence" to refer to erectile problems, difficulties, or dysfunction in order to better analyze the current discourse on erectile dysfunction from a social-historical point of view. The position that is assumed in this chapter does not aim to defend a medical or a psychological point of view but to understand the social consequences of the evolution and changes in the definition of this condition. Defending a psychological or a medical conception of male impotence would represent an endorsement of one professional position in the field, which is not the aim of this chapter. Finally, one can observe that this chapter deals mostly with male sexual problems and the consequences of males' sexual conduct. A lot has been written on women's sexual issues and much less about men, and female sexualities have evolved in a different way throughout the twentieth century. Most of the discussions about women were about reproductive issues (contraception and abortion), and it is only recently that the possibility of a medical enhancement of female sexual function came across the agenda with the pharmacological treatment of hypoactive sexual desire disorder.

HIV/AIDS PREVENTION

The various techniques developed for preventing HIV infection provide us with one of the most important examples worldwide of the medicalization of sexuality during the twentieth century. The major aim of the fight against HIV infection has been, and still is, to modify sexual behavior by convincing people to adopt protective measures so as to avoid transmission of the virus. This attempt to change behavior patterns is underlined by a scientific and medical rationale and by an understanding of public health. From the viewpoint of public health, campaigns against HIV infection have been undertaken by working with risk groups and using methods based on communication, education, and counseling.

The emergence of the HIV/AIDS epidemic at the beginning of the 1980s led to major changes in the field of sexuality. On the one hand, scientific and medical knowledge has not yet led to a vaccine or efficient remedy against the virus, which is mainly transmitted through sexual intercourse including penile-vaginal, oral, and anal contacts. This situation obliged the development of strategies for risk reduction aiming at decreasing rates of sexual activity. In the absence of a major medical discovery, the only way of avoiding the infection has been to use condoms, safer sex methods, abstinence from any sexual relations, and reduction in numbers of partners. On the other hand,

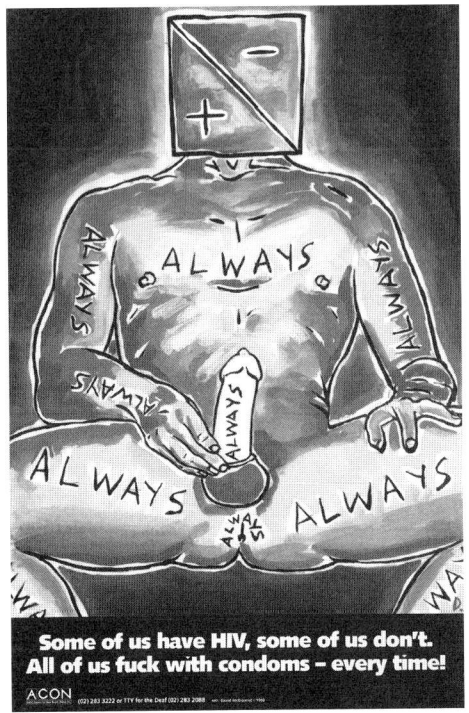

FIGURE 6.4: A man with a square head bearing the HIV positive and negative sign sits holding his erect penis with the words "Always" written across his body. The message is to always use a condom with little regard for other sexual/preventive options. Color lithograph by David McDiarmid, 1992, for AIDS Council of New South Wales. Wellcome Library, London.

the epidemiological, sociological, and psychological knowledge of sexuality increased significantly because of the many surveys undertaken in a large number of industrial and developing countries.

The main change in sexual activity in the so-called era of AIDS has been the use of the condom. In the mid-1990s many studies gave evidence of an increase of condom use considered as a major effect of prevention campaigns in modern industrialized countries.[38] The HIV/AIDS epidemic has thus contributed to the development of new representations of sexuality as an activity that may lead to serious and lethal consequences.[39] The relationships between sexual partners have changed because of the necessity to protect themselves against the risk of infection.[40] The medicalization of sexuality in the era of AIDS also opened a new perspective of research on anal sex and gay sex.[41] Safe sex promotion also appeared as a way of promoting non-reproductive and non-contaminating sexual practices. New or minority sexual practices—such as jerk-off parties and consensual sadomasochism—are now part of the agenda of safe sex promotion.

Sexual practices have been re-assessed in terms of their potential risk of infecting others with HIV, with distinctions being made between "safer" and "risky" or even "high-risk" behaviors. This ranking by risk is based on sexual practices, whether genital, oral, or anal, and the number of sexual partners. The meaning of sexual activities and relationships has evolved to the point of considering love to be a major risk factor for HIV infection,[42] insofar as most people do not feel that it is necessary to adopt protective measures in a relationship with someone whom they love. "Promiscuity" used to be a moral problem having to do with infidelity; nowadays, multipartner sexual relations are said to be a health risk factor. Attention has been devoted to gay men but not at all to lesbians, since they supposedly run fewer risks of HIV infection. This perspective has led to a concentration on insertive/receptive anal practices, which are classified as very risky. This stigmatization of anal penetration and the attempt to restrain such practices contrasts with the decriminalization of sodomy by the U.S. Supreme Court in 2003. Even as efforts were being made to limit anal practices for the sake of health, legal actions against those accused of sodomy were halted. The rationale of public health reintroduced medical norms where legal ones had been abolished. Sexual behaviors that are not mainstream—intercourse with commercial sex workers or group sex— have also become public health problems rather than legal or moral issues.

Approaches to fighting HIV/AIDS have targeted young people and persons with multiple sexual partners while overlooking the aged, the monogamous, and heterosexual married couples, all of whom are thought to run few risks of exposure to HIV.[43] As we can see, boundaries have been drawn around a set of risky sexual behaviors. Public health actions have targeted the latter while taking for granted that so-called "ordinary" sexuality, since it is not a risky practice, does not fall in the scope of public health interventions and recommendations.

The Turning Point in the Medicalization
of HIV/AIDS Prevention

Since the beginning of the HIV infection epidemics, the development of prevention has been based on the idea that individuals could be trained and educated to become aware of the sexual risks to which they can be confronted and that their rational attitude would be oriented toward the protection of their health and ultimately their lives. One can say that this political move was based on anthropological choice founded on the belief that human beings could adhere to the hegemonic rationality of health. This rationale was developed by the WHO in 1948, in the belief that people would accept suggestions to change their sexual behavior in the ways advocated by health and moral authorities around the world and inside their own communities. In this

FIGURE 6.5: Two black women hold a washing line to which condoms are pegged, advertising safe sex and AIDS prevention for a minority that was seen as particularly at risk. Black HIV/AIDS Network, London, 1990s. Wellcome Library, London.

perspective, the social and political responses to HIV infection have been based on education, on the increase of individual awareness toward sex, and on the development of consciousness toward the malignant effects of risky sex. Repressive policies, such as the incarceration and relegation of HIV-infected individuals that occurred in Cuba during the mid-1980s, were unanimously condemned around the world as inefficient and above all as threats to human rights. Sweden also took some similar measures and criminalized HIV transmission. In France, the Conseil National du Sida did not support the project of criminalizing individuals who were supposed to have contaminated their partner.[44]

Unfortunately, at the beginning of the twenty-first century, this state of affairs appears to have been much less efficient than it was supposed to be. Prevention efforts did not lead to the reduction of the epidemics. HIV infection is on the rise in most of the countries of the so-called developing and developed countries, among men and women, gay men and heterosexuals. The underlying rationality of HIV prevention and behavior modification is challenged by the development of barebacking (having voluntary and conscious unprotected anal sex) attitudes among gay men of the first world. New prevention strategies are also being developed in the developing world and especially in some areas of sub-Saharan Africa, where it has been suggested that male circumcision could help to reduce the rates of HIV infection.[45] We are observing a major change in the underlying philosophy of HIV prevention. Since democratic and educational prevention seems to be unable to dramatically reduce rates of HIV infection, public health and political managers are tempted to develop authoritarian prevention measures: men should be persuaded to accept circumcision with no need for an explanation as to the reasons behind the operation. In other words, the medicalization of sexual activity based on the development and awareness of men, which was proposed during the first twenty years of the HIV infection, was no longer being applied. After the relative failure of this initial approach, political and public health managers started developing authoritarian methods. The old colonial times of mandatory vaccination, without informed consent, in Africa and other areas may develop again under the control of democratic nongovernmental organizations.

THE EVOLUTION OF IDEAS AND CONCEPTIONS
OF MALE IMPOTENCE

The evolution of ideas and conceptions of male impotence is marked by a progressive evolution emerging from judicial conceptions. In the eighteenth century, impotence was considered as a civil offense treated in court.[46] In the nineteenth century, impotence included erectile problems and male sterility. Treatments were aimed at the recovery of both genital ability and fertility.[47] Impotence was also a supposed consequence of masturbation. Its etiology was physical, environmental, and psychological.

In the early twentieth century, conceptions of impotence shifted to psychosociogenic explanations. Stekel considered male impotence as a disorder of the self in society:

> The majority of cases of impotence started with emotional disorders that can be completely cured by psychotherapy. … The frigid woman and the impotent man are the products of a sick era. Impotence is a social disease that can be understood only in a specific historical period and through this period.[48]

Later on, Masters and Johnson represented a different perspective: male impotence was understood mainly as a disorder of the couple, and treatment necessarily involved both members of the couple in a behavioral and relational perspective.

> It should be emphasized that the Foundation's basic premise of therapy insists that, although both husband and wife in a sexually dysfunctional marriage are treated, the marital relationship is considered as the patient. Probably this is best expressed in the statement that sexual dysfunction is indeed a marital-unit problem, certainly never only a wife's or only a husband's personal concern.[49]

Masters and Johnson built a theory in which impotence is explicitly understood inside the dynamics of the married couple and grounded on objective and measurable criteria (failure of erection in 25 percent of the attempts of coitus). Impotence and premature ejaculation are thus dissociated, which was not the case in the early conceptions of male sexual dysfunction. It is also important to note the moralistic point of view of Masters and Johnson related to the fact that marriage is considered as the locus of sexual intercourse. Sexual disorders were not treated per se but as symptoms of a "dysfunctional marriage."

At the end of the 1980s, urologists started to propose definitions of male impotence in the medical field. The papers were published in the *New England Journal of Medicine* and not in sexological or psychological journals. In their paper "Impotence," Krane, Goldstein, and Saenz de Tejada defined impotence as "the consistent inability to achieve or sustain an erection of sufficient rigidity for sexual intercourse."[50]

These authors estimated that ten million American men are impotent. They concluded:

> The chief advance in the understanding of impotence in the past decade has been the appreciation that the state of contraction or relaxation of corporal smooth muscles regulates blood flow in the corpora cavernosa, determining whether the penis will be flaccid or erect. The ability to manipulate corporal smooth muscles tone by the intracavernosal administration of pharmacologic agents has led to the development of new diagnostic procedures and therapeutic options for impotence.[51]

This statement condenses the link between scientific advances, medical conceptions of etiology based on pathophysiology, and guidelines for treatments. The main shift is thus from social, psychological, and relational conceptions toward a biological etiology. In these definitions, impotence is strictly related to the organic functioning of the penis, and the functioning of the penis is strictly aimed at heterosexual intercourse, while other sexual practices are excluded. The definition reinforces and emphasizes the distinction already established by various sexologists between impotence, libido disorders, premature ejaculation, and orgasm.

The 1993 U.S. National Institutes of Health Consensus Conference proposed to abandon the term "impotence" and to replace it with "erectile dysfunction," which reinforces the reduction of the condition to erectile function regardless of other dimensions of sexual functioning. The conference proposed a new definition of erectile dysfunction as "the inability of the male to achieve an erect penis as part of the overall multifaceted process of male sexual function."[52] The attribute of "consistent" that was included in the 1989 definition was thus abandoned in this new definition. This change in definition represents a major shift. Impotence was thus transformed from a disorder of the global person and the self, which could be treated by psychological or psychosocial approaches, to a simple organic disorder, limited to a single organ: the penis.

The issue of the definition of degree and frequency appears to be an important issue at the clinical level for the purpose of diagnostic evaluation and for the construction of epidemiological data. Some authors would later define it as complete or persistent,[53] while others would qualify it as continuous.[54] Some authors would include the issue of degree (severe, moderate, minimal).[55] These changes in definitions will continue to play an important role in the social construction of epidemiological data.

The Evolution of Epidemiological Data

Since the early 1950s, epidemiology has started to play an important role in the definition and legitimization of public health policies.[56] The strong anchorage of epidemiology in public health revealed that epidemiological categories are not only strictly medical and scientific categories but also social and political ways of categorizing individuals and groups. These categories reflect the societal attitudes toward some individuals and groups. Changes in definitions and categories represent important challenges, since they contribute to the increase or decrease in the prevalence of a condition—that is, when one changes a category one can easily increase or decrease the numbers and the percentages.[57]

The Kinsey report estimated that *erectile impotence* affected 1 percent of men under nineteen and 25 percent of men above seventy-five years old.[58] The Kinsey data show that impotence is clearly related to age. In a study carried out among one hundred "normal couples," the authors established a distinction between the "difficulties in obtaining an erection" that affected 7 percent of the men and the "difficulties in maintaining an erection" that affected 9 percent of the men.[59] This study raised the issue of a precise definition of the erectile disorder and further questioned the essence of erectile disorders. In a critical review of the incidence and prevalence of sexual dysfunction, Spector and Carey observed that studies completed with community samples indicate a current prevalence of erectile disorder at between 4 percent and 9 percent among the male adult population.[60] Before the beginning of the 1990s, the epidemiological consensus on the prevalence of male impotence was around 10 percent of men overall, with an increase in prevalence with age.

In the beginning of the 1990s, a series of community and general population studies were performed. We can observe in these studies: (1) a change in the phrasing of the questions including degrees and frequencies of occurrence of erectile disorder, (2) important discrepancies in the estimates of prevalence, and (3) a dramatic increase in the estimates of the prevalence of male impotence in some studies.

The Massachusetts Male Aging Study (MMAS), which was the most widely quoted study, gives the highest estimates of prevalence of male impotence. This is one of the first studies based on the introduction of self-estimates of degrees of impotence: mild impotence: 17.2 percent; moderate impotence: 25.2 percent; total impotence: 9.6 percent. All together these percentages represent about 52 percent of men forty to seventy years old.[61] The same authors use

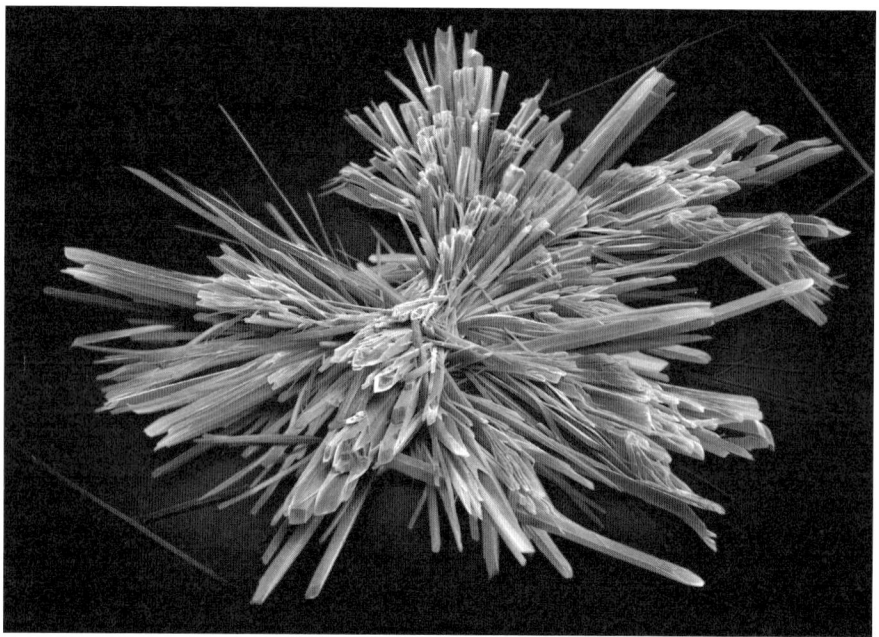

FIGURE 6.6: Sildenafil is the active ingredient in Viagra tablets, a medicine developed for the medical treatment of impotence but often used for sexual stimulation by others. Wellcome Library, London.

different aggregates of their data according to the purpose of their subsequent studies. For example, in an incidence study based on the same MMAS cohort, the authors include all degrees of impotence in their calculation to reach a prevalence of 52 percent of men, which represents eighteen million Americans forty to seventy years old.[62]

The U.S. National Health and Social Life Survey (NHSLS), a national population based study of sexual behavior, did not include any estimates of degree or frequency of occurrence of impotence. The results produced with this method gave a much lower estimate than those obtained in the MMAS study. The question was phrased as follows: "During the last 12 months has there ever been a period of several months or more when you ... had trouble achieving or maintaining an erection?" and found this to be true among 10.4 percent of men eighteen to fifty-nine years old.[63]

It is interesting to observe that two major studies undertaken at the same period in the United States reach such different estimates of the prevalence of erectile disorders by using different methodologies. The French National Survey on Sexual Behavior (ACSF),[64] based on a representative sample of the adult population eighteen to sixty-nine years old, introduced the criteria of the self-estimated frequency of occurrence of absence of erection. The question was phrased as: "Have any of the following ever happened to you? You do not have an erection (Impotence)"[65] 7.5 percent of the men responded "often"; 12.1 percent "sometimes"; 28.3 percent "rarely." All together, this equals 47.9 percent. The results of the French ACSF based on the self-estimates of the frequency of absence of erection give a comparable picture to the U.S. MMAS.

Degrees of self-estimated frequency used in the French ACSF survey are similar to the degrees of self-estimated severity of the condition used in the MMAS study. As a consequence, any introduction of degrees in the estimates of prevalence, whether related to frequency or to severity, increases the global prevalence.

Surveys performed in Scandinavia, using different phrasing of the questions, produced different global estimates of male erectile dysfunction. For example, the FINSEX (Finnish Sex) study used the following question: "It is not uncommon that a man cannot enter into sexual intercourse because he cannot get an erection or his penis becomes flaccid right when sexual intercourse is started. In the last year, has something like this happened to you?" This question gave two estimates: 49 percent of the men experienced problems related to erection difficulties "at least to some extent" and 6 percent "fairly frequently" during the last twelve months.[66]

In a secondary analysis of the 1996 Swedish sex survey, Fugl-Meyer and Sjogren Fugl-Meyer found much lower estimates with the use of the following question: "It happens that the man's penis does not become rigid or gets flaccid during intercourse. Has this happened in your sexual life during the last 12 months?" (The responses: "quite often," "nearly all the time," and "all the time" were judged as denoting that the subject had a sexual disability). The estimates were that 5 percent of men aged eighteen to seventy-four (and about 7 percent of men aged thirty-five to seventy-four) were considered to have an erectile disability. The Fugl-Meyer and Sjögren Fugl-Meyer study introduced an original measure of subjective evaluation of the trouble caused by the erectile disorder. According to this measure, they estimated that erectile disability is experienced as a problem by 69 percent of men and that 75 percent of those experiencing it as a problem are not satisfied with their sexual life.[67]

This brief review of epidemiological studies gives evidence that the estimates of the prevalence of male impotence are clearly dependent on the way the questions are phrased. These differences in estimates are not only explicable by different scientific conceptions across the world, but also by the extent to which self-estimated degrees of frequency or gravity of erectile disorders are considered as constitutive of the condition. The MMAS study seems to consider that a minimal degree of erectile dysfunction can be included in the definition of the condition, whereas the Fugl-Meyer and Sjögren Fugl-Meyer study did not include such minor degrees of erectile dysfunction in their definition of erectile disability.

The process of the medicalization of sexuality has been illustrated through the example of the evolution of conceptions of male impotence and its implication for the estimates of its prevalence. First of all, we observed an attempt to replace the term "impotence" with the term "erectile dysfunction" to represent the shift between psychogenic and organic etiologies of erectile disorders. Nevertheless, the term "impotence" is still used as a synonym of "erectile dysfunction" in the major papers in the field and even among those who argue most strongly for the abandonment of the old term "impotence." The term "impotence" was related to a more global conception of sexual functioning including psychological and relational dimensions and to a certain extent to the global identity of the man who is affected by such a condition. The new term "erectile dysfunction" appears to be more restricted to the biological and physiological aspects of the functioning of the penis and is considered as something external to the man and out of his control. The psychological dimension, and especially the psychological etiology of impotence, is currently in the process of being replaced by an organic etiology. One can observe a similar process concerning the concept of depression, now considered as a biological condition. As a consequence of the change in definition, the estimates of the self-declared prevalence of erectile dysfunction have dramatically increased. Erectile disorders, which are the most common problem in men's sexual lives and which might be dealt with through a variety of strategies such as changing partner or use of erotic or pornographic material or of an aphrodisiac, are now considered as a disease clearly defined in the *DSM-IV* and the WHO—*ICD* (International Classification of Disease) 10. This evolution seems to be related to the evolution of scientific knowledge and the advent of new medication. One of the major issues in terms of the professional implication in the treatments of male impotence will be the question of the relevance of psychological treatments of this condition by nonmedical health professionals, who in most countries cannot prescribe medication. The other issue will be to consider if any erectile disorder represents a serious condition or only a temporary or partner-related failure. In an interview published in the *New York Times Magazine* Irving Goldstein, the famous urologist who contributed to the social and scientific development of Viagra, declared: "Unless you don't have a treatment, you don't have a condition."[68] But we should remember that Aids is a devastating condition that had no treatment for a long time. This quotation reveals the importance of the professional implication in the social construction of disease. It is assumed that the recent introduction of "a novel effective oral therapy for male erectile dysfunction" will have important consequences for the practice of sexology and sex therapy and for the conception of sexual dysfunction.[69] This new medication appears to be part of important pharmacological developments including new medication for male and female sexual dysfunction.

CONCLUSION

The HIV/AIDS epidemics and erectile dysfunction drugs, such as sildenafil/Viagra and other more recent brands produced by the pharmaceutical industry, involve two complementary approaches to the medicalization of sexuality. On the one hand, the HIV/AIDS epidemic has led to an approach of limiting and stigmatizing some forms of sexual practices and relationships (anal practices, homosexuality, group sex, multipartnership) that are deemed to represent major health risks. HIV-prevention campaigns have mainly sought to reduce

FIGURE 6.7: "AIDS Is Beautiful. Protect Yourself This Summer," 1990s. AIDES France.

what is thought to be excessive or deviant in relation to heteronormative values (heterosexuality, marital relations, monogamy, and genital intercourse). In the case of Viagra, the objective is to restore, even stimulate, forms of sexual activity that are thought to be normal, though inhibited, and to reinforce normative heterosexuality. Despite the different means used—prevention and education in the one case, drug prescriptions and clinical interaction in the other—the intention is to re-establish a so-called normal functioning of sexuality by restraining it when it is deemed excessive or by stimulating it when it is deemed insufficient.

The process of the medicalization of sexuality goes far beyond the domain of medical and psychological therapeutic intervention: it takes places in a wider context of redefining the meaning of sexual experience by redefining what is normal and what is not normal by relating it to the notion of health. In this perspective, it is quite interesting to note that those who have criticized the process of medicalization in relation to Viagra did not use the same intellectual tools to understand the development of HIV/AIDS prevention, which is almost never interpreted as an enterprise of medicalization.[70] It is as if the dramatic situation related to the HIV/AIDS world epidemic gave more legitimacy to professional interventions in sexual behavior modification.

The twentieth century has been a period of major transformations of sexualities from different vantage points. On one hand, science and medicine, along with psychology and public health, chirurgical practice, and endocrinology have been involved in an enterprise of normalization of sexual activity, as in the cases of the HIV/AIDS epidemics and the treatment of erectile disorders, but also with the development of the contraceptive pill. On the other hand, different social movements endorsed the question of sexual identities in order to promote human and social emancipation of those that were considered deviant and stigmatized. We could conclude with the notion that science and medicine, when they are applied to sexuality, although often used for the sake of normalization, can also be used for the sake of emancipation.

CHAPTER SEVEN

Sex, Popular Beliefs, and Culture

FRANZ X. EDER

Popular sexual beliefs and cultures in the West were subject to swift and, at times, radical changes during the twentieth century. New sexual images, norms, and identities affected peoples' attitudes and influenced their erotic fantasies and sexual knowledge. During this period, changes in popular culture effectively became peoples' day-to-day life-world experiences.[1] At the same time, potential for communication increased, supported by expansion of educational institutions and growing mass media, which opened up further sexual ideas, fields of knowledge, and images to an ever-increasing audience; the educational institutions reached out to a broader range of social classes; and the extensive distribution of mass media such as books, newspapers, magazines, and the development of new media such as movies, radio, TV, and the Internet reached even more. Therefore, the twentieth century saw the term "popular sexual culture" evolve to refer to a culture "which is widely disseminated and consumed by large numbers of people."[2]

Media-based communication resulted in traditional procurers of values and knowledge—such as parents, teachers, and priests—losing their pedagogic importance and being replaced by new knowledge informers, such as sex researchers, guidebook authors, politicians, writers, or movie directors. However, conventional understandings that had up to then been conveyed by closed life-worlds were not substituted altogether. Social and cultural traditions continued, passed down via gender-specific education, socialization within the peer group, value conveyance within the professional realm, and group-specific ideals relating to love, partnership, and family. More often than not, they were concurring with the generally advanced knowledge about sex and the eroticizing images displayed by the media. This productive tension within the sexual culture of the twentieth century called forth relentless and emotional public debates, contributing in turn to changes in behavior and thought within just a few decades.

In this chapter, the history of popular beliefs and cultures of sex comprises various approaches: First, it combines opinions on and views of sex as revealed in contemporary surveys, in sex scandals exploited by the media, in autobiographical writings, and in popular marriage how-to manuals. Second, it includes an examination of the period's thriving and diverse popular sex culture from early forms of erotic photography via mass production of sex education literature and pornographic movies to places such as sex shops and the virtual sex realms of the Internet. Third, it explores how sexual discourse and images such as scientific or pornographic photographs grew to be part of the popular sex culture and ended up shaping the genesis of sexual scripts; this, on the one hand, was partly due to relaxing censorship and the development of a (semi-)public sexual language and, on the other hand, was a result of the rise of the consumer society (mainly due to technical innovations) that granted common access to terminology, texts, and images that had previously been available only to a selected few. Last but not least, a history of popular culture must address the genesis of the material culture that has resulted in a flood of objects and products onto the mass market that significantly influenced sexual practices (such as safe and low-priced condoms) and what generated them in the first place (such as telephone sex or erotic movies).

Many years of debate around the question of methodology for the study of popular culture have resulted in an unproductive hierarchical polarization of high and low culture. Therefore, the following presentation of the popular sex culture of the twentieth century will concentrate on norms, interpretations, impacts, discourses, and ideologies in detail and will focus on their respective social circumstances. This will also include the construction of individual and social identities and the way they have found their way into the narration of (hi)stories or into mythologies and normative models.

MAKING SEX SPEAK (1920S AND EARLY 1930S)

In Europe and the United States, World War I not only triggered political upheavals, social eruptions, and economic crises but also gave rise to continuous commotion within the traditional sex culture, seen in the increasing number of abortions, the uncontrollable spread of venereal diseases, and the rapidly increasing divorce rates. For the average (married) couple, the war called their attention to family planning issues and to consideration of deliberate and safe contraception. As a result, the Western nations' birth rates plummeted and, after picking up temporarily during the post-war period, remained moderate all through the 1920s and the Depression of the 1930s.

To have a small family had come to be regarded as a virtue by the West's bourgeoisie as early as the nineteenth century. An example can be seen in the French family—the French population having been shrinking since the 1850s—which was adopted as a beacon of modern family planning. By the turn of the century, demand for contraception had increased so much in various social groups, such as the urban working classes and trades people, that deliberate family planning did not merely conform to a self-determined marital life but also to a Christian one.

Eventually, the decrease in marital and extramarital fertility rates in Europe and the United States in the wake of World War I was incontrovertible. It resulted from varied social and cultural reasons,[3] including the dwindling influence of traditional moral and value authorities of the church and family on sexual conduct. Particularly in the cities, improved schooling and education systems resulted in increased literacy. Attitudes changed from aspiring to a life of divinely ordained destiny within a Christian family toward striving for an individually and personally designed life. In addition, from the time of the fin de siècle, the lower classes had increasingly adopted bourgeois family ideals and embraced the anonymity of city life, which quickly helped to expunge rural traditions.

Among the rural population, having many children was desired or accepted, and families remained integrated in the village's socio-regulative context. For most of the twentieth century, country people trusted in a life ordained by God, and their children served as workers and the future's safeguards. As a result, information on, and availability of, modern contraceptives spread slowly. Among the non-rural population, the working-class continued to have the highest birth rates. Officials and employees either considered applying, or did apply, birth control as early as the nineteenth century. In general, contraception was far more accepted in the cities. Capitals such as Paris, Berlin, London, Vienna, Stockholm, and Hamburg had soon reached a fertility rate of fewer than two children per woman. Vienna's and Berlin's fertility rates reached their lowest point during the interwar period, reaching only around 5–10 percent of their maximum fertility potential during the 1930s, with both cities called the world's most unfertile.

Religious distinctions, too, had their impact on attitudes toward individual birth control. In Protestant areas, people tended to deliberately restrict their fertility more readily than in Catholic areas, owing to Protestantism's potential to motivate individuals to choose a private, conscience-guided attitude to family planning. Consequently, their approach to fertility—after having given birth to a number of children—included sexual abstinence or the introduction of contraceptives. That said, bourgeois married couples in Catholic France had actively practiced birth control as early as the second half of the nineteenth century as new social values and moral concepts emerged.

Those who were prepared to control their own fertility selected from different methods of contraception. Importantly, the highly unreliable techniques of coitus interruptus (withdrawal) and post-coital vaginal douching (the second most popular method after abstinence) were now being replaced by increasingly safer and thinner condoms and diaphragms like the Mensinga diaphragm and spermicidal vaginal suppositories, all of which were sold as inconspicuous toiletries.

Nevertheless, as German medical doctors discovered through surveys, people in the countryside still knew little of the existence of new contraceptive products or of how to use them. As far as these sexual devices were concerned, prevailing embarrassment and unease kept married and unmarried couples from discussing them. In order to be able to make use of devices for vaginal douching that went by the names of "female syringe" or "injection" in the United States and in England, one required financial means and access to the selling market as well as a healthy attitude to one's own body.

To have a diaphragm of metal or rubber fitted, one had to see a doctor. Condoms were regarded revolting and indecent, the "rubber johnnys" having once been mainly used as protection against venereal diseases during sexual intercourse with prostitutes.[4]

All in all, the general problem of contraception was not solved until the pill. Even outside prudish England, the topic was avoided as being most indecent. Some countries' legislations bowed to this attitude by inflicting penalties on marketing and on distributing contraceptives. Nevertheless, educational sex firms were being created during World War I attempting to persuade soldiers to wear condoms, mainly as a protection against venereal disease. After World War I, in the face of increasing difficult predicaments in which women found themselves, a growing number of medical doctors and representatives of the feminist movement took to focusing on sexual problems such as illegitimacy and life-threatening illegal abortion, especially among the lower classes. While the first wave of the feminist movement had focused on elective franchise and access to education, now propaganda supported the right to be in charge of one's

Hygienic Whirling Spray Syringe

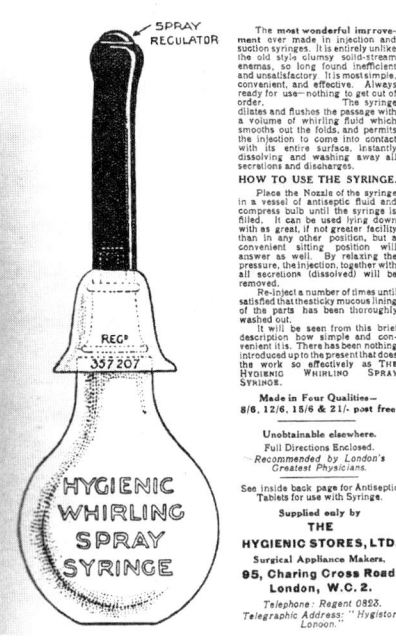

SPRAY REGULATOR

The most wonderful improvement ever made in injection and suction syringes. It is entirely unlike the old style clumsy solid-stream enemas, so long found inefficient and unsatisfactory. It is most simple, convenient, and effective. Always ready for use—nothing to get out of order.   The syringe dilates and flushes the passage with a volume of whirling fluid which smooths out the folds, and permits the injection to come into contact with its entire surface, instantly dissolving and washing away all secretions and discharges.

HOW TO USE THE SYRINGE.

Place the Nozzle of the syringe in a vessel of antiseptic fluid and compress bulb until the syringe is filled. It can be used lying down with as great, if not greater facility than in any other position, but a convenient sitting position will answer as well. By relaxing the pressure, the injection, together with all secretions (dissolved) will be removed.

Re-inject a number of times until satisfied that the sticky mucous lining of the parts has been thoroughly washed out.

It will be seen from this brief description how simple and convenient it is. There has been nothing introduced up to the present that does the work so effectively as THE HYGIENIC WHIRLING SPRAY SYRINGE.

Made in Four Qualities—
8/6, 12/6, 15/6 & 21/- post free

Unobtainable elsewhere.

Full Directions Enclosed.

Recommended by London's Greatest Physicians.

See inside back page for Antiseptic Tablets for use with Syringe.

Supplied only by

THE
HYGIENIC STORES, LTD.
Surgical Appliance Makers,
95, Charing Cross Road,
London, W.C. 2.

Telephone : Regent 0823.
Telegraphic Address : " Hygistor Lonoon."

REG?
357 207

HYGIENIC WHIRLING SPRAY SYRINGE

FIGURE 7.1: Hygienic Whirling Spray Syringe. Hygienic Stores Ltd, London 1929. Wellcome Institute for the History of Medicine. See also in Roy Porter and Lesley Hall, *The Facts of Life: The Creation of Sexual Knowledge in Britain, 1650–1950* (New Haven, CT: Yale University Press, 1995).

own body and the right to use birth control and access to contraceptives. In the United States, it was owing to Margaret Sanger that family planning rose to be a topic of discussion in spite of the Comstock Laws.[5] These had been in effect since 1873 and prohibited any advertisement of contraceptives and prevented the distribution of sex educational literature. In Britain, Marie C. Stopes spread information on contraception[6] with her book *Married Love* (1918), which sold around half a million copies within six years of publication. The thousands of letters that Stopes received from her readers confirmed the huge demand by people from all social classes for more information on contraception.[7] Unsurprisingly, Mother Clinics and Women Welfare Centres that opened in England in 1921 were filled with thousands seeking advice. Similar consultation centers in other European countries soon followed and offered advice and support for all sorts of sex-related problems in addition to information on contraception.

Many church representatives feared that the debates and consultations on contraception would contravene the ethics of Christianity. It was all the more surprising, then, that the Lambert Conference of Anglican Bishops came out in favor of liberalizing marital birth control in 1930. Non-marital intercourse, however, as well as the marketing and distribution of contraceptives, were to remain out of bounds. In Evangelic Lutheran Sweden, the socialist government was one step ahead with their 1930s sex reform and permitted public information on contraceptives as of 1938. The Catholic Church emphasized that the sole purpose of sexual intercourse was marital reproduction. In 1930, Pope Pius XI declared in the encyclicals *Casti connubii* that coitus must not serve any purpose other than procreation and that therefore any kind of contraception was against God's will.

Letters from Catholic believers poured in to Abbé Viollet in France, clearly expressing feeling that Rome had failed them in advice on contraceptive practices. Their comments marked the first cracks between official Catholic dogma on sexual morals and the church members' needs regarding contraception, a gap that was to widen in the decades to come. As one anonymous writer put it: "I feel that what the church asks is unrealisable ... This prohibition comes from a human and not a divine church ... It is neither happiness nor the wisdom of God. I feel that I weaken, I even worry about the strength of my faith ... The Blessed Father no longer appears to me as I feel he is, in other words perfectly just and good."[8]

Until the middle of the 1930s, such letters voiced sex-related questions of people who were—in comparison with today's knowledge of sexuality—entirely naive and forced to resort to gossip and myths to obtain any understanding of sex. A twenty-five-year-old woman from Nantes asked: "Maybe it is wrong and I will say something stupid and ridiculous, but it makes me crazy with fear to ask myself if one kiss could be enough to get pregnant. If you would tell me that I have nothing to fear and that other things are needed, you will deliver me from such torment."[9]

During the interwar years, there were still vast numbers of unwanted pregnancies and abortions in spite of improved sex counseling and education. Following the world economic crisis at the end of the 1920s and the beginning of the 1930s, the numbers of illegitimate births continued to rise rapidly. For this reason, the topic of abortion found its way into political debates. Conservative Christian circles insisted on interpreting abortion as an expression of society's poor moral condition. In addition, it was suspected that abortion might present a danger to the national population balance. Christian parties still regarded the working class as sexually permissive and blamed them for the majority of unwanted pregnancies. Supported by the church, Christian groups therefore attempted to provide the lower classes with a moral (and sexual) education. Conservatives demanded a tightening of the law and intensified prosecution of anyone involved in abortion—women seeking abortion as well as their obliging medics and backstreet abortionists. Left-wing parties, on the other hand, regarded the regulations on abortion as socially unjust, bringing poor people to court while discreetly ignoring more affluent citizens' offenses. In the face of failing family planning, many working-class families were trapped by pregnancies and turned to abortion as a last, if dangerous, resort. Politicization of sexual behavior was turned into a question of social hegemony and was therefore of concern to national politics. In Germany, western Europe's most liberal law was passed in 1926/1927, treating simple abortion as an offense and calling for a penalty of several months' imprisonment. Medical involvement was no longer subject to prosecution as of 1927.

In the 1920s and 1930s, researchers from the fields of medicine, psychology, and biology succeeded in affecting political debates by popularizing their findings. The British Society for the Study of Sex Psychology was founded in 1914, and their publications included the widespread works of Havelock Ellis and Stella Browne.[10] Popular guidebooks increasingly addressed explicit questions about techniques in the art of love for married couples. Marie C. Stopes' groundbreaking aforementioned work *Married Love* (1918) was the first to give practical advice on how couples could obtain and enjoy conjugal pleasures. Most popular, though, was Theodor Van de Velde's *Ideal Marriage: Its Physiology and Technique* (published in 1926; English edition in 1928), focusing on the eroticization of marital life and describing men and women as equally desiring and equally capable of experiencing orgasm, while claiming it to be the man's duty to sexually arouse his partner and make her reach orgasm. Van de Velde identified mutual sexual satisfaction as being essential to any marriage's emotional success. He listed "male inadequacy" in terms of impotence or *ejaculatio praecox* as the most common cause for failed marriages.

Van de Velde also popularized image techniques, such as arousal curves, making them permanent tools of the twentieth century's Western sexual culture. These images described the sexual act to the general public without having to resort to obscenity or verbal elaboration. They acted as a template for normal coitus, depicting simultaneous orgasm as the ultimate goal. After the discovery of the female ovarian hormone in 1912, popular sex guides increasingly referred to allegedly automatic biological or endocrinological processes that were presumed to govern our sexual lives—a tendency that would, within sexual biology, grow stronger in the decades to follow World War II.

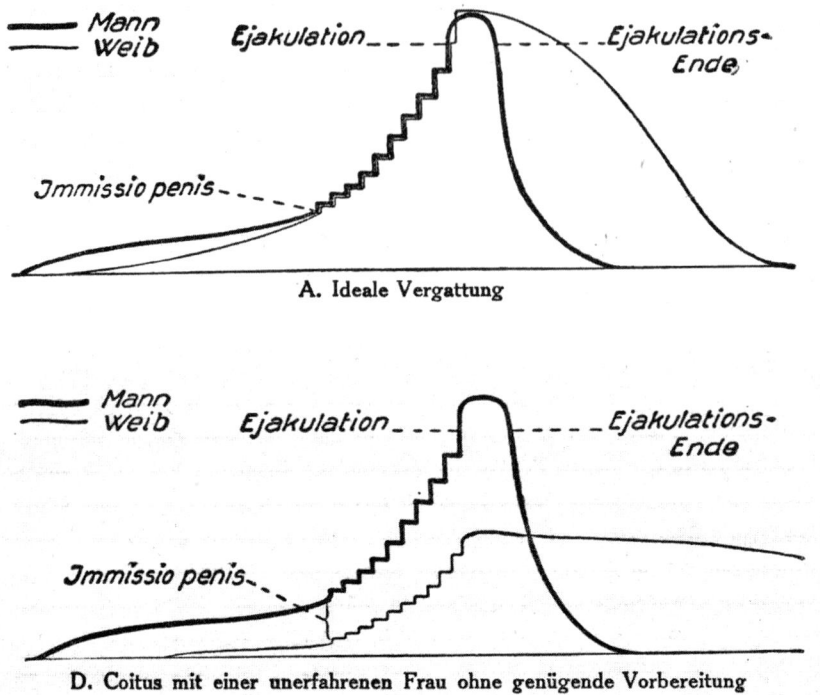

FIGURE 7.2A AND 7.2B: Male and female normal and deviant arousal curves during sexual intercourse, the first image showing complete sexual equality and the second "coitus
with an unexperienced woman without sufficient preparation." In Theodor H. Van
de Velde, *Die vollkommene Ehe* (44th ed.; Leipzig, Germany: Montana-Verlag/Press
Benno Konegen, 1932).

Censorship laws were used broadly, not only to suppress pornography but
also to prevent the selling and distribution of serious but potentially offensive
educational literature. In the 1920s, some Western countries reinstalled state
censorship with the intention of banning images that might violate public morality, above all with the intention of protecting children and adolescents. In
Germany, this approach was pursued with the Law to Preserve the Youth from
Pulpy and Pornographic Literature (1926). However, according to the law,
scientific sex education literature was also liable to be put on a nationwide
"trash index." Such works were banned from being offered for sale, advertised,
ordered, or sold to underage persons. Bookstores and libraries were prohibited
from storing indexed works unless under special conditions and delivered to
specific authorized persons.

Several feature films were produced during the interwar period that caused
scandals.[11] Initially, naked (female) body parts could be depicted within

classical artistic poses only—one pioneering example was Annette Keller-
mann's *Daughter of the Gods* (1915), in which breasts remained partially
hidden behind water and hair. More likely to arouse indignation were films
in which women not only showed skin but played sexually active characters;
vamps like Greta Garbo, Marlene Dietrich, and Mae West, and erotically radi-
ant sinners like Jean Harlowe, found their ways into the generation's collective
memory. Ardently discussed, censored, and partly prohibited was the Czech-
Austrian movie *Ecstasy* (1933), in which Hedy Kiesler(owa)/Lamarr, sur-
rounded by natural symbols like rutting horses, appeared completely naked
and acted as a sexually provocative married woman. In the United States,
the relevant scenes were cut owing to the Hays Office's intervention. As early
as 1920, leading American movie producers had developed a self-regulating
authority that saw that potentially indecent parts were removed from Hollywood movies by precensors. This measure was necessary mainly owing to the
legal censorship requirements of the United States, where by 1921 no less than
36 states had passed articles on censoring films. With the infamous production code, the Motion Picture Producers and Distributors of America submitted in 1930 to an elaborate list of issues and topics, headed by eroticism and
sexuality, and subjected themselves to a (self-)censorship that subsequently
remained in use—with modifications—for approximately thirty years. British
and French movie industries also resorted to similar voluntary self-control
authorities. Another victim to the censors was the film *Different From The
Others,* produced by Hans Oswald in 1919 in Berlin. It featured a story of
love and friendship between an aging music teacher and his pupil, who was
destroyed by a blackmailer. In the movie, the music teacher, was also convicted of perverse fornication (§175). Magnus Hirschfeld himself made an
appearance in the movie and called attention to the problematic life situation
of homosexuals and lesbians caused by prosecution and public discrimination.
This film, however, was not prohibited on grounds of depicting homosexual
eroticism or sexual acts, but because it allegedly reported homosexual love in
too much of a positive light.

In many Western nations, a multifaceted homosexual subculture developed
in the 1920s and early 1930s. Following World War I, the new freedom of
opinion, of press, and of assembly led, particularly in large cities, to a regular boom of related organizations, magazines, and clubs. Most notable was
Berlin, which blossomed into a regular El dorado for gays and lesbians.[12]
Organizations, such as the friendship unions, and friendship papers offered
opportunities to step out of anonymity, to gather at music or hiking clubs,
to meet kindred spirits, and potentially to find love and sex partners without

having to resort to police-controlled parks and public toilets. In the big cities, relevant bars and vaudevilles came to be the pinnacle of homosexual culture, where all tastes were catered for. The scene's magazines described gay and lesbian lifestyles and identities and for the first time addressed the concerns of transgenderism and transvestism. But in spite of new hair styles such as the bob or *garçonne,* and fashionable androgynous chic, the masculinization publicly now displayed by some lesbian women was perceived as being a distortion of gender distinctions. Unsurprisingly, the same question arose that had been asked of gay men some decades previously—were lesbian women to be considered as perverts or merely as people committing perverted acts? These questions of homosexuality resulted from a general insecurity concerning gender differences, mainly the issue as to what constituted a man on a sexual level and what legitimized his social ascendance.[13]

The sufferance of the homosexual scene must not, however, belie the fact that the public and private sexual lives of gays and lesbians in many European countries were still threatened by police harassment and penal prosecutions. In Great Britain, Germany, Austria, Finland, Portugal, and the United States, homosexual acts were prohibited by law,[14] while other Western countries repeatedly resorted to regulations around obscenity and various protective clauses (age, abuse of authority).

As a result, fighting the penal law remained at the top of the agenda even during the Golden Twenties, though now representatives of the social democratic and communist parties came out in favor of an abolishment of the prosecution of consensual homosexual acts between adults. This did not imply, however, that left factionists were of a different opinion.[15] Significantly, left parties employed the stigmatization of homosexuals as a political weapon, as when they denounced Ernst Röhm's Storm Troopers as a network of homosexual men. This was also one of the reasons why the stereotype of the potentially homosexual Nazi spread rapidly and became an integral part of left-wing propaganda. Toward the end of the 1920s, the fascist parties' attitude regarding homosexuals grew more obvious—they intended to eradicate them or at least impose heavy penalties on homosexual desires and acts.

Prostitution, too, was a topic of discussion after World War I. It was now obvious that the vice squad's surveillance of prostitutes had no positive effects and that women merely avoided registering or regular health check-ups for venereal disease. Milieu surveys reported that prostitutes lived and worked under inhumane conditions and that compulsory treatments against venereal diseases (mainly with the arsenic-containing Salvarsan) proved to be of no avail. In an attempt to combat venereal diseases, laws and regulations therefore

mostly exempted prostitution from punishment but at the same time constituted health check-ups and treatment of infected men and women as mandatory. Prostitution, however, remained an offense in England under the Criminal
Law Amendment Act (1922), which imposed sanctions against running a
brothel, or as in Holland, where both pandering and brothels were prohibited
as of 1911. Prostitution was not regarded as a legitimate female professional
occupation. A more lenient attitude was taken by newspapers and magazines
who not only allowed explicit advertisement markets for prostitution but also
permitted personal ads from heterosexual and homosexual backgrounds.

Although sex seemed very much in the public realm in the 1920s and 1930s,
did this result in a change of peoples' sexual attitudes in Europe and the United
States? The evidence is inconsistent: on the one hand, in spite of all the sex
education and improved contraceptives, people continued to perceive sexuality
mainly as burden and menace. More often than not, ignorance, shame, and a
lack of terminology turned sex lives into anxiety-provoking terrains. On the
other hand, there was a growing positive attitude toward everything sexual.
Biographical interview studies and surveys showed that the sexual reform of
the 1920s was of vital importance to the development of sexual education.
More and more juveniles and married couples acquired knowledge on sex and
attempted to put it into practice—eroticizing their own sex lives.[16] Contrary to
former generations, juveniles now found the physical and psychological processes of puberty less menacing and saw sexual morals as being less restrictive.
Premarital intercourse ceased to be generally condemned, providing it involved
potential spouses. Masturbation prior to, and during marriage, met greater
tolerance, and petting experiences increased.[17]

STATE INTERVENTIONISM, CONSERVATIVE FAMILY VALUES, AND COMMERCIAL EROTICIZATION (LATE 1930S UNTIL EARLY 1960S)

Propelled by the Great Depression of the late 1920s and the early 1930s, Western countries embraced conservatism in their developing sexual morals and
cultures. Franco's Spain, Salazar's Portugal, and Stalin's Soviet Union under-
went a Puritan change. Fascist governments of Italy (as of 1922), Germany
(as of 1932/1933), and Austria (as of 1934), and subsequently of all countries
occupied by the Germans, made sexuality an essential part of their ideological
quest.[18] Consequently, one's personal sex life was no longer a private matter
but was turned into a topic of debate regarding nationalism and race. Supported by pronatalist measures, the supposedly pure and high-grade (Aryan)

segment of the population was encouraged to expand. Measures included symbolic awards to women who joyfully had given birth many times, tax benefits for large families, the displacement of women from the labor market, the re-establishment of men as heads of the family, and a harsh penalty placed on contraception and abortion. In the long run, these measures failed to generate any substantial change in sexual conduct. Other countries, too, began to upgrade their public health departments and medical counseling centers, and as a consequence their medical competence. Their institutes offered anamneses (patient case histories), (marriage) counseling sessions, and answers for questions on pregnancy, venereal diseases, impotence, genetic diseases, and sex life.

The fascists' cult of the body made nudity socially acceptable, transporting it into racist, nationalist, and aesthetic concepts. Bodies steeled by gymnastics and sports symbolized strength, discipline, and the eagerness to procreate, and at the same time allowed for the publication of nude pictures without them being stigmatized as pornography. As a consequence, an inadvertent mass reproduction of nude photos took place decades prior to the sexual revolution. The sexualization of images was, however, two-sided: the beauty of the pure body was counteracted by so-called degenerate art depicting undisciplined sexual craving and the menacing art of lecherous Jewish, homosexual, and black artists. The same applied to erotic glamour girls displayed in French and American magazines and in photos and postcards sold under the counter. In general, fascist regimes tended to assume a prosexual attitude as far as premarital and extramarital relations were concerned. Apparently, the image of the presumably sex-averse Nazi regime was one of the myths materializing in the late 1960s and the 1970s in the wake of the so-called struggle to come to terms with National Socialism.[19]

The era's prostitution did, in fact, evoke ambivalence: on one hand, it was generally accepted that a man could occasionally frequent professional prostitutes, provided he did not contract any venereal diseases; on the other hand, the ubiquitous probability of infection made prostitutes a threat to the whole population, not just families and the military. In addition, homosexuals were seen as a menace to moral purity through their employment of seduction techniques and the ensuing contagion. The fascist regimes' homophobia resulted partly from the problematic demarcation of homosocial and homoerotic male relationships within their own—usually unisexual—organizations. Homosexuality was suspected to be a contagious disease spreading rapidly within male and youth organizations, and particularly so within the armed forces of the Third Reich. Consequently, threats of penalties, the banning of relevant magazines, and the policing of gay and lesbian subcultures increased.

FIGURE 7.3A AND 7.3B: Male and female nude images during National Socialism. In Wilm Burghardt, *Sieg der Körperfreude* (Dresden, Germany: Verlag/Press Geist und Schönheit, 1940).

Homophobia reached a state where neighbors, colleagues, and even family members volunteered to denounce suspected homosexuals. At the same time, during the 1930s, the Nazi regime utilized the population's anti-homosexual resentments when attacking government critics—for instance, when employing political purges upon church representatives and aberrant party members after incriminating them by claiming they had committed homosexual offenses.

During World War II, restrictive attitudes toward sexuality were on the rise as distress and dearth left their mark. Contraceptives were scarce to obtain, abortion rates skyrocketed, and venereal diseases spread. Married couples became alienated after long separations. Military officials therefore recommended sex during home leaves, seeing it as essential to the troops' morals. Military brothels—often abusing women (mainly forced laborers and concentration camp captives)—served the same purpose. Women in general faced increasing sexual violence: countless forcible rapes were committed by members of the German Wehrmacht in their occupied territories and by members of the Allied forces, particularly the Russian soldiers, in Germany and Austria in 1945.[20] These traumatizing experiences had dramatic effects on those involved but were hardly acknowledged after the war. Many of the women were scarred for life from the enforced physical and mental assaults, and their sex lives was permanently affected by the ordeal. Marriages frequently failed, as women could not explain their feelings and experiences to their husbands, or because their husbands considered the sexual assault of their wives to be conjugal infidelity.

Numerous voluntary sexual relations between German/Austrian women and Allied soldiers took place in the occupied territories. German-occupied areas in western and northern Europe, for instance, remained largely undisturbed by acts of war until the Allies' invasion. Because people could continue to live a civil or everyday life, there were more sexual contacts, as reported in France, Belgium, the Netherlands and Norway. After the war, many of those women were seen as collaborators and labeled as Germans' whores; along with their children, they were stigmatized and frequently attacked. Attitudes toward Allied occupiers were similarly ambivalent. GIs in particular represented a new type of man, who seduced women with offers of food and extra rations. They were popular with the local young women who, after years of wartime deprivation, wanted to have a good time; others acted out of sheer monetary need. Regardless of their motives, the so-called *Amiliebchen* ("GI mistress") had to bear her neighbors' contempt while being suspected of prostitution. At the same time, GIs gained a bad reputation in England. They were attacked for being "overpaid, oversexed, and over here,"[21] suspected of being the driving force behind the venereal disease epidemic, and were blamed for the alleged moral decay of young women and their sexual permissiveness.

A sexual crisis developed. Owing to the long separations, spouses drifted apart. Women had grown more independent, and men had returned changed or were broken by war trauma. Divorce rates increased as rapidly as illegitimacy, abortions, and venereal disease. Couples who were reunited often lacked the contraceptives necessary for having sex without fear. From 1947, Beate Uhse, the eponymous founder of the future worldwide sex company, realized the situation and started distributing information on contraception in a brochure marketing the Knaus-Ogino temperature method; this enabled couples to calculate a woman's fertile and infertile phases. As a second bestseller, she republished Van de Velde's *The Perfect Marriage* in 1949.

Young people developed a craving for adventurous sexual experiences, while facing an imbalance in the ratio of women to men because of the war's death toll. With the loosening of censorship, educational and advice literature came onto the market, supplemented with erotic magazines styled in the U.S. manner; the latter depicted pin-up girls, which had been part of every Allied soldier's field kit during the war.[22] Meanwhile, venereal diseases lost much of their threat once penicillin was introduced after the war.

The evident liberalization of sexual attitudes during and after the war was confirmed by surveys conducted in several countries at the end of the 1940s. They revealed that contraception was by now widely used and premarital sex was indeed accepted, if only with prospective spouses. Opinions on abortion, prostitution, and masturbation varied, but people remained largely antagonistic toward homosexuality. A healthy sexual relationship was now regarded as being essential to a successful marriage. Yet, in spite of these liberal tendencies, for the most part, sexual activities remained more acceptable for couples who were already married. As the so-called Little Kinsey Mass Observation report found in England in 1949, even in supposedly prudish countries, a sexual language developed that enabled conversation on such topics outside of the bedroom.[23] Meanwhile, churches maintained their considerable influence on moral standards: "Churchgoers are in consequence the only group which, when confronted with a sudden question on, say, prostitution or divorce, tends to be ready with a preconceived and preconsidered answer."[24] However, contemporary observers commented that most English people's views on sexual morality were "more rigid than their personal practice."[25] The result of the surveys indicated that sexual knowledge was more advanced than previously thought and found that many people derived erotic stimulation from books and magazines.

The Kinsey reports based their findings on a vast amount of collected data. Kinsey revealed that numerous American men and women masturbated, that a third of the population committed adultery, and that many people had homosexual experiences at some points in their lives. In short, he found that moral ideals and sexual practice diverged wildly. Furthermore, the reports discovered considerable differences between Europe and the United States, particularly concerning premarital intercourse: in the United States, premarital intercourse was not much approved of, whereas heavy petting (until reaching orgasm) was well accepted. American women explained their aversion to premarital coitus as a result of individual moral scruples (yet not necessarily conforming to definite religious or legal norms), as a lack of sexual desire, and as fear of both pregnancy and of the opinion of the public.[26] The double standard was obvious: while many men assumed a positive attitude toward premarital intercourse and actively pursued it, they expected women to enter into matrimony as a virgin. In the eyes of Europeans, the Kinsey reports exposed how American uptightness, which had generated ideas on sexual morals and legislation, diverged even more from actual sexual practice than in the UK.

The postwar 1940s and early 1950s, saw a clamp-down in reaction to the perceived sexual chaos: sex was once more regarded as something only to be conducted between married couples. The neoconservative (nuclear) family ideal was at the heart of this moral reconstruction. Sex manuals published clear definitions of a woman's role: "The job description of the housewife included being a willing and enthusiastic sexual partner."[27] Sexual freedom was curtailed, and sex became a quintessentially private and non-political act. The sexual fidelity of a woman was considered a highly treasured value. Traditional family role assignment was intended to stabilize economic reconstruction—the Fordist economical model that had been so successfully realized in the American way of life was focused on consumption. Its aspiration meant that young people rated marriage, family, and a home (and a secure income) much higher than any other asset, and this was reflected in rising marriage rates and the baby boom.

Premarital restraint and sexual integrity headed the Christian prescription for a future love match and a happy matrimonial life. Contrary to men, women were seen to be more emotional, eager to procreate, and sexually passive by nature. Among approved sexual ideals for adolescents were virginity, restraint from masturbation, and a stable heterosexual orientation. In European countries, sexual education was regarded as the responsibility of the parents, but brochures and films gained territory as commercial interests increased.[28] German and Austrian pornography laws came out around 1950 aimed at preventing the distribution of pulpy and pornographic literature. Marketing and distribution of contraceptives were subjected to strict regulations, resulting in soaring sales through discreet ordering services.

Several sex problems of the war and postwar period, such as sexually transmitted diseases and prostitution, became less significant in the wake of medical advance and the stabilization of the family system. And even though rates were somewhat higher than in the 1930s, the topic of illegitimacy and abortion also faded into the background. As economic prospects began to brighten, many illegitimate children, often conceived by long-time couples who had postponed marriage in the hope of a more stable economic future, were legitimized by fast marriages. Homosexuality, on the other hand, largely remained an indecent topic, yet the predicaments of—mainly male—homosexual life managed to reach the public via press releases on sensational arrests and legal proceedings.

In the United States, homosexuals were put on the index of political suspects during the cold war as being debauched and vulnerable to political blackmail. Persecution and discrimination peaked during the McCarthy years as homosexuals fell victim to political paranoia: "Already believed to be morally enfeebled by sexual indulgence, homosexuals would readily succumb to the blandishments of the spies and betray their country rather than risk exposure of their sexual identity."[29] Homosexuals were seen as the antithesis of the heterosexual married couple; Finland's media became particularly concerned "when the issues of family, motherhood, and women's employment were also very much in the forefront."[30] The statements of medical doctors, psychologists, lawyers, and politicians reinforced prejudiced stereotypes, even in countries where they did not strictly prohibit homosexual acts. In France, homosexuals were blamed for refusing to procreate and were equated with Nazis and Arabs.[31] More open discussions were taking place in Britain with the establishment of the British Wolfenden Committee (1957), which suggested decriminalization of consensual homosexual acts among adults (over twenty-one years of age) and same-sex prostitution.

The 1950s and early 1960s can be perceived as a period of conservative sex morals, yet they were also marked by a media-hyped boom of eroticism. A commercialization of sex took place in popular culture, particularly in the music and movie industries, as investors realized the potential value of sex. Elvis ("the Pelvis") and other rock 'n' roll musicians began to attract the attention of young people. Wild dancing styles opened new opportunities to young men and women to express themselves more openly than had their parents from the frugal and sacrificing war generation. Sexy movie idols such as James Dean in

Rebel without a Cause (1955) played angry and rebellious yet highly attractive young heroes. Bikinis and so-called atomic boobs adorned the female body on magazine covers. Beauty contests became the 1950s' platform for marketing and adapting erotic body ideals to national and regional styles. Smut and men's magazines, such as *Razzle* and *Playboy* (1953), published articles along with pictures of pin-ups (including the famous Vargas Girls) in glamour shots. Such American-style movie, music, and youth magazines conveyed gossip and fashion to the new teen market. Everyone who had the opportunity went to see one of the new scandalous erotic movies showing naked actresses. Françoise Arnoul shed her clothes in *L'Epave* (1949) and *Le fruit défendu* (1952) and Hildegard Knef stepped naked (if only for a couple of seconds) in front of the camera as an artist's model in *The Sinner* (1950). The female characters in Western filmmaking remained firmly stuck with three types: Marilyn Monroe, lascivious and at the same time naive, forever luring men into extramarital pleasures; Brigitte Bardot, whose half-dressed body appeared like a vision of nature on screen; and the Virgin Queen, Doris Day, after tumultuous erotic banter awaiting prospective sexual fulfillment in the conjugal bedroom. The average teenager's sexual desires were directed primarily into the private, nonpolitical

FIGURE 7.4: A lascivious Marilyn Monroe in the German youth magazine *BRAVO*, 35 (1957).

family life, promising connubiality along with economic stability and the prospect of consumption. Parents' adverse reactions to the media's sex symbols made them all the more appealing to their teenage children and ensured their attraction to the forbidden erotic culture. When Ingmar Bergman's *Tystnaden* (The Silence, 1963) depicted scenes of masturbation and sex scenes devoid of love or affection, the media cried out in protest, yet few people resisted going and marveling at the sensation: some ten million spectators made the movie a great commercial success.

A REVOLUTION, OR CATCHING UP ON LIBERALIZATION (MID-1960S TO 1980S)

Sexual lives in the Western world had, in fact, been revolutionized decades prior to the so-called sexual revolution of late 1960s and the 1970s; public moral standards and attitudes merely trailed behind established practice. What we refer to as the sexual revolution is therefore not so much a swift and radical change of sexual conduct as a culmination of a lengthy process. From the mid-1960s onward, this process was widely discussed in Western societies and within a few years had led to a liberalization of attitudes and sex-related norms. In a strictly historical context, therefore, one should perhaps refer to a sexual liberalization rather than a revolution. Without a doubt, the discourse on liberalization via media, politics, and youth and student movements contributed to convincing more and more people to adopt the new liberal approach, eventually making them standard. Yet the sexual liberalization's entire impact was not entirely revealed until the 1970s, when politicians succumbed and modified provisions of the law that had been valid for decades or even centuries. The new sexual culture showed itself in continuously decreasing marriage and birth rates. In devout Catholic countries such as Italy, Spain, or Portugal, the sexual revolution came a few years later. However, Spain, immediately following the end of Franco's dictatorship in 1975, was flooded by a radical sex and porn wave.

During the 1960s, rapid economic development saw the change from productive to consumption society that made sex a positive asset of culture and society. For the first time people were able to forget the years of deprivation and poverty and turn their attention to consumption and experience. Even in countries most affected by the war, the economy turned from demand oriented to supply oriented—more goods and services were available than demanded. Marketing and advertisement soon utilized sex as a communication tool to support products' and media's competitive edge.[32] Although the traditional sex norms of the church were still in place, certain laws were relaxed: business investors quickly took advantage of the opportunities that had opened up to make money from trading in erotic and sex-related products. Meanwhile, while sex was still widely considered a dirty secret by their parents' generation, young people happily absorbed any information on the subject. Yet sexualization was not a phenomenon restricted to youth and student culture. It was widespread, having initially emerged among the working class and lower middle class before reaching better-off juveniles and students.

Furthermore, liberal attitudes were supported by political and democratic developments such as feminist and antiracism movements. Increasing individualization also had its impact, allowing people (young people in particular) to develop their own and very private living space—such as a room of one's own for adolescents, either in their parents' houses or in single flats for young adults—and as a result more space for sexual activity. This private space became more widely accepted as a realm where one had a right to pursue one's sexual pleasures (provided they were within the law). In some countries, several years passed before governments changed their laws and fell in line with popular practice—for instance, in the United States following the Supreme Court's decision on *Griswold vs. Connecticut* in 1965, which protected "the sanctity of a man's home and the privacy of life against all government invasions."[33] In Holland, it was the Catholic and Protestant clerics who advocated a positive approach to sexual life and sexual questions regarding education or marriage—including contraception and divorce.

One of the prevalent factors propelling the change in attitude toward sexuality was, indubitably, the popularization of sexual knowledge provided in guidebooks and educational movies. They shifted attitudes from focusing on marital intercourse as an imperative to the pursuit of one's own individual experimental experiences. Compared to titillating works such as David Reuben's *Everything You Always Wanted to Know about Sex (But Were Afraid to Ask)* (1969) or Alex Comfort's *The Joy of Sex: A Gourmet Guide to Love Making* (1972), sex manuals in Europe presented themselves as being quite conservative and uptight. Professional sex science and psychiatry remained, for the time being, dedicated to sexual pathology, reaching only a small circle of interested intellectuals.

Schools also eventually opened up the topic for debate: Sex education classes were discussed for years before finally being put in place in the 1970s. This move also revealed the need to first educate the school teachers who were to teach the subject, not only on the social and cultural aspects of sex life but also the biological ones. When William H. Masters and Virginia Johnson published *Human Sexual Response* (1966) and *Human Sexual Inadequacy* (1970), they paved the way for a medical and biological comprehension of sexuality, facilitating public debate in the process. Both "became the iconic representatives of an international scientific and social movement that sought to demystify sex, employing 'objective' scientific observation along with political and philosophical debate to liberate human sexual pleasure from the shackles of political, religious and social conventions."[34] As a result of Masters and Johnson's investigations, it was obvious that sexual science "discovered a responsive, sexually capable and potentially autonomous female body underneath social and expert myths of feminine passivity."[35]

With the abolition of the Hays Code in Hollywood any legal obstacles that had blocked the way to eroticizing commercial U.S. movies disappeared. The U.S. Supreme Court abolished the Comstock Law in 1945, legalizing marketing and distribution of contraceptives and educational literature and paving the way for extensive discussion on the pill and sexual education. From the middle of the 1960s onward, magazines depicting half-naked female bodies eagerly reported on various ways and practices of physical lovemaking. At the same time, the first modern educational movies, such as Oswalt Kolles's *The Miracle of Love* (1967), *Your Wife, the Unknown Being* (1968) and *Your Husband, the Unknown Being* (1969), were produced. Erotic movies sold sex by disguising it as educational material of a Kinsey sex report fashion.

From 1970, the commercial exploitation of the sexualized—mostly female—body served the basis for movies such as *Schulmädchen-Report* (Schoolgirl Report, UK: Confessions of a Sixth Form Girl) and *Hausfrauen-Report* (Housewife Report), viewed by some twenty-five million spectators all over Europe.

For the media's sex industry to live up to its potential, however, pornography laws first had to be abolished. Denmark was the first to legalize distribution of classical erotic literature: In 1979, pornographic literature could be produced and sold to anyone aged sixteen or older. Two years later, all prohibition of depictions of erotic images and objects was dropped. In October 1969, Copenhagen hosted the world's first erotic fair, attracting national and international—mostly male—visitors of all social classes. Sweden overturned its pornographic laws in 1971 and advanced quickly to be a dominant supplier of related products. By the middle of the 1970s, pornography was available to all adults in most other European countries.

Representatives of the new feminist movement criticized the sexual objectification of the female body and objected to the pandering to men's power-obsessed domination fantasies. Nonetheless, the market for erotic and soft-core porn magazines such as the so-called weekend magazines flourished, and hard-core pornographic images and movies began to appear, concentrating on showing the sex act at the expense of a proper plot line. Television, now the leading medium during the 1960s, eventually fell in line; even in Catholic Austria, bare breasts were seen on TV for the first time on April 11, 1969—in a report on a cinema film. One year later, the sensation could be marveled at live—if covered by a transparent blouse—during prime time in the entertainment show *Wünsch dir was*.

The birth control pill made a huge impact on popular culture The first hormonal contraceptive to be produced in the United States was Enovid-E in 1960, to be followed by Anovlar in Europe a year later. By the middle of the 1960s, advertising and press reports had generated sufficient publicity for the oral contraceptive to be prescribed and purchased on a larger scale. A survey from 1989 revealed that around 75 percent of all English women born between 1945 and 1959 were using the pill, lifting the threat of unwanted pregnancy from their sex lives.[36] For the first time, young women could take control of their sex lives without requiring their partner's support; the pill was also reliable, relieving much of the anxiety of unwanted pregnancy. Meanwhile, feminist movements voiced their concerns over the lack of surveys on long-term use and possible adverse reactions and suggested that women had once again ended up with yet another burden of unshared responsibility.

The youth movement was another force propelling sexuality into public debate. Striving to confront their authoritarian parental generation and the capitalistic consumerism they represented, young people banded together to establish alternative lifestyles involving flower power, beat music, and drugs. They introduced the concept of free love, the message "Let's Spend the Night Together," proclaimed by the Rolling Stones, acting as the leitmotif for popular youth culture and their leading medium, rock music. The spirit of freedom in the Summer of Love in 1967 was seized by the youth movement as the beginnings of a new time of sexual liberation in expectation that a revolution of general social standards would follow. The most prominent example was Berlin's Kommune 1, whose members conveyed their criticism of society via sex scandals. "Make Love, Not War" was their motto, aimed especially against the Vietnam War. Wilhelm Reich and Herbert Marcuse supplied them with the theoretical ammunition to develop a sex-based explanation for the bourgeois repression of sexuality. According to these authors, liberalization of sex was mandatory in order to create a more just and nonrepressive society. The limitations of the youth and student movements was exposed by the women's liberation movement of the 1970s, which equated social dominance of men with phallic dominance in bed and put a noisy end to the "Myth of Vaginal Orgasm."[37]

As a result of public debate, laws against abortion were abolished. In Germany, for instance, hundreds of women in a spectacular campaign of *Stern* magazine (1971) admitted they had had abortions, pointing out the uselessness of the law. In the wake of the protest movements and their exposure in the media, the laws were changed in various countries, and abortion was permitted within the first three months of pregnancy or under special circumstances agreed on by the doctors (German Democratic Republic, 1972; Austria, 1973–1975; Sweden, 1974). On a practical basis, however, it took years to supply the required number of doctors and medical outpatient clinics sufficiently equipped to undertake the demands for abortion.

The 1970s saw the liberalization of regulations regarding family and divorce, both for contracting and dissolving marriages of two (heterosexual) partners based of their mutual consent alone. Civil contracts were allowed, devoid of any religious ceremony. Gays and lesbians vehemently demanded legal and social emancipation, with the Stonewall Riots attracting considerable media attention: on June 27, 1969, for the first time homosexuals openly rebelled against police harassment and discrimination after a raid at the Stonewall Inn located on New York's Christopher Street. Many hours of upheaval in the streets of Greenwich Village ensued.

In other Western countries, gays and lesbians made their voices heard in demonstrations and demanded change. Laws against homosexuality were annulled, but different regulations concerning age of consent, matrimony, hereditary, and adoption remained unchanged for decades to come. The cultural identity of gays and lesbians, however, did change during the 1970s. Traditional role concepts of effeminate men and masculine women faded, to be replaced by so-called normal homosexuals who increasingly adopted their own genders' identities. Most homosexual couples now socially positioned themselves akin to heterosexuals, and formerly marked age differences between same-sex couples diminished. A normalization of homosexual desire was established by the American Psychiatric Association in 1973, when it concluded that homosexuality was not a mental disease.

Comparative studies on German students confirmed the shifting of attitude toward homosexuality. Between 1966 and 1981, they increasingly tolerated homosexuals, while their own heterosexual orientation became more fragile. At the same time, heterosexualization became further entrenched in the 1970s and 1980s, seen in decreased homosexual contact during adolescence.[38] This was a result of co-education and better sex education. All those having sexual contact with another person of the same gender were now forced to contemplate the possibility that they were homosexual and would be subject to stigmatization as homosexuals. In general, as far as sexual behavior and attitudes of conservative groups (of which students were a part) were concerned, sexual attitudes and behavior changed rapidly. As had been the case with young working-class members during the 1950s and 1960s, premarital sexual intercourse now grew to be standard among other classes, and the number of sex partners and frequency of intercourse increased. The employment of a variety of sex techniques became a sexual imperative, just as did the acceptance of masturbation prior to and during partnership or matrimony. This progress was most obvious among women. Premarital virginity ceased to be regarded as a virtue; young people mostly rejected the sexual double standard as a relic from their parents' generation. Supported by the feminist movement, by sex guidance literature, and by the media, more and more women actively demanded that their specific sexual desires should be satisfied. The message failed, however, to reach the booming sex film industry of the 1970s: in and out of Hollywood, women were still portrayed as sexual objects.

SEX BETWEEN NEGOTIATION, RISK, AND VIRTUALIZATION (1980S TO PRESENT DAY)

As a result of liberalization in the late 1960s and the 1970s, sex was soon fully integrated into the commercial supply of the Western market. Products and services were sold in the media as sexual promises. This oversexualization rapidly reduced the effect of sexual stimuli, forcing the advertising industry to push back the boundaries of what could or should be explicitly depicted.[39] Visual sexual stimulation was easily obtained in the rapidly expanding market of erotic and pornographic magazines and movies, offered for sale at every kiosk or video store's adult section. This gave birth in the 1980s to a feminist movement named PorNo, fighting against the pornographization of the female body and the accompanying violent sex fantasies. At the peak of the sex war in the middle of the 1980s, the battles involved "the regulation of pornography, the scope of legal protection for gay people, the funding of allegedly 'obscene' art, the content of safe-sex education, the scope of reproductive freedom for women, the extent of sexual abuse of children in day care centres, the sexual content of public school centres, and more."[40] Alternatively, so-called porn for women voted for a different kind of eroticism and pornography that would cater to the needs of women.

A satisfactory sex life had now come to be a requirement for (post)modern men and women. Terms such as "performance," "innovation," and "technique" entered the sexual arena, aimed at improving one's own and one's partner's pleasure. Sex manuals suggested remedies for impotence and suggested how to work on lack of sexual interest. Therapists and sexual medical doctors offered their services, and in the middle of the 1990s, Viagra came to the aid of those suffering from impotence. "Sexual health and pleasure are endlessly promoted everywhere and appear to be keys to 'life' itself."[41] Those who did not manage to act out their fantasies and desires with a lover or sex partner would soon find substitutes in new technology such as telephone or Internet sex. Increasingly, masturbation came to be regarded as a separate autoerotic sexual realm offering uncomplicated sexual satisfaction or simply relaxation.

In the face of affordable, easily obtainable, and, most importantly, safe contraceptives, sex was no longer tied to procreation. Meanwhile, new reproduction technologies (such as in vitro fertilization) detached procreation from sexual desire. Sexually transmitted diseases lost some of their threat, owing to effective remedies. During the 1980s, however, AIDS, became the new fear but was then thought to affect only a marginalized minority. Moralizers even claimed the so-called gays' pest to be a divine retribution for the promiscuity of homosexuals. Nevertheless, the AIDS panic only held up the increasingly liberal approach to homosexual men and women for a short while. Intense coverage of homosexuality in the media even opened up new insights into the social and relational cultures of gays and lesbians, with it came an increase in tolerance and acceptance. During the second half of the 1980s, it became evident that unprotected heterosexual intercourse had led to a rise in the spread of venereal disease, putting an end to sex without worries and unprotected sexual liberty.

During the 1990s and the early twenty-first century, horrifying cases of pedophilia, child pornography, and sexual murder of children were exposed. Although the number of such cases had not increased—most assaults on children still occurred within the circle of family and acquaintances—the number of occurrences that were uncovered did increase, mainly owing to a higher sensitivity to these offenses. The highly emotional media coverage did, however, opened the debate on age of consent and possible sexual dependencies between adults and children/adolescents. For some groups of migrants, sexual liberalization went beyond their realms of tolerance, which were defined by their traditional cultures' approaches to gender and sexuality matters. Violent assaults on members of the gay community were reported from some of the new European Union member states, where after 1989 latent resentments erupted as new homophobia.

In the 1990s for adolescents and young adults, solid relationships and sexual fidelity also grew more important, again as a reaction to a culture that had abandoned traditional sex morals and replaced them with negotiation or consent morals.[42] The desire to experiment in promiscuous relationships was increasingly replaced by a need for closeness and safety in a relationship. Now male youths increasingly connected sex to love and emotional ties, and young women and girls demanded sexual pleasure more actively.[43] Using contraceptives was by now commonplace, yet first sexual contacts often still took place without protection, mainly because of embarrassment. In comparison with the sexual revolutionists of the 1960s and 1970s, both men and women had come to perceive sex as a rather nonmythical and undramatic part of life, with no requirement for liberations or attachments to a political utopia. This does not necessarily imply a sexual counter-revolution. The rigid attitude that had prevailed prior to the sexual liberalization never reestablished itself.[44] But in comparison with the liberal 1970s, some people displayed less tolerance to promiscuousness, to pre- and extra-marital sex, and to homosexuality, particularly in the United States in the 1980s and 1990s: "This ending of liberal advance might reflect a homeostatic cycle of reform or a reaction to problems created by liberalism in general or sexual permissiveness in particular (in other words, increases in sexually transmitted diseases and non-marital births was possibly a desire for commitment rather than casual recreational sex)."[45] Also in the United States, new right-wing parties and conservative religious circles joined together to wage a so-called war on sex, employing measures such as the Abstinence Until Marriage campaigns in schools.[46] In Europe, the fuelling of sex panics repeatedly proved useful in introducing neoconservative and restrictive moral standards to everyday political discourse.[47]

The mass production of sexual cultural images and texts has had the effect of blurring gender and sex identities. Beyond polarized heterosexuality and homosexuality, today there exists a wide range of sexualities: hetero-, homo- and multi-sexuals, androgyny, queer and transgender sexualities, and so forth. Homosexual desire is widely accepted within the normal range of sexualities—which is one of the reasons why sexuality has ceased to be a suitable basis for the constitution of a specifically gay or lesbian identity. According to today's confessional TV shows, everybody should or could be a little perverted. The fetishizing of images of sex has not stopped at normalizing perversion. Currently, the Internet offers a conglomeration of diverse sexual practices, some of which, only a few decades ago, would have been subjected to penal law or, at the very least, investigation by psychiatrists Furthermore, intimate bodily contact had been replaced by cybersex, the auto-erotic pleasures of steel prostheses nipple-claps, and machine-generated stimulation such as the Sybian (a masturbatory device for women), but such cold technology failed to take hold.

After the sexual liberalization of the 1960s and 1970s and the gender revolution of the 1980s, the 1990s saw a radical change in relationship culture—matrimony decreased and long-term cohabiting partnership rose. The preferred sexual relationship is now one in which both partners communicate on an equal basis.[48] Whether the relationship endures or not is influenced by mutual compatibility, which includes, as a central factor, excitement and satisfaction in one's sex life. As was the case in the romantic love partnership of the eighteenth and nineteenth centuries, sex is now being integrated into the overall vision of a loving relationship. Instead of gaining only satisfaction in sex, a rounded loving relationship is being sought—yet sex is only one component of consumption, leisure, and individualism, an everyday experience along with many others. But the egalitarian, emotion-oriented, and soothing sex ideal misjudges vital constituents of sexual desire, such as difference in power relations and sexual tensions, and this may be one of the reasons why sexual desire decreases instead of increases.[49] Also, in most Western countries, criticism of sexual liberalization is increasing, with rising authoritarianism eradicating freedoms gained since the 1960s and 1970s. Recent surveys have revealed that the number of people who are dissatisfied with their sex lives is rising—possibly a result of the growing gap between the media-produced ideal, in all its glossy variations, and the unvaried everyday bedroom practices between spouses or partners. Compared to the other increasing differentiations in the world of consumption, Western capitalism has not diversified the average citizen's sex life, but has instead restricted it[50]: In the past two decades, normalized heterosexual monogamy has gained momentum, leaving promiscuous, homosexual, or prostitute sex practices far behind. Prior to the sexual revolution, Europeans and Americans practiced sex in every way they pleased regardless of the law or moral reprobation. Now, it seems, the highly sexualized Western contemporary culture ignores the practices and forces us to make use of whatever sexual images and fantasies are available to us.

CHAPTER EIGHT

Prostitution

MARIE-LOUISE JANSSEN

Throughout Western history, many stories circulated about prostitution, giving rise to myths and fears about prostitutes. Within Christian morality, prostitution has always been viewed as a manifestation of evil, sexual impurity, and deviance. Prostitutes were seen as immoral women who formed a threat to public health. In Victorian Britain, for example, prostitutes were considered vectors of diseases and blamed for widespread epidemics, such as the plague or syphilis, a common venereal disease in those days. Historical narratives tended to present prostitution as a result of poverty or pathology, leaving working-class women particularly vulnerable to stigmatization. The pervasiveness of these dominant narratives lends support to a continued representation of prostitutes as poor and helpless women instead of as individuals who think for themselves, make choices, and might even enjoy such work in preference to other jobs.

In most Western societies today, prostitution is treated as a social problem that has to be eradicated from society. Depending on how prostitution is defined and analyzed, various solutions are articulated and implemented, but prostitutes have always been excluded from major policy decisions. As prostitutes find themselves marginalized, alienated, criminalized, or victimized, the causes of prostitution are explained, standpoints arise, discourses emerge, and policies are imposed without their voices.

The French strike in 1975 marked a decisive point in the contemporary Euro-American history of prostitution, when 100 to 150 prostitutes occupied

one of the main churches in the centre of Lyon in protest against police harassment. For the first time in Europe, prostitutes started to speak up in great numbers in public spaces and were listened to. This collective action by prostitutes
marked the beginning of a new political movement and had a decisive impact
on the course of prostitution policies in Western countries.

When we look at the twentieth century, we see two opposing standpoints
in the debate on prostitution: the abolitionist movement and the prostitutes'
rights movement. Both movements are currently operating on the political
level and they have become the two main discourses. The first perspective is
put forward by the abolitionists, who consider prostitution to be a form a
sexual violence against women. According to this point of view, sexual relations with customers are by nature demeaning and harmful for the prostitute,
so they campaign for legislation against prostitution. The second is expressed
by politically mobilized prostitutes, supported by prostitutes' rights activists,
libertarians, and pro-sex feminists, who approach prostitution through labor
law and decriminalization of the sex industry, emphasizing individual choice
and the right of self-determination. From this perspective, prostitution should
be treated like other kinds of work. The problem is not the work itself but the
stigma attached to it and the lack of good legislation and protection of prostitutes against violence, abuse, and exploitation.

The prominence of both discourses forces us to engage in a historical examination and to unravel the underlying assumptions about sexuality and gender.
Dissecting some of these conceptions allows us to understand the complexity
and barriers to fully grasp the meaning of prostitution in the twentieth-century
Western world. By giving a short overview of the policy developments regarding
prostitution and identifying the different forms prostitution has taken, this
chapter attempts to put the lives of these women and men in a sociohistorical
and political context. First, I will analyze the rise of the dominant discourses
and the ways in which prostitution has been articulated. By examining the
different prostitutes' organizations that have been established in the course of
the twentieth century, a greater insight can be gained in the lives of prostitutes
and the issues they face daily. I will continue by focusing on the developments
that have been taking place in the sex industry toward the end of the century,
culminating in two opposite political models of prostitution, the case of the
Netherlands, which has legalized prostitution, and the case of Sweden, which
has criminalized the clients. Within this latter model, clients are seen as a particular kind of person with a deviant personality—an idea that has given rise
to the identity of a sex client, like Foucault's homosexual in the nineteenth

century. Finally, the accomplishments of prostitutes' organizations will be addressed, and I will discuss what the future may hold, including relationships with general labor unions.

INCREASED REGULATION OF PROSTITUTION

Western societies are characterized by a Christian tradition in which reproduction is seen as the primary criterion of sexual morality—sex is permitted, but only within the boundaries of a heterosexual marriage. Women who offer sexual services to a high number of different men violate these sexual taboos and are therefore morally condemned as "whores" or "sluts." Since the nineteenth century, our perception of human sexual behavior has largely been shaped by medical science. Within the medicalization of sexuality, all non-procreative sexual activities, like masturbation, homosexuality, and prostitution, were taken to be manifestations of bad habits and lack of education, and as signs of unhealthy and pathological behavior.

In the medico-sexological discourse, sex came to be understood as one of the key determinants of human personality, particularly so in relation to prostitution, since it was considered a deviant form of female sexuality. In historical studies, prostitutes have been mainly depicted as a homogeneous category of women to whom all kinds of negative personal traits were attributed. In Victorian England, for example, prostitutes were portrayed as promiscuous, lustful women with dissolute habits. They were thought to be depraved women who were naturally more inclined to prostitution than others because of their wanton sexual desires. Expressions such as "once a harlot, always a harlot" conveyed prominent beliefs about prostitutes, and this dominant image mainly derived from police reports, prison records, and cemetery registers in which prostitutes appeared as criminals and pathological figures.[1]

Sexual conduct, and its possible consequences, came to be seen in terms of critical political issues, since it involved the health and strength of the nation. This medical interest in sexuality was dictated by wider social anxieties. Sex was problematized in a new way, now linked to economic and social problems. It was now recognized that most prostitutes came from the poor labor class and engaged in prostitution out of economic necessity. Hence the medical profession was an influential pressure group that provided the intellectual rationale for state intervention in working-class culture. It was no longer thought that penal law alone should prevent immorality and create socially acceptable sexual standards but that medicine, education, and social hygiene should play a part.

In Britain during the nineteenth century, calls for chastity mounted, and with them came an increase in moral indignation about prostitution. This shift was connected to other developments that took place in society, such as the rise of the abolitionist movement, an international movement supported by Christians, socialists, feminists, and doctors, who defended public morality and strived for the abolition of slavery. A strong moralistic section of this movement was the antiprostitution movement, which considered prostitution a form of female sexual slavery, which had to be combated. This line of thought was also a reaction to the introduction of the French system of the regulation of prostitution. In the early nineteenth century, Napoleon had established the first mandatory health examinations in a system of registered prostitutes and tolerated brothels.[2] As a consequence, systems of registering prostitutes and compulsory medical examination were implemented throughout Europe. In 1811, the Netherlands followed suit, and in the 1860s, Italy, England, and Germany introduced variants of the French regulatory system.

Gender and class were key variables in the organization of sexuality. This became clearly visible when The Contagious Diseases Acts were introduced in England and Ireland in 1864 to control the spread of venereal disease (VD) among men in garrison towns and ports. These acts authorized the British police to pick up any morally suspect woman who might be a prostitute and have her physically examined. Infected women were interned in specially designated hospitals wards. The abolitionists and middle-class feminists in the Victorian period had several objections against the regulation of prostitution and considered the Acts an example of class and sex discrimination.[3] The Acts not only deprived poor women of their constitutional rights and forced them to submit to a degrading internal examination but they officially sanctioned male vice. While the male bourgeois could visit prostitutes without fear of punishment, these women were submitted to mandatory health controls and hospitalization. Tolerating and regulating prostitution suggested that for men, going to prostitutes was inevitable because of their natural need for sexual satisfaction. These feminists strongly opposed this law and the double standard of sexual morality that was implicit in it, and criticized the misogynist rationale for regulated prostitution, which imposed repressive controls on prostitutes. Largely due to the mobilization of this first wave of feminism, the Acts were finally repealed in 1886.

In comparison with England, Scotland developed a more interventionist ideology.[4] During the 1920s, Scottish local health authorities implemented measures to regulate and contain the spread of VD that were increasingly targeted not just at professional prostitutes but also at young sexually active women in general. The vicious habits and unresponsiveness of young women—commonly designated as problem girls or loose women—were viewed by Scottish health officials as both immoral and unclean. "Their promiscuity was perceived as central to the continuing spread of VD and a serious threat to the health and stability of family and community relationships."[5] Besides the more primitive notion of women as reservoirs of infection, such a view shows how anxieties and assumptions fuelled public health debate over sexually transmitted diseases, such as contemporary fears over female immorality and vice. "Even when demoralization of women had been caused by male exploitation, it was the loss of female chastity that was central to the spread of disease."[6]

CLANDESTINE BROTHELS

The abolitionist movement in Britain spread to the Netherlands and made an abrupt end to the liberal age. Over the course of the nineteenth century, contraception had become more widely available, especially for middle-class couples, which lead to increased toleration of those sex practices, such as prostitution and homosexuality, which fell outside of the legitimated boundaries of heterosexual monogamy and marriage. Brothels in the Netherlands were officially recognized until far into the nineteenth century. However, at the turn of the nineteenth century, prostitution, and its medical regulation, became a highly contentious subject. Thousands of people from different ideological backgrounds mobilized in the struggle against prostitution and campaigned for stricter sex laws.[7] In the early twentieth century, the method of systematic regulation broke down and was finally abandoned. This was legally reinforced by the Ban on Brothels in 1911, a law that forbade the exploitation of prostitution. The prohibition of brothel-keeping was part of a set of Morality Laws, whereby all sex outside the context of marriage, reproduction, and love was deemed immoral. Besides tighter regulations on prostitution, this law prohibited same-sex acts between adults and minors under twenty-one years, and banned pornography, contraceptives, and abortion.

Despite the prohibition of brothel keeping, prostitution proved impossible to eradicate. On the contrary, the new sex laws that were meant to improve public morality and ensure the closure of the brothels resulted in an increase of illegal brothels and street prostitution.[8] The big, luxurious brothels, which

FIGURE 8.1: Bordello disguised as tobacco shop,
Amsterdam 1920s. Since 1911, making money
from prostitutes had been forbidden in the Netherlands, but prostitution itself was legal. Therefore,
brothels were illegal. In P. J. De Bruïne Ploos van
Amstel, *De Prostitutie door alle eeuwen* (Amsterdam: Mulder & Co., 1929).

had been mainly populated with foreign girls, disappeared, but prostitution
itself did not decrease;[9] it merely took on other forms. Prostitution became increasingly integrated in the catering industry, noticeably in bars; women would
go in under the pretext of having a drink while casually looking for clients.
Another ruse was for women to position themselves by the window as way of
self-advertisement. With the closure of the brothels, this type of window prostitution increased enormously.[10] Also the massage parlors, the art-dealing (for
the wealthier clients) and the tobacco trade served as effective covers for prostitution.[11] The women stood in the doorway of the tobacco shop and solicited
potential clients. In 1936, almost half of all female prostitutes in Amsterdam
were streetwalkers, one-third received clients at home, and the rest of the prostitution took place in clubs and bars or was occasional.[12]

One of the negative consequences of the Ban on Brothels was the inter-weaving of prostitution with criminality and the emergence of the pimp, a protector and exploiter of a prostitute, often her lover or husband.[13] By 1920, people were calling for the regulation of prostitution, but the state of affairs lasted until 1960 when it became clear that the Ban on Brothels was violated on a large scale.

MORAL PANIC

In the course of the twentieth century, the idea that thousands of women were being captured and sold into prostitution as so-called white slaves gained increasing public attention and caused an international panic. The earliest use of the term "women trafficking" referred to the white slave traffic at the end of the nineteenth century and primarily described rural white European women who were recruited and coerced into prostitution. In Paris on May 18, 1904, the first international agreement was signed, International Agreement for the Suppression of the White Slave Trade, which aimed to combat "the procuring of women and girls for immoral purposes abroad."[14] This was followed in 1921, by the League of Nations' Committee on the Traffic in Women and Children and in 1949 by the United Nations' General Assembly adoption of the convention for the Suppression of the Traffic in Persons and of the Exploitation of the Prostitution of Others.

At the turn of the twentieth century, Russia was also characterized by an abolitionist stance against prostitution. The provisional government that emerged in February 1917 considered prostitution a major social and political problem and declared its abolition. The Bolsheviks also rejected regulation, like other socialist theorists, considering prostitution a transient symptom of industrial capitalism.[15] Prostitution, however, did not disappear. During the Civil War of 1917–1922, authorities treated prostitutes as labor deserters, but a more laissez-faire attitude emerged during the New Economic Policy (1921–1928), with its toleration of private trade. Under the presumption that prostitutes could be rehabilitated through manual labor, the Soviet government dispatched former prostitutes to sanatoriums. Yet authorities still associated prostitutes with disease and disorder, and repression became the practice.

The anti-prostitution stance was also reflected in the program of the World League for Sexual Reform (WLSR). This organization was established in 1928 in Copenhagen, aimed at sexual reforms based on sexual science, and was focused on four themes: women, abortion, contraception, and homosexuality. One of the ten demands of the league was directed at the prevention of

FIGURE 8.2: Prostitution at the Oudekerksplein in
Amsterdam, 1920s. In P. J. De Bruïne Ploos van
Amstel, *De Prostitutie door alle eeuwen* (Amster-
dam: Mulder & Co., 1929).

prostitution and was supported by its members at conferences in Copenhagen
in 1930 and in Brno in 1932.[16] Despite the moral panic surrounding prostitution, it was nevertheless tolerated in most American and European cities.

From the 1970s, there was an increase and commercialization of the sex
industry. As a result, the abolitionist discourse surfaced again. This time, it
was mainly put forward by a group of radical feminists, such as Catherine
MacKinnon, Kathleen Barry, Andrea Dworkin, and Sheila Jeffreys. According
to this radical feminist view, sexuality is defined by patriarchal institutions,
and, as such, it is oppressive to women. Women's sexuality is seen as the
result of a long period of male domination in which men, who had greater
power over women, defined and controlled women's sexuality. The scholars
advocating this theory argue that in patriarchal, capitalist societies, sexuality
is a tool used by men to dominate and oppress women through their sexual
objectification. This means an attack on compulsory heterosexuality and pornography, as became clearly visible in the anti-pornography movement of the

1980s in the United States.[17] The American feminist Robin Morgan became well known with her phrase "Pornography is the theory: rape is the practice," in which she makes an explicit connection between pornography and sexual violence against women.[18] Under the radical feminist interpretation, prostitution is hardly different from marriage and is part of a general system by which men gain sexual access to women. Within this perspective, both are inherently oppressive practices and always happen under constraint.

MALE PROSTITUTION

Besides female prostitution, male prostitution also became a topic of concern for the authorities. In 1900, in cities such as Berlin, London, Paris, Amsterdam, and New York, male prostitutes were walking the streets, both young queens in drag and more masculine straight young men such as soldiers. They catered to different clienteles: the drag boys focused on a straight working-class public, and the straight youngsters focused on older queens. Often they walked the same routes as female prostitutes. For these working-class youngsters, prostitution served as an important source of their income. Kerwin Kaye analyzed how the meanings and practices of male prostitution changed dramatically over the course of the twentieth century. These changes were transformed by new discourses of homosexuality, which influenced middle-class and working-class culture. "What most concerned many of the early sexologists, [and what continues to concern many contemporary commentators,] are not the daily living conditions of men who trade sex for cash, but rather how one might characterize the sexual orientation of the participants."[19] The male prostitute posed a problem for the theories of inversion: was a man homosexual if he engaged in sex acts with other men for money? Kaye focuses particularly on the ways in which the emergence of a homosexual identity decisively shaped the social patterns of exchange that characterized male prostitution in the United States, turning it from something engaged in by straight clients into something only queer men practiced. Since the term "homosexual" became widely known in the 1920s and 1930s, many working-class men felt they were no longer free to pursue commercial sex with fairies (feminine-acting homosexuals) or transgender workers.[20]

With the ongoing rise of the hetero/homo dichotomy, fewer and fewer straight men were willing to pay for commercial sex with other men, even if the worker was clearly identified as a fairy. Increasing cultural suspicions that the clients of gay prostitutes were themselves homosexual slowly drove away business, and the figure of the fairy became an increasingly marginalized figure

FIGURE 8.3: Cartoon on male prostitution from *Simplizissimus* (not dated, 1920s) with caption: "Have a look, Bella, that sailor—is he a client or competition?" In Magnus Hirschfeld, *Geschlechtskunde* IV. *Bilderteil* (Stuttgart Püttmann, 1930).

among male prostitutes. "While previously a wide-cross section of the straight male working-class had been willing to trade sex for money, by mid-century only the most marginalized were willing to deal with the stigma associated with gay identity. They were [being] associated with 'deviants' or 'hoodlum types' that engaged in prostitution as a means of obtaining spending money."[21]

As a result, young men stopped engaging in passive sex acts and taking on the effeminate mannerisms and clothing that had previously acted as signals of homosexual availability.[22] Instead, a growing number of often straight prostitutes who were "aggressively masculine in their self-presentation" took up the sex trade.[23] This transition, occurring in New York during the 1930s, marks the final passing of widespread cruising of fairies for heterosexual men. A new type of brothel in which straight men provided services for a mostly gay clientele, known as "peg houses,"[24] was rapidly on the rise.[25]

All over the Western world, prostitution of straight male youngsters remained widespread and an important source of homosexual outlets until the 1960s. This market again crumbled with the rise of gay liberation. Now gay men had places to go for sex among themselves and could stop relying on straight hustlers for their pleasures. Instead, gay-identified hustlers working in bordellos and from escort-services and participating in a variety of acts and roles took over.[26] With Internet and mobile phones, the last male brothels collapsed after 2000, leaving the market to escorts and independent hustlers.

PROSTITUTION IN NAZI GERMANY

The nineteenth-century medico-sexological discourse, in which prostitutes were considered mentally ill and sexually deviant, found its strongest expression in the way the Nazis treated prostitutes. Besides a brutal repression and mass arrests, prevailing negative notions of mental illness, deviance, and race were reflected in their policies. The Nazis endorsed ideas about prostitutes that had circulated in the preceding decades and feared the degenerative affects of venereal diseases. They established a registration system and set up their own practices, starting with incarceration of prostitutes in hospitals and forced sterilizations.

The historian Julia Roos places the Nazi attitudes toward prostitution in the light of pre-1933 developments. In 1927, Germany introduced the Law for Combating Venereal Diseases. This nationwide abolition of state-regulated prostitution meant an end to compulsory medical examinations of prostitutes as well as to numerous other restrictions on their freedom. Until then, regulated prostitutes were treated as "social pariahs."[27] Now they were banned from major public areas, could only reside in lodgings approved by the police, and had to obtain permission if they wanted to travel.

The prostitution reforms in the Weimar Republic became a central target of Nazi propaganda and triggered a powerful right-wing backlash during the early 1930s.[28] The period from 1933 to mid 1934 was characterized by the Nazi's effort to appeal to conservative concerns about immorality and to present themselves as "defenders of established notions of sexual propriety."[29] Prostitution was a key concern of the religious right, and the Nazis and religious right found themselves together in the fight against immorality. In 1933, the Nazis effectively outlawed street soliciting. Massive raids on streetwalkers took place between 1934 and 1939.[30] In 1934, the council of ministers decided to root out every form of prostitution. An investigation department *(Fahndungsdienst)* was set up to search for, and arrest, prostitutes and deport them to

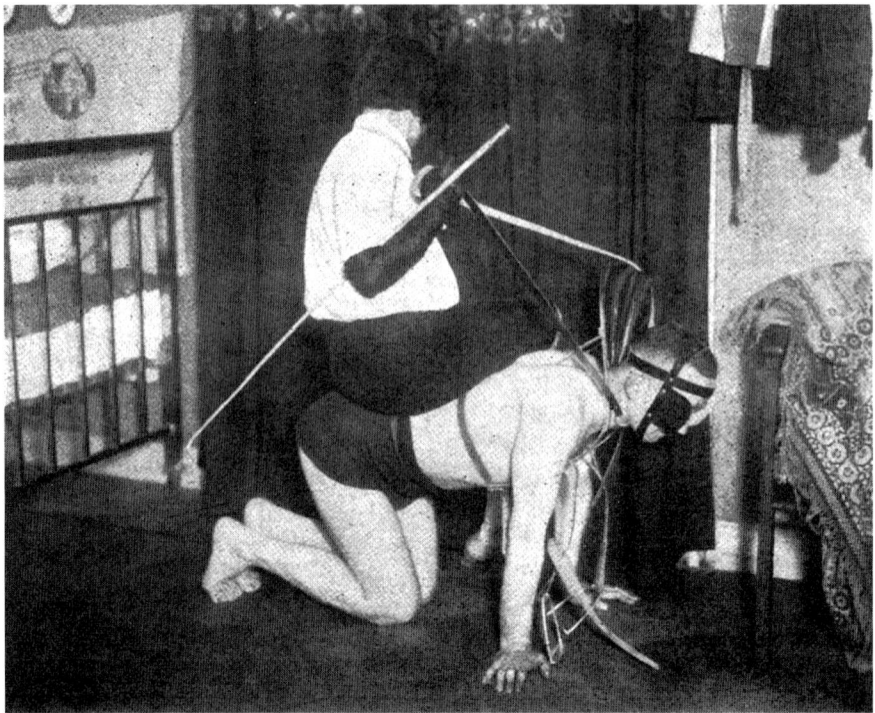

FIGURE 8.4: A so-called massage salon in Berlin offered services like this mixture of sadomasochism and zoophilia. The city was in the 1920s a major attraction for tourists who looked for all kinds of sexual pleasure. This ended with the establishment of the Nazi regime. In Magnus Hirschfeld, *Geschlechtskunde* IV. *Bilderteil* (Stuttgart Püttmann, 1930).

concentration camps where they were placed together with the political criminals. This investigation department was based on collaboration between the government and its citizens. Local inhabitants put together lists of people who were suspected of working in prostitution and passed this on to the police.[31]

Although Adolf Hitler saw prostitution as a moral and racial danger, state-regulated prostitution increased dramatically under Nazism. Especially during wartime, the regulated brothels became a key institution of Nazi sexual policy. "After 1939, the Nazis finally abandoned all efforts to accommodate the religious Rights and launched a massive campaign to set up brothels throughout the Reich."[32] From then on, prostitutes were not eliminated, but were instead forced to work as prostitutes in the brothel barracks where they were superintended by the SS. The use of a condom was obligatory.

What was new about the Nazi system of *Reglementierung* was the attempt to use the state in a direct way to create a certain form of human sexuality.[33]

The concentration camp brothels during World War II provide evidence that the Nazis tried to radically alter human sexual behavior.[34] In a speech before SS commanders in 1937, the *Reichsführer SS*, Heinrich Himmler, defended the use of female prostitution as a weapon in the fight against male homosexuality:

> it is possible to regulate all kinds of things by means of the state and through police measures. One can organize the question of female prostitution … which by comparison with this question [of male homosexuality] in principle is completely harmless, in a way that is acceptable for civilized people.[35]

At the same time, the persecution of prostitutes intensified. The brutality of the suppression of prostitution in Nazi Germany marked an important break with older forms of state-regulated prostitution, along with the racialization of

FIGURE 8.5: Poster for the prevention of venereal diseases among the U.S. troops in Italy, ca. 1944. All armies were affected by and had to deal with rampant sexually transmitted diseases. Wellcome Library, London.

Nazi regulationism. German soldiers were only allowed to visit full-blooded German prostitutes in order to ensure the preservation of the "purity of the German blood"; to secure this aim, Hitler ordered the establishment of special brothels for foreign prostitutes.[36] German women who had sexual contacts with Polish prostitutes (who occupied together with the Russians the lowest ranks within the Nazi racial hierarchy) were sent to prison or to a concentration camp in addition to humiliating public shaming.[37] In this way, regulated prostitution played a crucial role in upholding racist hierarchies between Germans and nationalities the Nazis considered racially inferior.

THE DEMAND SIDE

A wave of moral reform swept through Europe in the course of the twentieth century, but its restrictive vision concerning prostitution did not result in a decrease of demand for commercial sex. In many European countries, visiting a prostitute was a common way of sexually initiating men[38]; "In France, in cohorts born before 1937 one man out of 10 had his first intercourse with a prostitute. The number of men, who reported having ever paid for sex, ranges from 6.6 per cent in Great Britain to 38.6 per cent in Spain."[39]

The American sexologist Alfred Kinsey surveyed men and prostitutes in the United States in the period between World War I and II, and examined the reasons for visiting prostitutes, rates of clients, and the sorts of sexual gratification or actions different males prefer from their encounters with prostitutes.[40] The research revealed that the frequency of male intercourse with prostitutes was much lower than formerly believed. About 69 percent of the total white male population had some experience with female prostitutes. Many of these males, however, never had more than a single experience or two, and only 15 or 20 percent of them indulged in such activities more than a few times a year, over as much as a five-year period in their lives. This means that nearly a third (31%) of the American population never had any sort of sexual contact with prostitutes. The main motivations that Kinsey found for the purchase of sex were insufficient alternative sexual outlets, the desire to have sexual activities not easily available with their partners (such as oral sex, sadomasochistic sex, or group sex) or inexperience with sex. Other reasons included the fact that having sex with a prostitute was easier and cheaper than courting a girl, the possibility of avoiding the attached responsibilities of a long-term relationship, and the impossibility of finding partners in traditional ways. He also found patterns of clients related to age and education. According to Kinsey, men with lower education had a higher frequency of visits due to his limited need for emotionally interactive coitus. Males with an upper-level education were unsatisfied with prostitutes because of the lack of affection in the relationship that left them emotionally unsatisfied.

Although it can be questioned whether education or social status made a difference to the kind of sexual experience male customers desired, Kinsey's research is an interesting example of early research that focuses on learning who these clients are. The outcome of research like Kinsey's shows the pressing need for more empirical data in understanding more about the motivations and experiences of clients. Despite the fact that there was little prostitution in the first half of the twentieth century in the United States, we see increasing efforts to eradicate prostitution in the United States.

THE EMERGENCE OF THE PROSTITUTES' RIGHTS MOVEMENT

At the same time, a subversive discourse on prostitution emerged. With the arrival of the sexual revolution in the 1960s, we see the development of a freer sexual morality and a more tolerant attitude toward deviant sexual behavior, such as homosexuality, pornography, and prostitution. Since the 1970s, prostitutes started to organize and to respond to police violence and discriminative laws against them.

On June 2, 1975, more than 100 French prostitutes occupied the church Saint-Nizier in Lyon. The occupation was based upon the grievances of prostitutes who had experienced much harassment, repression, and imprisonment at the hands of the police. The revolt can be considered "a huge historical marker in the self-actualization and assertion of prostitutes' right to work without harassment and fear of arrest."[41] While prostitution was legal in France, the actual soliciting of clients was not, and prostitutes were being fined and jailed for their actions. On top of these grievances, a serial killer in Lyon had been murdering prostitutes, and the prostitutes were angry that police were not paying enough attention to catching him. In order to combat their own harassment and to concentrate the police's inattention on the murders, prostitutes filed a formal complaint to governmental officials and the press. Their complaints were ignored, so in order to gain more media and governmental attention, a group of prostitutes occupied the Saint-Nizier Church.

The prostitutes presented themselves in the first place as mothers and emphasized their motherhood. In a public letter to the population, they wrote: "We are mothers talking to you. Women trying to bring up their children alone as best they can, and who today are scared of losing them."[42] This was also

FIGURE 8.6: Metalwork in front of window brothel in Amsterdam, the first illustrating coital heterosexual sex, the second oral heterosexual sex, and the third a nude woman. Such public art work shows the greater freedoms after the sexual revolution. Photo: Gert Hekma.

clearly expressed in a banner that was hung over the church façade, which said: "Our children don't want their mothers to go to prison."[43] While the complaints of the French prostitutes centered on their dignity as women and mothers, the legitimacy of the work itself was not mentioned. This can be explained by the strong abolitionist position of the French authorities and of their allies, such as the social workers and feminists, who were vehemently against prostitution.

This was the first public demonstration to assert the rights of prostitutes to be treated as full citizens before the law. Among the main catchwords was the exposure of *"L'Etat Maquereau"* (the pimp state) since prostitutes had to pay taxes without benefiting from any advantages, especially the social security system.[44] The revolt of Lyon had an immediate impact on the rest of the country, extending to cities, such as Marseille, Grenoble, and Nice. Almost a week later, prostitutes in Paris invaded the St. Bernard Chapel in Montparnasse. The revolt finished on June 10 when at five o'clock in the morning the police entered the church in Lyon and brutally ended the occupation.

The church occupations were an enormous success and had, and still have, a great symbolic value for prostitutes worldwide. Appearing for the first time as a distinct and autonomous group, prostitutes managed to bring their concerns and worries into the public space, through their own voice.[45] As Margaret Valentino and Mavis Johnson of the English Collective of Prostitutes conclude: "the greatest victory of the French strike was the birth of many prostitutes' organizations all over the world, and strengthening of those already in existence."[46] The flame of the collective revolt spread out quickly:

> Some of us, having heard about the French strike, got together. We were determined to do something about our situation. We knew we could do it—the French strike was a proof—but it was hard to begin. We called ourselves the English Collective of Prostitutes after the French Collective, and later the New York Prostitutes Collective was formed. For us, it was the possibility of building an international network with other prostitutes' organizations.[47]

Another organization, which developed around the same time, was an American organization named COYOTE, an acronym for Call Off Your Old Tired Ethics. In 1973, a group of prostitutes came together in San Francisco to fight for equal rights. The focus of COYOTE was to reform the laws dealing with prostitution and to end the stigmatization of prostitutes and their profession. The organization wanted, and still fights for, the repeal of laws concerning pimping, or the controlling and living off the earnings of a prostitute.

Unlike the French movement, which claimed the dignity of prostitutes, COYOTE began with a focus on the civil rights of prostitute by first asserting the right to work rather than the conditions of work. The use of civil rights as a foundation was further supported by the recent gains made by both the women's movement and the gay liberation movement. The aim was to reconstitute the right to privacy and free expression, the right to choose your own work, and the right to free sexual contact between consenting adults without government interference. This last point became the banner under which COYOTE began, and it spread to the ultimate struggle to end the criminalization of sex work. COYOTE served as the pioneer collective to stand up for the rights of prostitutes and paved the way for other collectives to develop across North America beginning in the late 1970s. Among these were Prostitutes of New

FIGURE 8.7: Painting by Hans van Norden of prostitutes in Amsterdam's Red Light District, 1960s. Collection Amsterdams Historisch Museum.

York (PONY), Associated Seattle Prostitutes, and Seattle Prostitutes against Rigid Rules over Women (SPARROW).[48]

THE NOTION OF "SEX WORKER"

The history of organizing sex workers who demand recognition of prostitution as labor and their rights as workers began with the restructuring of the language used to build solidarity and by explicitly contending that sex work is a legitimate profession. By framing sex work as *work*, the fight for rights could be approached through the labor movement, which emphasizes decriminalization and improving labor conditions. Language was a key determinant in asserting the right to sell sexual services without legal and social stigma. However, in order to claim the right to work, the work itself must not be criminal.

In 1973, the concept of *sex worker* was introduced by Carol Leigh, alias Scarlot Harlot, a prominent figure in the U.S. prostitute rights' movement. The strategy of employing the term "sex worker" in reference to persons who used to be considered hookers and whores, was a deeply significant transition into civil and labor rights paradigms. Within this approach, prostitution could be seen as a form of work based on consent and choice. As an international movement, sex workers sought to remove the victim label through decriminalization and law reform. Sex workers did not want to be seen as helpless victims anymore but as independent individuals who make choices and decisions for themselves.

Since the 1980s, sex workers started to organize themselves in many places around the world, such as in England (1976), Ecuador (1982), Uruguay (1982), Thailand (1985), the Netherlands (1985), and New Zealand (1987). This period also saw the development of international committees that were founded to target the harmful laws and negative image of sex workers. One such association was the International Committee for Prostitutes' Rights (ICPR), a federation of sex workers' organizations created in 1985. The ICPR now fights for the human rights of sex workers by developing a public discourse, which states that sex workers are "autonomous and responsible" adults who are able to make their own decisions about their personal and professional lives.[49]

At the first international sex workers' conference, held in 1985 in Amsterdam, the ICPR developed the World Charter for Prostitutes' Rights, which called for the decriminalization of "all aspects of adult prostitution resulting from individual decision."[50] According to this charter, laws that uphold human rights, such as the freedom to travel, immigrate, work, speak, and marry, should be honored and developed. The charter also advocates the creation of public educational programs to change the negative image that the public has of sex work and sex workers and to highlight the role of the client in the transaction.

PROSTITUTION AND MIGRATION

The sex industry in contemporary Europe and the United States is characterized by a high mobility of sex workers, many of whom are immigrants. During the last three decades of the twentieth century, migrants from different parts of the world were an important part of the European sex industry.[51] At the end of the 1970s, exotic women from Southeast Asia, especially from Thailand and the Philippines, became very popular among European clients. This wave of immigrants was a consequence of the development of sex tourism to the Southeast Asian region in the aftermath of the Vietnam War and the continued stationing of U.S. military troops in the region.

Since the 1980s, a second wave of immigrants followed, arriving from Latin America, mainly from the Dominican Republic, Colombia, Brazil, and

Ecuador. A few years later, many West African women followed suit, mainly coming from Ghana and Nigeria. From 1989, the European sex industry saw a constant increase of women migrating from Central and Eastern Europe, from Ukraine, Macedonia, Armenia, Poland, Czech Republic, and Albania, among others.[52] There is also a growing number of male immigrants engaged in European prostitution, mainly coming from Morocco and Romania. Since the 1990s, the number of transgender immigrants has also increased, especially those from Thailand, Ecuador, and Brazil.[53] At the end of the twentieth century, immigrants in many countries in Western Europe, such as the Netherlands, Germany, Belgium, Spain, Italy, Austria, and Switzerland, made up a large number of all sex workers. The number of immigrants working in the European sex industry is estimated to be between one-third and one-half of all sex workers.[54] Within the European Union, the number of foreign sex workers is in many areas larger than the number of local sex workers.[55]

This strong representation of immigrants in the European sex industry can be explained to a great extent by poverty and unemployment in the countries of origin. In many Western European countries, the majority are economic immigrants who have left their home country driven by the hope of a better life for themselves and their families back home. In general, they are usually from lower socio-economic classes, with only a few years of education. The sex industry is one of the few informal labor markets in Europe, besides domestic work and care for elder people and children. Because of their financial contribution to the family, they earn a respected position in their countries of origin. For many of these women and men, this therefore makes prostitution in Europe an important instrument for achieving upward economic and social mobility.[56]

Besides economic motives, gender-specific and emancipatory reasons can underlie the decision to migrate. Some women come from violent relationships and situations in which they have little or no decision-making power. Working in European prostitution can offer them the possibility to break free from these relationships and start to live independently, while still pursuing their goal of financially supporting their children and seeking a better future. In these cases, migration can offer an opportunity to escape from a situation of oppression and the cultural restrictions of a traditional gender role.

This longing for more personal freedom is clearly manifested with the transgenders who are strongly represented among the Latin American sex workers in Europe.[57] At the end of the 1980s and beginning of the 1990s, we see an increase of the number of transgenders. This tendency is particularly noticeable in the street prostitution in the bigger European cities, such as Paris, Rome,

Madrid, and Barcelona. Besides male transvestites, who exclusively dress up as women during work, the majority of this group consists of male-to-female transsexuals who want to adapt themselves as much as possible to the female gender by means of hormone treatment, silicon implants, and surgical intervention. A high proportion of these transgenders come from Ecuador, Colombia, and Brazil.[58] Many transgenders have experienced discrimination and rejection by their families. The climate of relative tolerance in many European cities regarding homosexuality and transsexuality has encouraged them to migrate with the hope of building an independent life and to further develop their gender identity. The money they are earning in the sex industry, and the work itself, offers them the opportunity to experiment and explore their body and sexuality during the transformation process.

HUMAN TRAFFICKING DISCOURSE

With the increase in migration and the globalization of the sex industry, human trafficking became a major political concern in Western Europe by the mid-1980s. We can speak of human trafficking as a situation when a person is forced into work by means of violence, deception, or abuse, for the benefit of economic exploitation. Often, women are trafficked for the purpose of prostitution, but people are trafficked into other kinds of labor, such as the domestic service, agriculture, horticulture, the mining industry, or in sweatshops. During the postwar period, there was little discussion of this issue, and it did not appear on the international agenda again until the 1980s.[59] Since then, many international nongovernmental organizations working on the issue of human trafficking have demanded the revision and replacement of the UN convention of 1949. One of the great shortcomings of this convention was that it lacked a specific definition of trafficking—it aimed to stop trafficking, but it did not define the term. It called on all states to suppress not only trafficking but prostitution, regardless of whether it occurred with the consent of the woman involved—no distinction was made between forced and voluntary prostitution or with human smuggling. Third parties who coerced women into prostitution were as "liable" for prosecution as those who facilitated the voluntary migration of adult sex workers.

Before the 1980s, UN instruments against trafficking were abolitionist, but from the mid-1980s there is an observable shift toward a more liberal discourse on prostitution. Since the adoption of the UN Vienna Declaration on the Elimination of Violence against Women (1993), the majority of the international agreements denote forced prostitution and trafficking, rather than prostitution itself, as violence against women and a violation of human rights. Another important change in the human trafficking debate is the further broadening of the concept: it is not only about women, but also about men and children.

Since the last decade of the twentieth century, the discussion on human trafficking in Europe and the United States has been placed in the framework of combating crime. Many new regulations have been put in place, such as stricter border control, repressive migration policies, and the restriction of women's freedom of movement, in order to combat organized forms of crime. At the end of 2000, the United Nations accepted a new protocol on human trafficking that was signed by many countries, but only a few countries have ratified it. Within this protocol, for the first time a broad definition of human trafficking was introduced that includes all forms of forced labor and slavery-like practices into which people, male and female, can be trafficked, no matter which industry. This protocol offers an important basis for national legislation, but it also generates ambiguity for the definition of trafficking.[60] On the one hand, the protocol penalizes all third parties who use force to obtain labor, including sex work. On the other hand, the protocol also applies to non-forced or even consensual activities. So it is unclear whether prostitution is always regarded as a form of exploitation. Besides, there is no clear position on the relationship between prostitution and trafficking, and consequently all persons who migrate and engage in sex work will automatically be treated as victims who have been forced into their work. This means that the old problems attached to the anti-trafficking framework have not disappeared. Instead, they have returned with full force, in particular the preoccupation with the morality of the people concerned and the conflation of trafficking with prostitution.

In policy making on prostitution and human trafficking in Europe almost no attention is paid to the rights of the sex workers. Questions as to how we should deal with situations of abuse and exploitation in the sex industry remain unresolved. The fact that only a part of all migrants is forced into sex work does not appear in the policy against trafficking. Most policies only target one part of the spectrum: the fight against criminality and illegal migration is of primary concern, whereas the status of the sex worker is a secondary concern. This denial of sex workers' rights has made many sex workers increasingly critical of antitrafficking campaigners and human rights activists.

THE ISSUE OF CONSENT

Whether women are working voluntarily or are forced into the sex industry is a subject that causes worldwide disagreement within the international human rights debate, feminist activism, and in academic work on this issue. The fundamental difference of opinion concerns the question of whether or not a person can choose prostitution as a profession. In other words: Is prostitution inherently coercive? For abolitionist feminists, consent to prostitution is irrelevant because prostitution is always a coercive sexual practice. Sex workers are irrelevant "instruments of male pleasure and sexual commodities" and are always sexually exploited.[61] Therefore, the policy here should be directed at the abolition of prostitution.

The new law on the criminalization of clients in Sweden in 1999 is a clear example of this line of thinking. The Swedish model means criminalization of the male clients, regardless of whether the sex is consensual or not. The explanation of this can be found in the official Swedish perception of prostitution as a form of violence against women. Sex workers are seen as female victims and clients as male perpetrators. By punishing the buyer, society would make it clear that the purchase of sexual services is deemed immoral in Sweden. Within this radical feminist view, prostitution degrades all women and forms a threat to gender equality. The law was passed in the Swedish parliament under the guise of feminism. The government argued that the law reflected a need to strengthen the position of women in society in general. By criminalizing and pathologizing the buyer of sexual services, sexual behavior was connected to the Swedish national character, which abides by a "normative national sexuality" grounded in love and gender equality.[62] As a result, being a client became more of an identity on the basis of sexual practices, and can form a reason for organization.[63]

Since the law has been in effect, official Swedish reports on the subject merely state that street prostitution decreased when the law came into force, but there is no evidence that the law in itself resulted in a decrease in the amount of prostitution. The majority of the street workers did not quit the sex business. Rather, the law forced them to organize the business in other ways in order to reach clients who have been scared off the streets by the police. Many sex workers have started working in illegal brothels run by pimps or on their own from illegally rented apartments on the outskirts of the town. For those who have not been able to move their business indoors, life has become much more difficult because of the law. The threat of being caught gives street workers less time to choose and negotiate with their clients before getting into the car. When arresting clients, the police collect evidence of payment as well as of sex. This means harassment of both sex workers and their clients; filming both parties having sex is seen as a method of collecting evidence, which means that sex workers, even if they are not committing a criminal offence, are subjected to police actions that violate their integrity. It is apparent that the main concern of the lawmaker here is not the well-being of sex workers but rather to end all prostitution through criminal law and a concern to promote so-called equal sexuality. The implications of this legal framework is an increase in illegal prostitution, less visibility, and more pimp-governed business, which leads to an increase in women's vulnerability and more risks in terms of personal safety and sexual health.

Liberal feminists, on the contrary, argue that consent *is* important because not all sex workers are victims of sexual violence. Here, a distinction is made between forced prostitution and prostitution based on the choice of the individual. The newly implemented laws on prostitution in the Netherlands in 2000 fall in line with this second line of thinking, with its legalized brothels and strict rules imposed on hygiene and condom use. The aim of the government was a pragmatic one, namely to regulate and to control the sex business. The legalization of prostitution consists of two sets of criteria. The first

FIGURE 8.8: Rooms for rent in the Amsterdam's Red Light District, 2009. Indication that only EU citizens can rent rooms and also of the prices for half-day shifts. Photo: Gert Hekma.

concerns a system of licenses; the owners can lose their license if they have minors (under eighteen) or illegal migrants. The second concerns the interior of the building, such as running water and dimensions of the room. The new legal situation regulates voluntary prostitution, punishes more severely forced and illegal prostitution, and gives all local councils the right to make their own policies within the framework of the law.

However, Dutch sex workers still cannot see the benefits of the new law and are disappointed with the results of the legalization. Although officially sex workers now have rights, it is still difficult to secure them. An important reason for this is that the social stigma attached to prostitution has remained. For example, several banks and insurance firms have openly refused mortgages to prostitution-related businesses. Furthermore, the Dutch government has failed to facilitate the labor emancipation process of the sex workers. The sex workers have not properly been informed about the new law, nor their rights and duties. Instead, the legal change has led to more control and restrictions and to a deterioration of the position of non-European sex workers. Most measures are connected to residence permits.[64] As a consequence, many undocumented sex workers have moved from publicly visible windows to the less visible escort services, phone sex, or Internet sex.

CONCLUSION: FROM SEXUAL DEVIANTS TO POLITICAL ACTORS

The debate on prostitution in the twentieth century is polarized between the abolitionist approach and the sex workers' rights position. From the late nineteenth century to the beginning of the twentieth century, we can see an important shift in Western discourse that has influenced ways in which we view prostitution today, and we have seen a call for an end to the regulation system.

During the second half of the twentieth century, a victim discourse emerged, in which prostitutes were considered victims of poverty and unrestrained male lust. However, for the first time in history, this century has witnessed the emergence of a social movement of sex workers who have started to publicly speak out. Since the 1970s, the dominant sexual morality and the victim discourse is moving aside to make way for the voices of the sex workers. Without legitimacy, sex workers cannot enter the political domain to make themselves heard. Their participation in the debate on prostitution is therefore essential for improving their living conditions and daily security.

Besides the claim for labor and human rights and decent labor conditions, an important aim of the sex workers' rights movement is the fight for citizenship rights. During the history of prostitution in the West, it has become clear how prostitution has been used to determine what is considered normal sexual behavior and what is good sexuality. In this case, sexuality becomes a determining factor of the allocation of citizenship rights. In many places in Europe, sex workers still do not have a full right to citizenship because their sexual behavior is considered deviant. In Greece, for example, sex workers are not allowed to marry, and in Portugal, they lose custody of their children to social services or family courts solely because of their occupation.[65]

At the end of the twentieth century, many Western governments have opted for more control and restriction of prostitution. However, repressive measures, such as excluding migrant groups from the prostitution market, cannot stop abuse and exploitation in the sex industry. On the contrary, these measures make sex workers depend more on abusive recruiters and force them underground, where they are further marginalized and stigmatized. This shows the importance of empowering sex workers, especially immigrants, and of giving them the legal tools to establish conditions that enable their capacity to determine their own labor conditions.

In reaction to current government policies, a number of associations of sex workers have emerged to form official unions to fight for acceptance of sex work as a legitimate form of employment and the professionalization of sex work. The accomplishments of sex workers' organizations have resulted in a growing online movement to fight for both the civil rights and labor rights of all persons engaged in the sex industry. By utilizing the legacy of the labor and civil rights movements, sex workers have substantial models on which to claim the right to assert agency in their lifestyles and occupational choices.

CHAPTER NINE

Erotica

KELLY DENNIS

The greatest impact on erotic imagery in twentieth-century visual culture arguably has been the rapid development and mass dissemination of visual communication technologies, from photography to cinema, from VHS to HD video, and from computers to the World Wide Web. Technology and its commercialization attended the increasing democratization and internationalization of Western cultures and fed growing tensions among classes, ethnicities, sexualities, and genders in the struggle for sexual expression and political self-representation. Increasingly democratized access for women and ethnic minorities to the public sphere, including suffrage, civil rights, and international human rights, called into question the long-held conventions of eroticism in art—particularly the female nude—but also the repression or exclusion of the sexuality and erotic ideals of sexual, ethnic, and cultural minorities. Indeed, the categories of art and culture themselves, traditionally the provenance of elite white males, were increasingly complicated by developments in mass reproduction and cultural democratization.

Twentieth-century erotic imagery was also heir to the kinds of disciplinary classification and study begun in the nineteenth century that historian and philosopher Michel Foucault characterized as the discourse on sexuality.[1] Indeed, by mid-century, for the industrialized West, sex and sexuality were scrutinized, medicalized, and performed in venues ranging from psychoanalysis to pop psychology, from women's liberation and feminist consciousness-raising to the sense of inadequacy or sexual failure if a woman was not multiorgasmic, and from incontinence to erectile dysfunction. By century's end, the discourse on sexual functioning in its physical and emotional manifestations increasingly became the subject of magazine advertising and nightly television commercials during the family dinner hour. Perhaps most notably, the clinical definition of homosexuality, a medical term coined in the nineteenth century, became in the twentieth century the discursive model for sexuality as identity rather than as object choice,[2] a model that extended beyond the definitions of hetero-, homo-, bi-, and transgendered to contribute to what Foucault called the proliferation of the discourses on sex.[3]

Insofar as Foucault claimed that the West produced no *ars erotica*, only *scientia sexualis*, the task of identifying erotic imagery is far from a simple matter. After mid-century, misguided legal efforts to regulate nude imagery throughout Western Europe and the United States served to conflate even the previously mundane family photographs of naked infants and toddlers with child pornography and the sexual abuse of children.[4] In the prudish yet prurient United States, especially after mid-century, virtually any image of the naked human body could be claimed to be erotic, pornographic, or sexually explicit. As a consequence, issues of pornography and censorship perhaps inevitably inflected the production of erotic imagery across media and cultures.

This chapter can only gesture toward some of the many manifestations of erotic imagery in the twentieth century, and the reader will no doubt identify any number of lacunae. What is more, although an attempt has been made to provide specific cultural manifestations of erotic images across varying media, as categories these manifestations are far from discrete and overlap inevitably among the various topics treated. To provide what can ultimately function only as an arbitrary frame by which to narrow its focus, this chapter will first focus on the role of erotic imagery in early twentieth-century art and then move to the impact of technologies on erotic and pornographic representations of sex and sexuality within different mediums, consistently attending to the role that censorship played in their definition and dissemination.

EROTIC DEPICTION AND AVANT-GARDE TRANSGRESSION

At the beginning of the twentieth century, eroticized and sexualized imagery comprised one of several fronts on which avant-garde artists launched an oppositional attack on mainstream culture and by which they attempted to shock the middle class (*épater le bourgeois*). In some instances, artists attacked, parodied, or rendered grotesque previous conventions of eroticism in art, such as the reclining female nude, in order to expose its conventions. Such avant-garde attacks targeted the tradition of idealizing the female body through the eradication of pubic hair, which inevitably aestheticized and eroticized the body at the expense of its sexuality. In other instances, erotic or overtly sexualized imagery was depicted not only to shock viewers from complacency but to criticize attitudes about sex and sexuality constrained by religion, marriage, reproduction, and, indeed, by politics, economics, and ideology.

Groups of artists in Europe experimented with the bright, non-realistic use of color and with gestural, expressionist styles of painting deemed primitive, both of which had been pioneered by Vincent Van Gogh and Paul Gauguin. Also at this time, artists in Europe gathered in communities in urban and rural locals, united in their rejection of the social alienation caused by industrialization and urbanization. Their art often constituted a denunciation of the staid values of the middle-class who had gained economic and political ascendancy in the nineteenth century. In France, Fauvism, although a short-lived artistic movement (1905–1907), had a significant impact in spite of having had few exhibitions. *Les fauves,* or the "wild beasts," used exaggerated color and rough gestural brushwork to depict scenes of sensual abandon. Nude figures relaxing in nature, as in Henri Matisse's *Luxe, calme et volupté* (1905), represented an expression of joie de vivre at odds with the middle-class work ethic. Like Gauguin's work before it, Fauvist imagery disturbed middle-class sensibilities about propriety, dress, and sexual behavior, and it disrupted mimetic expectations with pink skies and yellow grasses.

In a related fashion, primitivist artists in Germany, including such groups as Die Brücke (The Bridge) in Dresden and the Viennese Secession in Austria, also used highly sexualized imagery rendered in bright colors and expressionist styles to tweak middle-class sensibilities. Ernst Kirchner's *Bathers at Moritzburg* (1909) crudely depicted male and female figures bathing together nude at one of the countryside spas popular at the time. In Vienna, Gustav Klimt's student Egon Schiele's delicate yet violent pornographic depictions of nudes, including several self-portraits representing the subject masturbating, offended many, as did the artist's reputation for seducing underage girls.

Like earlier Fauve artists, cubist artists Pablo Picasso and Georges Braque collected African and Oceanic objects and borrowed stylistically from the visual culture of the global south. Considering such cultures primitive and thus untouched by modern urbanization, the avant-garde, while rejecting middle-class mores, nonetheless celebrated, perhaps unconsciously, European imperialism. Pablo Picasso's infamous *Desmoiselles d'Avignon* (1906–1907), for example, depicts a brothel scene of nude women in the artist's distinctive geometrical style, and in a gesture that simultaneously referred to black ethnicity and to reigning stereotypes about the hyper-sexuality of African women, features an African mask for one woman's face to further eroticize the scene.

The use of erotic imagery in avant-garde painting took a more overtly critical turn during World War I. *Neue Sachlichkeit* artists Max Beckmann and George Grosz utilized highly sexualized images, especially of prostitutes, as symbols of German society's moral degradation. Beckmann's biting and claustrophobic depiction of religious allegories and Grosz's collaged paintings incorporating mechanical gears in lieu of body parts caricatured German nationalism, religion, duty, technological progress, and, above all, the capitalist profiteering these artists deemed responsible for the Great War. Grosz was also part of the Dada movement in Germany. In France, Dada artists such as Marcel Duchamp, Francis Picabia, and the American photographer Man Ray concocted eroticized machine imagery in order to liberate the machine from its equipmental servitude to capitalist production. Picabia's highly detailed engineering drawings and pen and ink illustrations, such as that of an automobile spark plug, titled *Portrait d'une jeune fille américaine dans l'état de nudité* (*Portrait of an American Girl in a State of Nudity,* 1915), both opaque and evocative, invited endless associations between femininity, nascent automobile culture, materialism, technology, and phallic sexual excitation.

Entre-guerre French surrealist artists looked to Freud's theories of dreams and the unconscious in order to channel repressed sexual desires and taboos as a means to *épater le bourgeois*, and several dadaists joined this later, loose international coterie of artists and writers. Surrealist photographers such as Man Ray and Hans Bellmer attempted to expose Freud's theory of the sexual "return of the repressed" as revealed in everyday objects: Man Ray's men's and women's hats (*Untitled,* 1925) featured folds or points resembling female or male genitalia. Bellmer's *Poupées* (1930s) depicted bulbous, multilimbed and even multibreasted children's dolls. Surrealist imagery has been criticized by some scholars for violently fragmenting, even dismembering the female body. Yet such images by the Belgian surrealist René Magritte—as in his painting *Le Viol* (*Rape,* 1934), which features a nude woman's torso as though the breasts were eyes and the pubis her mouth, and *Eternal Evidence* (1930), in which the various body parts of a standing female nude are depicted across five separate, framed, vertically arrayed canvases into a whole—seem to acknowledge if not indict the objectification of the female body throughout the entire history of art. Indeed, female surrealist artists, such as Lee Miller and Meret Oppenheim, sometimes served as the nude, eroticized models for many of Man Ray's photographs and created art in their own right. Miller became a highly celebrated

fashion photographer and photojournalist. Oppenheim created highly eroticized compositions of found objects, such as a pair of white high heels trussed
together, heels topped with poultry frills and served on a silver platter (*Ma
Gouvernante*, 1936). Perhaps most infamously, Oppenheim's (*Le Dejeuner en
fourrure*) (*Luncheon in Fur*, 1936)—a teacup, saucer, and spoon lined with
Chinese fur—invokes cunnilingus through its tactile inducement to sip
warm liquid from the lip of a fur-lined teacup.

During this same period in the United States, artist Paul Cadmus, who like
many at the time worked for the federally funded Public Works of Art Project (PWAP), created several paintings including isolated fey figures among otherwise stereotypically masculine figures. Notably, his painting, *The Fleet's In!*
(1934), featuring sailors enjoying a raucous shore leave with numerous women,
was condemned by naval officials and ultimately removed from exhibition.
Yet the painting was ultimately controversial less for its unflattering if perhaps
apt depiction of the sailors' rambunctious carousing and sexual harassment of
women than for an anecdotal depiction of one sailor accepting a cigarette from
a stereotypically depicted homosexual figure.[5] As would often be the case in the
United States throughout the twentieth century, censorship of the painting led to
heightened media attention and resulted in far more people seeing the forbidden
work in reproduction than might have viewed it had it remained on exhibition.

FIGURE 9.1: Meret Oppenheim, *Le Dejeuner en fourrure* (*Luncheon in Fur*, 1936).
© 2010 Artists Rights Society (RS), New York/Pro Literris, Zurich. DIGITAL IMAGE
© 2010, The Museum of Modern Art/Scala, Florence.

FIGURE 9.2: *Entartete Kunst* catalog cover, 1934.

Although perhaps lost on audiences today, the success of avant-garde artists' use of erotic and sexualized imagery to challenge mainstream values prior to World War II can be said to have been confirmed by the display and subsequent destruction of many of these works under Nazi Germany. Confiscated from museums and art collections, primitivist, expressionist, cubist, Dada, and surrealist works, among others, were publicly displayed in an exhibition titled *Entartete Kunst* (*Degenerate Art*) in 1934 as examples of sociocultural degradation, madness, sexual promiscuity, semiticism, and negritude. The most widely attended exhibition of the twentieth century, *Entartete Kunst* sensationalized the very art that the Nazis considered a threat to the values they cynically promoted to control women and their sexuality—*Kinder, Küche, Kirche* (children, kitchen, church)—on the road to a nationalist war and economic power.[6]

PHOTOGRAPHY, ART, AND MASS CULTURE

This period also saw a rapid increase in the production and dissemination of visual mass culture, which placed it on a collision course with art as traditionally defined. By the turn of the twentieth century, development of the half-tone process, which allowed newspapers and periodicals to reproduce photographic images directly rather than through engravings, permitted a greater mass dissemination of visual images. The increasing availability of such visual forms of mass reproduction as photography and film hastened the democratization of culture and, as some argued at the time, facilitated its manipulation by the culture industry.[7] Indeed, some of the earliest eroticized imagery was seen in advertising, which quickly adapted avant-garde and high-modernist photography styles to fragment and fetishize the female body for fashion advertising and to create visual juxtapositions that generated and exploited consumer desire.

Photographers associated with Alfred Steiglitz's Photo-Secession group in New York were conscious both of developments in abstraction in European art during the opening decades of the twentieth century and of the need to extricate photography from its long-held position as a mere mechanical recording device if it were ever to be seriously considered as an artistic medium. In the shift to straight photography, Steiglitz and such photographers as Edward Weston and Imogen Cunningham each photographed the nude body as a formalist abstraction, deploying such techniques as lighting and cropping in order to defamiliarize the body, which often appeared as a landscape.

In France, Claude Cahun (née Lucy Schwob, 1894–1954), an artist and writer loosely associated with the surrealists, created photographic self-portraits in the 1930s that emphasized the ambiguity of gender. Having adopted the sexually ambiguous name "Claude," Cahun photographed herself with her head shaved in exaggerated feminine masquerade, in contradistinction to the elaborate feminine coiffures of the period, which made her appear "more powerful, even phallic."[8] Images such as these played on ideals of the androgyne or so-called third sex—neither simply male nor female—prominent at the time. Hungarian-born photographer Brassaï (né Gyula Halasz, 1899–1984) photographed sexual subcultures in *Paris de nuit* (*Paris by Night*, 1933). Among the evocative images published in this book are a series of same-sex couples, some adopting butch and femme dress, attending a "Homosexual Ball." Although Brassaï's photographs represented Paris nightlife and subculture not usually seen, images such as these also confirmed the growing acceptance of the clinical definition of homosexuality as identity formed by object choice. Pierre Molinier (1900–1976), who photographed himself in elaborate and often quite kinky drag, using prosthetic limbs and dildos, is reputed to having been too much even for the surrealists.

German photographer Wilhelm von Gloeden (1856–1931), a wealthy baron, photographed nude boys in Sicily. It is said that his homosexual lifestyle was tolerated not only because of his poor health, but because he so often (although not always) photographed adolescent Sicilian boys in classicizing garb—laurel wreaths, togas, sandals—and shared profits from the photographs with his models.

A "major player" in the Harlem Renaissance,[9] Carl Van Vechten (1880–1964), a wealthy white art collector, patron, and portrait photographer of artists and literary figures, also produced a considerable private oeuvre of racial and interracial homoerotic nude photographs. Van Vechten forged "interracial, erotic, and modernist ties" to avant-garde primitivism in order to "legitimate his negrophilic sympathies publicly and to satisfy his homoerotic desires privately, while simultaneously laying claim to an 'enlightened' engagement in contemporary notions of the primitive and, therefore, in the modern."[10]

The continued technological development in the twentieth century of photography represents perhaps the single biggest impact on visual culture generally and erotic imagery in particular. As the circulation in mass-market magazines increased, so did the market of erotic and pornographic magazines.

Erotic imagery often confirms sexual desires other than those generally acknowledged in mainstream culture and, in popular contexts, can serve as an isolated and closeted adolescent's first link to the gay community.[11] *Physique Pictorial* was one of the earliest magazines pitched directly toward gay audiences. Published initially in 1951, *Physique Pictorial* was loosely based on muscle magazines from the first half of the century, which featured photographs of nearly nude men posed to display their athletically sculpted bodies to best advantage. But physique magazines in the 1950s had to disguise their content from postal inspectors. As with von Gloeden's work earlier in the century, a little classicism went a long way toward legitimating display of the male body: along with carefully placed fig leafs, the magazines adopted such titles as *Grecian Guild Pictorial*, *Adonis*, and *American Apollo*, and they juxtaposed exercise- and health-oriented columns.

Late in the century, the work of photographer Robert Mapplethorpe gained considerable notoriety after an exhibition of his work in the Corcoran Gallery of Art in Washington, DC was censored in 1988, fomenting a debate in the United States regarding the federal funding of art. Originally trained as a sculptor, Mapplethorpe's homoerotic photographs of white and black men, often with sadomasochistic overtones, were highly aestheticized and rigorously formalist. Nonetheless, the would-be public display of homoerotic images unsettled conservatives in Congress as well as religious conservatives, who started a culture war. Ostensibly a war over traditional versus amoral values, the battle featured conservatives using federal arts funding as a public referendum not only on homosexuality but also on women's and minority rights and cultural visibility—all threats to the reigning patriarchal order. Indeed, at the opening of the twenty-first century, conservatives across industrialized nations continue using culture wars to distract citizens from the material effects of the neo-liberal market economy on the lives of the working poor and middle classes.

PORNOGRAPHY

Since its invention in the nineteenth century, photography has enjoyed a singular reputation for mimetic accuracy and as having an indexical relation to the depicted object, often despite evidence to the contrary. As a result, pornographic imagery occupies a liminal space between reality and fantasy from which it benefits and for which it is often condemned. Indeed, technologies of reproduction in the nineteenth and twentieth centuries, including photography, video, and digital-electronic media, were initially explored as erotic and pornographic imaging devices.

If pornographic production was dominated by France in the nineteenth century, it was dominated by the United States after World War II. *Playboy* magazine, begun in 1953, was an instant success. The magazine's combination of erotic female photography with such high-brow features as fiction by well-known authors, interviews with cultural and political figures and celebrities, and advertising pitched to an upper-middle-class or would-be wealthy consumer, proved to be a successful formula, and its iconic bunny logo is recognized worldwide. Despite its early emphasis on playmate models who looked like the so-called girl next door, *Playboy* soon faced stiff competition from such hard-core magazines as *Hustler*, with the latter's first issue published in1974. Larry Flynt's magazine broke prior taboos on showing pubic hair, and in subsequent decades pushed the subject further in featuring explicit photographs of female genitalia—but also of men's penises, thus raising the specter of homosexuality among its readers and detractors. Magazines aimed more explicitly at gay male audiences than previous physique magazines, including *Advocate Men* and *Honcho*, followed a formula similar to *Playboy*'s but also adopted *Hustler*'s more explicit, hard-core emphasis in their pictorials. What is more, in the 1980s, with the advent of AIDS, these magazines provided important health information and alternative safe sex options for masturbation. A product of the pro-sex, third-wave feminist movement, the hard-core lesbian magazine *On Our Backs*, begun in 1984, featured erotic and pornographic pictorials of models who did not always meet mainstream beauty ideals for women. Indeed, the title *On Our Backs* was an explicit parody of the radical feminist periodical, *Off Our Backs*, which began in 1970 and held a strong anti-pornography stance.

Such niche pornography exploded among magazines in the late 1980s and early 1990s but was quickly dampened by the easier dissemination of pornography on the World Wide Web. Although amateur computer users were the first to upload and download scanned erotic images from *Playboy* and *Hustler* magazines, corporate pornography quickly colonized the Internet with commercial pornography sites. However, throughout at least the first decade of the twenty-first century, a vibrant alternative pornography, or so-called alt. porn, subculture exists on the Web, providing legitimate amateur porn for free. Like the amateur, home-pornography VHS exchanges of the 1980s, alt.porn circumvents—for now—both mainstream body ideals *and* the efforts of corporate capitalism to colonize sexuality and user-generated content for profit.[12]

EROTICISM IN ART OF THE POST–WORLD WAR II ERA

In the post-World War II era, an American avant-garde developed, aspects of which were both homoerotic and antagonistic toward the much-touted machismo of earlier abstract expressionist artists. Artists such as Robert Rauschenberg, Jasper Johns, Larry Rivers, and Andy Warhol created works that indirectly critiqued both the masculinist iconography and the artistic style surrounding abstract expressionist painters. More wry and satirical than the paintings that typified abstract expressionism's apolitical withdrawal, the work of these painters evidenced a turn toward mass culture and even mass politics as sources. Following the 1948 publication of Alfred Kinsey's report on male sexuality, one in which male homosexuality was revealed to be much more prevalent and much harder to visually detect than had been thought previously,[13] the sexuality of these artists was known only among close friends and was not part of the public reception of their work. At most, it remained a topic of speculation and gossip.[14] Of the four artists, only Rivers painted male nudes in an expressionist style, while Warhol became doyen of an entire gay and bohemian subculture that largely escaped the notice of mainstream America. As we will see later in this chapter, however, in the context of film and art in the last quarter of the century, the artist's sexual identity became an explicit issue, one increasingly difficult to disentangle from issues of pornography.

During the American war in Vietnam, the grassroots anti-war movement, the sexual revolution and youth movement, the civil rights and women's movements, and the gay liberation movement all seemingly conspired to challenge reigning patriarchal paradigms and, for a moment at least, seemed to make possible a different definition of masculinity.[15] A fascination with an eroticized male image resurfaced in the 1950–1960s in film stars such as James Dean and Rock Hudson,[16] and in such music stars as Elvis Presley, Jim Morrison, Mick Jagger, and the androgynous David Bowie. Long-haired singers like Led Zeppelin's Robert Plant, in cropped shirts with pants slung low on narrow hips to expose a lengthy swath of thin torso, established a feminized erotics of the male body, one at odds with war-era hyper-masculinity and slated for patriarchal backlash in the 1980–1990s,[17] a backlash further complicated by the hyper-masculinity of black rap music stars and the misogyny of their lyrics.

Women artists in the United States, themselves influenced by the feminist movement, women's consciousness-raising groups, and the Kinsey report on female sexuality, which emphasized female masturbation and highlighted the role of the clitoris in female orgasm, sought to create and thereby claim erotic imagery outside of the previously phallicized norm. Joan Semmel painted highly intimate images from the perspective of herself in bed, framing the view down the length of her own and her lover's body, often with her own hand at her pubis. Performance art, a new medium without the centuries-old baggage of painting and sculpture from which women had traditionally been excluded, provided a significant context for women to explore their own sexuality as well as the kinds of patriarchal conditions of representation placed upon it. Austrian artist Valie Export conducted guerilla performances out in the general milieu. *Tapp- und Tast-Kino* (*Touch Cinema*, 1968–1971) saw the artist walk about the streets with a cardboard box around her upper body, its front an ersatz theater proscenium. Her fellow citizens were invited to reach through the stage curtains to touch that which was ordinarily mere spectacle in the movies. *Genitalpanik* (*Genital Panic*, 1969) saw the artist stride up and down theater aisles in a pair of crotchless pants and bearing a machine gun, demanding viewers to engage with a material woman versus the fantasy women on screen. In the 1980s, former porn star turned performance artist Annie Sprinkle, in less confrontational fashion, promoted a sex-positive agenda by hosting and starring in her own titillating yet didactic performances throughout the 1980s. *Bosom Ballet* (1987–1991) featured the artist manipulating her breasts to music in a lighthearted fashion quite antithetical to similar breast manipulation by dancers in strip clubs. More famously, in her *Public Cervix Announcement* (1989–1996), the artist, dressed first like a nurse and then in lingerie, douched on stage and then inserted a speculum and invited audience members to peer in at her cervix. Such eroticized feminist imagery paved the way for queer visual explorations during the last quarter of the twentieth century and on into the twenty-first.

FIGURE 9.3: Annie Sprinkle, *Yin-Yang Breasts*, 1987–1991.
Copyright Annie Sprinkle. Photo: Marc Trunz.

CINEMA, SEX, AND POLITICS

The role played by technological reproducibility in mass reproduction meant that those who worked in photography and film struggled for artistic recognition, and as these mediums became the primary representational forms of the masses, attempts to provoke a more sophisticated dialog about eroticism and sexuality were often condemned as obscene or pornographic. Thus, like photography before it, institutionalized forms of censorship followed quickly on the heels of cinematic innovation in, for example, Germany, as well as in the United States and elsewhere in Europe.[18]

As the first truly mass medium, film in the 1910s transitioned from the individual viewer of the nickelodeon to the group experience of the darkened theater. In the United States, white slavery fears of the period were fomented by lurid films on the theme. On the one hand, the burgeoning movie industry desired to feminize audiences in a bid for respectability; on the other, the screening of such exploitation films as *Traffic in Souls* (1914) and *Is Any Girl*

Safe? (1916) nonetheless reflected the conflicted response to the suffrage move-ment and to women's increasing participation in the public sphere. Thus, white slave films titillated with tales of the capture and ravishment of young white women. Such films identified the theater itself as a site for such white slavery abductions, and thereby stoked concerns about those same young women's conduct with young men in the darkened theaters themselves.[19]

White slave films clearly hit on a cinematic formula of sexually illicit subject matter that would be exploited in such early Hollywood films as *Baby Face* (1933), which featured Barbara Stanwyck escaping a life of prostitution in a speakeasy by sleeping her way to the top of New York's social elite. The Hays Code of 1930 temporarily put the brakes on such immoral subject matter in Hollywood films. In the post–World War II era, morally ambiguous themes were reintroduced in film noir, whose stylish cinematic look was influenced by German expressionist cinematography. Such noir films as *Double Indemnity* (1944), *Gilda* (1946), and *The Postman Always Rings Twice* (1946) combined sexy femmes fatales with hardboiled criminals and detectives and often meted out justice through grim ends in contrast with more formulaic Hollywood happy endings.

In the 1960s, avant-garde filmmakers pushed the boundaries of acceptabil-ity with experimental films about sex and sexual ambiguity. Jack Smith's *Flam-ing Creatures* (1963) featured hermaphrodites, drag shows, transvestites, and even vampirism in a surreal montage style in which both "imagination and desire are reaffirmed."[20] Andy Warhol's silent, thirty-five-minute film *Blow Job* (1964) was censored despite the fact that no nudity or overt sexual act was shown. The camera never moves from its tight cropping of the face of a young man presumably receiving the titular fellatio, stimulating a desire in the viewer to see what is visually denied and to confirm the exact moment of ejaculation.[21] Artist Carolee Schneemann made *Fuses* (1965) to counter what she perceived as Stan Brakhage's failed depiction of her sexual pleasure in *Loving* (1957) and *Cat's Cradle* (1959). Both intimate and graphic, Schneemann's film was anom-alous during a period in which U.S. feminists were attempting to distinguish between an acceptable erotica and an unacceptable pornography.[22]

Film adaptations of literature that had once been condemned for obscenity further pushed the still expanding boundaries of acceptability. The sexual revolu-tion of the 1960s provided the context for such filmmakers as Britain's Ken Rus-sell to feature a firelight nude wrestling scene between two men at a time when male genitalia could still not be shown in mainstream cinema. *Women in Love* (1969), Russell's adaptation of the D. H. Lawrence novel, is renowned for the sensualism of its depictions of its male and female stars. Stanley Kubrick's film adaptation of *Lolita* (1962), based on the titular novel by Vladimir Nabokov, despite only alluding to erotic activity in conformance with the Motion Picture Association of America (MPAA) codes, nonetheless met controversy due to its subject matter, pedophilia. Although the argument is often made that the difference between erotica and pornography is that the former leaves more to the imagination, clearly the imagination can be far more lascivious than any explicit sexual display since, in the controversial U.S. version, the scene wherein Lolita "seduces" Humbert Humbert is in fact truncated, in contrast to the UK version. At the end of the century, British director Sally Potter adapted Virginia Woolf's *Orlando* (1992) for the screen. Both the film and its star, Tilda Swinton, received wide acclaim for the lush sensuality with which the title character's androgyny was portrayed.

Fascist iconography in Germany, Italy, and Spain during and after World War II often emphasized so-called traditional values of family, maternity, religious morality, and patriarchy. Not unlike turn-of-the-century avant-gardes, postwar European film used erotic sexual themes as one means for undoing these often politically manipulated values.

Ossessione (*Obsession*, 1943), Luchino Visconti's version of James M. Cain's 1934 novel, *The Postman Always Rings Twice*, unlike its U.S. film noir counterpart, paired eroticism with desperation among the ordinary village people who characteristically populated what would become known as Italian neorealist film. Visconti, along with Federico Fellini, set some of their films (most notably, Fellini's *La strada*, 1954) among ordinary people, often villagers and Italian peasants. In contrast to the earlier fascist hypocritical romanticization of peasant life, Visconti, Fellini, and to an even greater degree Pier Paolo Pasolini, whose films centered on the proletariat, offended authorities by their depiction of an Italian peasantry otherwise disavowed at the roots of Italian society. But later films by these directors, including Fellini's *Satyricon* (1969), and Pasolini's *Decameron* (1971) and *Salò* (*The 120 Days of Sodom*, 1976), each based on Italian literary works, were satirical, bawdy, and sensual, their nudity often perceived as an assault on contemporary viewers. An outed homosexual, Pasolini's films and his politics were measured against his homosexuality, and his private life was sensationalized in the press, never more so than with the publication of police photographs of his brutally murdered corpse in 1975.[23]

Italian neorealist film influenced the Nouvelle Vague (French New Wave cinema), in which many films addressed controversial political and sexual issues. Alan Renais's *Hiroshima, Mon Amour* (1959), which focuses on an affair between a French architect and a Japanese woman, juxtaposes explicitly erotic scenes with those of the atomic destruction of Hiroshima. Jean-Luc Godard's *A Bout de Souffle* (*Breathless*, 1960) also concerns a transnational love affair between a French gangster and a young American woman who went shockingly braless throughout the film. François Truffaut's *Jules et Jim* (1961) traced the madness underpinning a love triangle between two men in love with the same woman.

In Germany, director Rainer Werner Fassbinder, associated with postwar New German Cinema, similarly affronted bourgeois mores with his film subjects and his personal life, both of which garnered controversy. Although homosexual, Fassbinder's films, including *The Bitter Tears of Petra von Kant* (1972) and *Fox and Friends* (1975) were criticized by straight and gay groups alike, often for the bleakness and brutality of their depiction of humanity. Similarly, director Paul Verhoeven's early Dutch film, *Spetters* (*Hunks*, 1980), and his later Hollywood erotic thriller *Basic Instinct* (1992), were criticized by gay and lesbian groups respectively for their violence and negatively eroticized depiction of homosexuals and thus of homosexuality itself.

Spanish director Pedro Almodóvar came of age during the later, postwar cultural *abertura* (opening) after Franco's death in 1975, and his films subverted many of the repressive ideals about motherhood, nunneries, family, class, and even bullfighting that had characterized Spanish cultural life under dictatorship between 1939 and 1975. Films such as *La ley del deseo* (*Law of Desire*, 1987), *Pepi, Luci, Bom y otras chicas del montón* (*Pepi, Luci, Bom and Other Ordinary Girls*, 1980), *Entre tinieblas* (*Dark Habits*, 1983), and *Matador* (1986), among others, featured baroquely eroticized homoerotic themes, feminine sexuality, and transvestitism as a means of destabilizing the traditional identities and iconographies of gender. Almodóvar's hyperbolic replication of many of the sociocultural changes experienced under the rapid liberalization of Spanish culture and of the world economy helped to exorcize Spain's repressive past, especially for its nascent youth culture, which embraced the films. Ironically, tepid critical reception in the United States helped to stimulate the films' popular reception there.[24]

Such foreign films, produced outside of the profit-driven Hollywood studio system, were stylistically different: nonlinear narrative, long takes, and obscured or off-center framing were often coupled with an overtly political negotiation of sexuality and of nationalism, especially in the context of the recent fascist histories of Germany and Italy. As a consequence, foreign films, relegated to smaller, art house venues in the United States, gained a curiously doubled reputation as simultaneously boring *and* licentious.[25] Particularly exemplifying this duality was the international production and reception of Italian director Bernardo Bertolucci's *Last Tango in Paris* (1972). Bertolucci had previously directed *The Conformist* (1970), a film deeply critical of fascist ideology. In *Last Tango in Paris*, Bertolucci cast American film star Marlon Brando in this scandal-making film of an anonymous sexual affair between a divorced American man and a Parisian girl. Most memorable is the infamous butter scene, in which Brando's character forces anal sex on actress Maria Schneider's character using the dairy product as a lubricant. Less often remarked is that the scene is also intended as an exorcism of the affianced girl's typically bourgeois mores, as Brando's character insists she intone the words "church, family, state" while being sodomized. Released the same year as *Deep Throat*, the first feature-length porno film, *Last Tango in Paris* was itself condemned as pornographic, and continues to enjoy a salacious yet somewhat exclusive and high brow reputation. Indeed, the 1967 Swedish film, *I Am Curious (Yellow)*, with its experimental narrative form and explicit sex scenes, was largely considered a pornographic film upon its 1969 U.S. release.

In 1969, four of the titles in the top-twenty box-office hits were X-rated, including director John Schlesinger's tale of a male hustler, *Midnight Cowboy*.[26] Although some American moviegoers after World War II sought out foreign films as an alternative to Hollywood cinematic boosterism, the sexual revolution of the 1960s–1970s fomented interest in art house films and helped to establish a context for mainstream pornographic films. Explicit sex in film, relegated during the first half of the century to private pornographic screenings of short films known as stags and smokers, saw its full-length cinematic realization in the early 1970s in such films as *Deep Throat* and *Behind the Green Door* (1972) and *The Devil in Miss Jones* (1973).[27] The reception of these films launched an era of semirespectability: a largely middle-class and mix-gendered audience lined up around the block to see them; the mainstream press—including mention in the *New York Times*—made them an acceptable topic of public discourse; and celebrities who admitted to having seen the films helped to establish "porno chic."

As visual communication technologies developed, pornography became ever more mainstream, as well as ever more entrenched within the domestic sphere in the form of rented VHS tapes and, later, DVDs and streaming video over the Internet. In the absence of a Western tradition of *ars erotica*, reactionary groups increasingly claimed a need for regulation and censorship, and were thus complicit with pornography's highly profitable reputation as illicit.[28]

EROTIC COMICS AND COMIC BOOKS

Like the Hays Code for the film industry, strict codes regarding imagery and subject matter deemed licentious or obscene enforced in the United States after World War II resulted after mid-century in the bulk of erotic image production taking place in Europe; such material in the United States enjoyed an underground revival in the 1960s–1970s.

Pre-code erotic comics in the United States include the underground Tijuana Bibles, produced soon after Prohibition and enjoying their greatest popularity during the Depression. These small (four by six inches), usually eight-page booklets were illicitly produced and circulated by hand, especially among soldiers, and featured caricatures of such film stars as Mae West and such beloved characters as Popeye, Mutt and Jeff, and Betty Boop. The trade in underground comics benefited from the fact that the 1930s were the golden age of mainstream serialized comics, which provided the fodder for Tijuana Bible caricatures rendering beloved characters in pornographic detail. Like the name "Tijuana Bible" itself, which derives from racist stereotypes about Mexico, these Bibles were often racist and certainly sexist, although in the tradition of pornography they also parodied political figures, including Mussolini and Stalin.[29]

In the United States, the widely held view that comics are primarily entertainment for children led to concerns that children could too easily encounter such pornographic comics. During the 1950s, fears that crime and horror comic books, with their attendant glorification of eroticized violence, were causing juvenile delinquency incited Congressional hearings in 1954.[30] As a result of the hearings, a restrictive code was implemented that resulted in less tight-fitting blouses on the *Archie* teen comics' Betty and Veronica characters and put most other titles out of business: Hajdu reports that between 1954 and 1956 the number of titles published diminished from 650 to 250,[31] a development that ushered in the underground "comix" movement in the 1960–1970s, spearheaded by such illustrators as (Robert) R. Crumb. Crumb's *Fritz the Cat* combined the erotic escapades of its title character with the author's subversive take on mainstream American culture and politics.

The postwar history of erotic adult comic books is predominantly European. The Italian comic illustrator Guido Crepax, who gained initial fame with the character of Valentina in 1965, is widely considered to have had a central influence on European adult comics. His international fame is also due to his sophisticated translation into black and white comic-book form of such erotic classics as Pauline Réage's *Histoire d'O* (1975), the Marquis de Sade's *Justine* (1979), and Leopold von Sacher-Masoch's *Venus in Furs* (1984); many of his comic books have been translated into Japanese and into multiple Western languages. Fellow countryman and comic book illustrator Milo Manera works in color, and is known for his comic *DECLIC* (*The Click*), featuring a man in possession of a device that sexually arouses women. Images from *DECLIC* can be found reproduced on postcards throughout Paris, and the comic book series was source for the 1980s film by the same name, which starred Florence Guérin.

FIGURES 9.4A AND 9.4B: Two Tijuana Bible images, 1930s.

Famed illustrator Tom of Finland (Touko Laaksonen, 1920–1991) can be considered as one possible heir to U.S. painter Paul Cadmus. Like Cadmus, the illustrator focused on stylized yet detailed depictions of secondary sexual characteristics—prominently rounded and cleft buttocks—as well as the heavily muscled torsos of homomasculine types: sailors, bikers, policemen, lumberjacks, and leathermen, all in tightly fitting attire. Whereas Cadmus's paintings for public consumption contained only hints at the erotic focus of many of his paintings and sketches for private consumption, Tom of Finland's work became a veritable icon of homosexual subculture, appearing first in U.S. muscle magazines in the 1950s and later in galleries and museums. Tom of Finland's figure illustrations and more overtly pornographic illustrations of homosexual liaisons, replete with outsized erections, became icons of post-Stonewall gay liberation in the United States, while their technical accomplishment has made them enormously popular among art collectors. Ironically, Tom of Finland's autobiography treats his experience in Finland's Axis army during World War II as a source for his eroticized images of jack-booted leathermen.

Gay comics also played an important role in the 1980s as a source of disseminating safe-sex information. *Safer Sex Comix*, published by the Gay Men's Health Clinic (GMHC) in New York City, depicted—in elaborately eroticized detail—condom-use as a regular part of the pornographic story lines of happily random sexual encounters between gay men.[32] Similarly, Gregg Bordowitz and Jean Carlomusto created a series of erotic Safe Sex Shorts (1989) for the GMHC, varyingly directed to gays and lesbians, but also to ethnic subgroups.[33] In Spain, Nazario's *Anarcoma* comic-book, although not explicit, depicts underground gay life through its transvestite detective character, while Juan Mediavilla's *El pase* addresses the controversial topics of drugs, sex, and violence. In England A.A.R.G.H. (Artists Against Rampant Government Homophobia), created a one-off comic anthology in 1988 to fight antigay legislation known as "Clause 28." German comic artist Ralf König's work, which includes an homage to Tom of Finland, has focused variously on his own coming out, on AIDS, on gay marriage, and, more whimsically, on gay dogs, and has been translated into fourteen languages and adapted for film.

VIDEO GAMES AND VIRTUAL REALITY

Although one hesitates to draw a straight line from the eroticized violence of U.S. comic books in the 1950s to more contemporary forms of adult entertainment, erotic comics clearly influenced late twentieth- and early twenty-first-century trends in video games, a technology dominated largely by U.S. makers.

Like comic books, early erotic and pornographic video games indulged a sophomoric taste for exaggerated anatomy and both evaded censorship and courted controversy by their very existence in a medium generally held to provide entertainment for children and adolescents. Early erotic video games designed for Atari in the 1980s, including the nightmarish castration-anxiety game *X-Man*, and the ethnically offensive and violently misogynistic *Custer's Revenge*, built on the primitive computer graphics model of ASCII-porn with similarly blocky results.[34] One long-running adult video game, *Leisure Suit Larry* (1980s–2000s), featured a nerdy protagonist charged with seducing attractive women. Notably, the game was among the first to introduce a multiple-choice test to confirm players' legal age, a test that experienced young gamers easily skipped by keyboarding Alt-X.

But the kinds of stereotypical erotic depictions that marked adult video games also invaded so-called mainstream games marketed to adolescent boys. One example is the well-endowed Lara Croft in the *Tomb Raider* series (1996–) and later embodied by film actress Angelina Jolie in the 2001 Hollywood film adaptation, *Lara Croft: Tomb Raider*. The violence and prostitution depicted in *Grand Theft Auto IV*, developed by the Scottish company Rockstar Games North and released in 2008, garnered many of the same sorts of parental objections and media attention as did 1950s comic books. By the early twenty-first century, an expanding spectrum of interactive adult video games, increasingly focused on VR (virtual reality), faced competition from on-line VR erotic gaming, particularly from such massive multi-user dimension object oriented (MUD and MOO) sites as Second Life. Here, as in sex-chat sites, users—called residents—adopted fictional identities, or avatars, that did not necessarily reflect their gender, ethnicity, or sexuality in RL (real life) in order to have or even sell sex online.

HOMOEROTIC AND DIASPORIC SEXUAL IMAGERY IN ART AT THE END OF THE CENTURY

What constitutes eroticism in imagery was increasingly contested after mid-century as sexuality and sexual identity were further polemicized, politicized, and marketed under globalization. As visual communication technologies made the overt erotics of pornography more easily available, what constituted the erotic—rather than its dissection or critique—became increasingly difficult to identify. Was feminist imagery critical of female objectification erotic? Was the confrontational genital parade of Judy Chicago's *The Dinner Party* (1974–1979) erotic? Was any image of the nude body inherently erotic or obscene? If it seems as though what was erotic in art was increasingly being defined within queer contexts, this was no doubt due at least in part to the fact that after Stonewall and with the advent of AIDS, gays and lesbians had more at stake mortally and politically in asserting positive and erotic images of sexualities long repressed by or conscripted to the patriarchal ordering of the visual culture of desire. As we consider art at the century's end, what is erotic is increasingly defined by those occluded from its definition at the century's beginning, and for centuries prior: lesbians, gays, Hispanics, and diasporic Africans and Asians. Homoerotic and diasporic erotic art will be touched upon in a variety of media.

During the postmodern era of corporate and consumer capitalism under its greatest global cultural hegemony, the United States nonetheless remained regressive on issues of sexuality, sexual identity, and erotic imagery, all fodder for the culture wars. In Marlon Riggs's documentary film, *Tongues Untied* (1990), the gay African American artist daringly proffered one of the earliest inquiries into black gay identity. Frankly homoerotic imagery of African American men combined with a more documentary focus on racial self-hatred in the gay community, which itself had displayed a white beauty bias. Like Mapplethorpe's photographs, Riggs's videos, which often aired on television on federally funded Public Broadcasting Service stations, were targeted by religious and political conservatives as an example of publicly funded pornography.

Video artist Richard Fung, a Trinidad native who lives and works in Canada, explored race, sexuality, and gender in a postcolonial, diasporic context. *Dirty Laundry* (1986) parallels the legendary Chinese quest for the source of the Yellow River with a less legendary but no less symbolic homosexual search for pleasure and positive sexual reinforcement from gay pornography. Mexican artist Guillermo Gomez-Peña performed in a parodic costume mix of Aztec finery, Mexican kitsch, and U.S. stereotypy about Mexicans that simultaneously reveals and fetishizes his body. His erudite, linguistic plays between English and Spanish, such as "CyberVato" and "Webback"—the racial slur of immigrant laborers as "wet backs" combined with the World Wide Web—highlight not only cultural difference but parody U.S. nationalism and its paternalistic and often hypocritical attitudes toward Mexico, particularly surrounding immigration and labor. Video performances such as *Border Brujo* (1988), and an online project in collaboration with Roberto Sifuentes, *The Temple of Confessions* (1995), exposed the exoticized eroticism that often underpins white fears and fantasies about Mexicans.

Until his death from complications due to AIDS in 1989, gay Nigerian photographer Rotimi Fani-Kayode juxtaposed the black male body with ritual

Yoruba artifacts in a gesture that simultaneously refers to primitivist imagery and its formalist modernity and reclaims the body's sensualism despite its diasporic fragmentation.[35] In a related fashion, artist Catherine Opie also photographed the lesbian body in ways that directly invoke homophobic stereotypes. A series of self-portraits from 1993 show the artist from behind: one, with the word "Dyke" tattooed on her neck; the other with a child's stick figure drawing of two women holding hands in front of a house carved by razor into her back, fresh blood still dripping, the image denoting the scars left by heterosexual childhood narratives. An arch series of closely cropped photographic portraits of drag kings from 1994 includes an ethnically diverse group of women with cropped hair, tattoos, and fake facial hair. An engraved silver tag on the frame identifies each by her drag king name: Papa Bear, Chicken, Chief. If the drag-king photographs demonstrated that masculinity is as much of a masquerade as psychoanalyst Joan Riviere famously claimed femininity is, more powerfully erotic is Opie's portrait series of Jake (1991) a shirtless and handsome young woman straddling a chair, chest concealed by the chair's

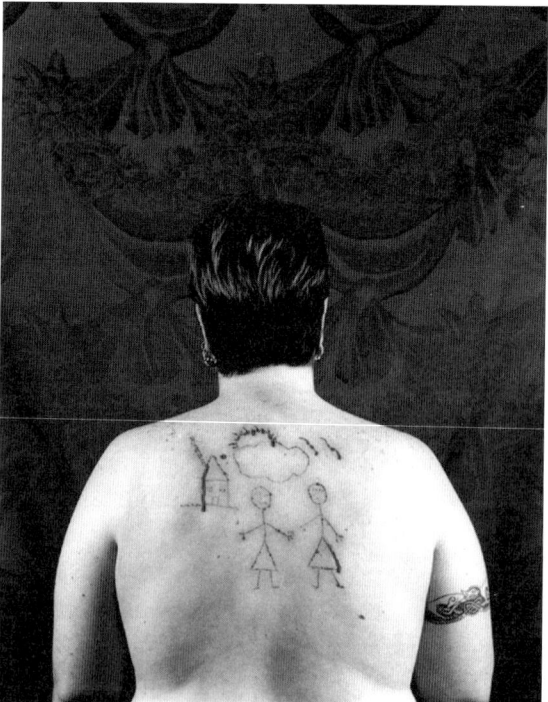

FIGURE 9.5: Catherine Opie, *Self-Portrait / Cutting*, 1993. Chromogenic print. 40 × 20 inches, edition of 8 Courtesy Regen Projects, Los Angeles.

back, and looking at the camera from under his/her fedora with an appealingly frank desire that simultaneously confirmed his/her own desirability despite the absence of clear gender signals. Intersexed artist Della Grace Volcano/Del LaGrace Volcano also uses photography to depict the subversive qualities of lesbian masculinity.

EROTICISM AND EXOTICISM: RACE, ETHNICITY, AND NATIONALISM

As an outgrowth of nineteenth-century imperialism, nationalism in twentieth-century Western cultures perhaps predictably relied on the stereotyped or exaggerated sexualization of countries and cultures deemed undesirable. The cultural and ideological disseminations of other nations' putative sexualized image production served, like French nineteenth-century orientalist imagery, to render the culture or nation in question alien and other, as well as to justify colonial conquest and imperialist rule. Longstanding rumors, for example, that sado-masochistic pornographic films were made in Hitler's bunker continued to fuel contemporary erotic imagination, and were exploited, for example, in U.S. advertising of the Rosselini film *Open City* (1946),[36] and subsequently ironized in Don DeLillo's 1989 novel, *Running Dog*. Thus, stereotypes of sexual perversity continue to function as weapons for othering national and cultural differences.

World War I propaganda imagery fomented nationalism by depicting white European women sexually defiled by black troops from other countries (including from the United States). After the war, ideological imagery contrasting good (middle-class) women and bad (working-class) women helped to stimulate the fascist suppression of the working-class Spartacist uprisings by the Freikorps, who later became Hitler's storm troops.[37] The perversity of other cultures is often contrasted with the wholesomeness of one's own cultural eroticism. In the United States, the pin-up girl—bathing-suit clad beauties such as actress Betty Grable—adorned posters sent to American GIs during World War II to remind them what they were fighting for at home. In a related fashion in the United States throughout 1910s–1960s, and in an extension of antebellum stereotypes about the hyper-sexuality of blacks, miscegenist fears were stoked by images of hyper-sexualized black men coveting or consorting with white women. Indeed, the African American boxer, Jack Johnson, was the first to be prosecuted under the 1910 Mann Act, ostensibly designed to prevent white slavery by preventing interstate transfer of women for immoral purposes. Such miscegenist images were recycled during the civil rights movement.

With the end of the cold war and the globalization of capitalism, Neil Jordan's *The Crying Game* (1992), initiated a "global taste" for queer films that

"mobilize" queer male desire in order to "relegitimize ... a new global hegemony around the different national masculinities and hegemonies set in crisis
by globalization."[38] The film's politics caused it to fail upon its initial release in
Ireland and the UK, but the main character's eroticized secret drew U.S. audiences. As queers and ethnicities are increasingly commodified and consumed,
such commodification seems strikingly at odds with the fact that sexuality and
sexual identity have consistently comprised elements of international border
control and provided reason for the exclusion of certain populations from immigrating, particularly into the United States.[39] Globalization has undoubtedly
exacerbated the global sex trade and is reflected in an explosion of Internet
sex sites focused on exoticized women in developing nations. Although the
military has a long history of promoting forced prostitution and providing a
market for prostitution in conquered or occupied nations,[40] the rapid growth
of the Internet has expanded the trade in global sex—chat rooms, exotic pornography, oriental and Russian brides. Such exoticized ideals about the sexual
availability of other nations and cultures is similarly evidenced in the panracial
ethnic characteristics featured by many online avatars adopted in on-line chat
rooms and in such VR sites as Second Life.

In the wake of the photographs of sexualized torture victims at Abu Ghraib
in 2004, it seems clear that sexualized imagery remains a potent means of othering ethnic national enemies. Characterized as an "imperialist mockery" that
nonetheless evokes a centuries-old tradition of pathos in art, reception of these
sexualized images of torture victims for some were diminished by the photographs' implication that the victims "[took] pleasure in their chastisement and
pain."[41] Colombian artist Fernando Botero (b. 1932), known primarily for his
stylized, Rubenesque figures inhabiting pleasant, pastoral scenes, shocked the
world in 2005 by applying his characteristic painting style to the widely disseminated images of the torture and sexual humiliation at Abu Ghraib. The depiction
of these horrifying scenes peopled by Botero's characteristically roly-poly figures
is jarringly dissonant and revives the ethical and sensory assault of the original
photographs, now muted by repetition and by U.S. political and cultural complacency. Although Botero's paintings will continue to be exhibited, the artist
refuses to profit from the events of Abu Ghraib by their sale or auction.

Do the Abu Ghraib photographs constitute pornography, as has so often
been charged? Some feminist critics have traditionally analogized lynching photographs of black men in the 1920s to the torture of women working in the pornography industry, and thus argue that pornography is evidence of a comparable
crime against women.[42] Sexism and racism remain rampant in Western culture,
but to equate images of ethnic torture, rape, or murder with pornographic

depictions of women is deeply problematic, leveling as it does actual physical torture and mutilation with the erotic fantasies of men *and* women.

That the Abu Ghraib images were exposed on the Internet is significant for more reasons than can be covered within the scope of this chapter. But their circulation on the Internet is surely perhaps one of the reasons they have been mischaracterized as pornography. Indeed, modern pornography has followed upon the heels of developments in technological mass reproducibility from the printing press to the Internet. As erotic imagery left the previously exclusive domains of art and its association with elite culture to represent the bodily based desires of the lower classes, the very mass circulation of erotic imagery became an unacknowledged aspect of pornography's definition.[43] Pornography, then, is one of the risks—and one of the benefits—of the democratization of culture. The confusion of pornography with other types of images—such as those of torture at Abu Ghraib—attests to the ongoing conflicts between the secular body and the embeddedness of Judeo-Christian tradition in Western cultures.

In the absence of a Western tradition of *ars erotica*, it is possible to assert that no genuine erotic imagery exists in Western culture outside of pornography. Distinctions between a high-art erotica and a technologically produced and disseminated pornography historically has served patriarchal and class privilege. Erotic imagery prior to the twentieth century largely confirmed patriarchal ideologies, and its deployment by early avant-garde artists frequently confirmed those ideologies under the auspices of questioning them. After mid-century such imagery was contested by feminists and ethnic minorities, and by century's end previously suppressed erotic realities had nearly displaced those images in both art and mass culture. Early in the twenty-first century, as artists as diverse as German photographer Thomas Ruff and American painter John Currin have borrowed liberally from Internet porn, it has also become increasingly difficult to distinguish between art and pornography. Such an elision between art and pornography demonstrates, as Dorelies Kraakman suggests, pornography's ongoing role in the "cultural transformation of sex."[44] Indeed, Kraakman characterizes pornography as a hybrid genre, one that historically partakes of medical and scientific discourses as well as of art and mass cultural forms. And although the "pornification" of culture decried at the ready accessibility of Internet pornography has been condemned by those who would defend culture, so, too, have representations of nontraditional sexualities—feminine, ethnic, queer, trans—been condemned as pornography. The difficulty in distinguishing art from pornography and pornography from erotica is symptomatic of representation's ability to confound our sense of where the raced and gendered body ends and sexuality begins.

NOTES

Chapter 1

1. For overviews, see John D'Emilio and Estelle B. Freedman, *Intimate Matters: A History of Sexuality in America* (New York: Harper & Row, 1988); Franz Eder, Lesley Hall, and Gert Hekma, eds., *Sexual Cultures in Europe*, 2 Vols. (Manchester: Manchester University Press, 1999); Lesley A. Hall, *Sex, Gender and Social Change in Britain since 1880* (London: MacMillan, 2000); Eder, *Kultur der Begierde. Eine Geschichte der Sexualität* (München: Beck, 2001).
2. Sigmund Freud, *Drei Abhandlungen zur Sexualtheorie,* 5th ed. (Leipzig, Germany: Deuticke, 1915); Jonathan Ned Katz, *The Invention of Heterosexuality* (New York: Dutton, 1995); Louis-Georges Tin, *L'Invention de la culture hétérosexuelle* (Paris: Éditions Autrement, 2008).
3. Terence Kissack, *Free Comrades: Anarchism and Homosexuality in the United States, 1895–1917* (Oakland, CA: AK Press, 2008).
4. Regina Kunzel, *Criminal Intimacy: Prison and the Uneven History of Modern American Sexuality* (Chicago: University of Chicago Press, 2008).
5. Alan Bérubé, *Coming Out under Fire: The History of Gay Men and Women in World War Two* (New York: Free Press, 1990).
6. Anthony Giddens, *The Transformation of Intimacy: Sexuality, Love and Eroticism in Modern Societies* (London: Polity, 1992), chapter 4.
7. Alan Sinfield, *On Sexuality and Power* (New York: Columbia University Press, 2004).
8. Sinfield, *On Sexuality and Power*; Gert Hekma, "The Drive for Sexual Equality," *Sexualities* 11 (2008): 51–55.
9. Karla Jay, *The Amazon and the Page: Natalie Clifford Barney and Renée Vivien* (Bloomington, Indiana University Press, 1988).
10. Thomas W. Laqueur, *Making Sex. Body and Gender from the Greeks to Freud* (Cambridge, MA: Harvard University Press, 1990).

11. Lisa Duggan and Nan D. Hunter, *Sex Wars: Sexual Dissent and Political Culture* (New York: Routledge, 1995).

12. Ariel Levy, *Female Chauvinist Pigs: Women and the Rise of Raunch Culture* (New York: Free Press, 2005); Susanna Paasonen, Kaarina Nikunen, and Laura Saarenmaa, eds., *Pornification: Sex and Sexuality in Media Culture* (Oxford: Berg, 2007).

13. Dagmar Herzog, *Sex in Crisis: The New Sexual Revolution and the Future of American Politics* (New York: Basic Books, 2008).

14. Edward O. Laumann, John H. Gagnon, Robert T. Michael, and Stuart Michaels, *The Social Organization of Sexuality: Sexual Practices in the United States* (Chicago: University of Chicago Press, 1994); Michel Hubert, Nathalie Bajos and Theo Sandfort, eds., *Sexual Behaviour and HIV/AIDS in Europe* (London: UCL Press, 1998).

15. Floor Bakker and Ine Vanwesenbeeck, eds., *Seksuele gezondheid in Nederland 2006* (Delft: Eburon, 2006).

16. For an overview, see Robert Aldrich, ed., *Gay Life and Culture: A World History* (London: Thames & Hudson, 2006).

17. Florence Tamagne, *Histoire de l'homosexualité en Europe. Berlin, Londres, Paris 1919–1939* (Paris: Seuil, 2000).

18. George Chauncey, *Gay New York: Gender, Urban Culture and the Making of the Gay Male World 1890–1940* (New York: Basic Books, 1994); Matt Houlbrook, *Queer London: Perils and Pleasures in the Sexual Metropolis, 1918–1957* (Chicago: University of Chicago Press, 2005).

19. Volkmar Sigusch, *Karl Heinrich Ulrichs. Der erste Schwule der Weltgeschichte* (Berlin: Rosa Winkel, 2000).

20. Karl Heinrich Ulrichs, *Argonauticus* (Leipzig: A. Serbe's Verlag, 1869), 87.

21. C. J. Pascoe, *"Dude, You Are a Fag": Adolescent Masculinity and the Fag Discourse* (Berkeley: University of California Press, 2007).

22. Times, 21–8-2008

23. Marcela Iacub and Patrice Maniglier, *Antimanuel d'éducation sexuelle* (Rosny: Breal 2005).

24. Thomas W. Laqueur, *Solitary Sex: A Cultural History of Masturbation* (New York: Zone Books, 2003).

25. Dagmar Herzog, *Sex after Fascism: Memory and Morality in Twentieth-Century Germany* (Princeton, NJ: Princeton University Press, 2005).

26. Gert Hekma, "How Libertine Is the Netherlands? Exploring Contemporary Dutch Sexual Cultures," in *Regulating Sex: The Politics of Intimacy and Identity,* ed. Elizabeth Bernstein and Laurie Schaffner (New York: Routledge, 2005).

27. Don Kulick, "Four Hundred Thousand Swedish Perverts," *GLQ* 11 (2005): 205–35.

Chapter 2

1. Jonathan Ned Katz, *The Invention of Heterosexuality* (New York, 1996).

2. Manfred Herzer (trans. Hubert Kennedy), "Kertbeny and the Nameless Love," *Journal of Homosexuality* 12 (1985): 1–25.

3. A lesser-known work of the same title had been published in 1844 by physician Heinrich Kaan, and was principally concerned with masturbation.

4. James G. Kiernan, "Responsibility in Sexual Perversion," *Chicago Medical Recorder* 3 (1892): 185–210.

5. Marc-André Raffalovich, "L'éducation des invertis," *Archives d'anthropologie criminelle de médecine légale et de psychologie normale et pathologique* 9 (Novembrer 1894): 738–40.

6. Penis envy, according to Freud, explains the attitude of feminists of his time: "Now, upon this penis-envy follows that hostile embitterment displayed by women against men, never entirely absent in the relations between the sexes, the clearest indications of which are to be found in the writings and ambitions of 'emancipated' women." Sigmund Freud, *"Das Tabu der Virginität,"* [The Taboo of Virginity], *Collected Papers Volume 4* (New York, Basic Books, 1918), 231.

7. A principle known in the United States as civilized morality, supported by organizations such as the American Purity Alliance, the Woman's Christian Temperance Union or the American Federation for Sex Hygiene.

8. Henry Havelock Ellis, *Love and Virtue* (New York: George H. Doran Company, 1922).

9. It has often been pointed out that an overwhelming number of homosexuals and Jewish people were involved in the fight for sexual liberation. The same is true for socialists of all factions, and it is easily explained: these are all categories of people who, naturally, felt alienated from the established order.

10. Herbert Marcuse, *Eros and Civilization: A Philosophical Inquiry Into Freud* (Boston: The Beacon Press, 1955).

11. Reich is often mentioned as having coined the expression "sexual revolution." Under this title, in 1945 he published an English edition of writings previously limited to Germany and Denmark: Wilhelm Reich, *The Sexual Revolution* (New York, Orgone Institute Press, 1945). However, the great psychoanalyst Otto Gross had introduced both the expression and the concept decades earlier, and James Thurber and E. B. White, *Is Sex Necessary?* (New York: Blue Ribbon, 1929) contains a chapter titled "The Sexual Revolution."

12. An account of the first two meetings was published in the 11th edition of *La Révolution surréaliste* (1928). Those of subsequent meetings came out only after André Breton's archives were made public. André Breton, *Recherches sur la sexualité - 4ème* volume des *Archives du surréalisme* (Paris, Gallimard, 1990).

13. José Pierre, ed., *Investigating Sex* (London: Verso, 1992), 10.

14. Pierre, *Investigating Sex*, 129.

15. James Mahoon and Christine Wenburg, eds., *The Mosher Survey: Sexual Attitudes of 45 Victorian Women* (New York: Arno Press, 1980).

16. Katherine Bement Davis, *Factors in the Sex Life of Twenty-Two Hundred Women* (New York: Harper & Brothers Publishers, 1929). It should be noted that K. B. Davis's work, as well as other investigations such as that of Gilbert V. Hamilton, were made possible through the support of billionaire philanthropist John D. Rockefeller Jr. and his Bureau of Social Hygiene, whose help was to be equally indispensable to Margaret Sanger.

17. R. L. Dickinson and L. Beam, *A Thousand Marriages: A Medical Study of Sex Adjustment* (Baltimore, MD: Williams & Wilkins, 1932); Dickinson and Beam,

The Single Woman: A Medical Study in Sex Education (Baltimore, MD: Williams & Wilkins, 1934).

18. See M. A. Macciocchi, *La donna nera. Consenso femminile al fascismo* (Milan: Feltrinelli, 1976). Victoria De Grazia, *How Fascism Ruled Women: Italy, 1922–1945* (Berkeley: University of California Press, 1992).

19. A. M. Fischer, *The Mass Psychology of Fascism* (New York: Orgone Institute Press, 1946).

20. Dagmar Herzog, ed., *Sexuality and German Fascism* (Oxford, NY, Berghahn Books, 2005); Herzog, *Sex after Fascism: Memory and Morality in Twentieth-Century Germany* (Princeton, NJ: Princeton University Press, 2005).

21. Simone de Beauvoir, *Le Deuxième Sexe* (Paris: Gallimard, 1949). Translated H. M. Parshley as *The Second Sex* (New York: Knopf, 1952). There have since been many alternative translations and subsequent editions.

22. *"La femelle humaine est une creation sociale: rien ne la prédestine â un rôle spécifique."*—["The human female is a social creation: no specific role is assigned to her."] Extract from an interview with Simone de Beauvoir on Radio Canada, 1959 (censured).

23. J. Money, J. G. Hampson, and J. L. Hampson, "An Examination of Some Basic Sexual Concepts: Evidence of Human Hermaphroditism," *Bulletin of the Johns Hopkins Hospital* 97 (1955): 301–19. "In place of a theory of instinctive masculinity or femininity, which is innate, the evidence of hermaphroditism lends support to a conception that psychologically, sexuality is undifferentiated at birth and that it becomes differentiated as masculine or feminine in the course of the various experiences of growing up."

24. This form of education only began to be organized in 1939, with the creation of the National Council on Family Relations and its journal, *Marriage and Family Living* (1941), later to become *Journal of Marriage and the Family* (1964).

25. Later developments in genetics showed this estimation to be relatively accurate: the proportion of children born to married women, and whose biological father is not the legal father, varies from country to country but is frequently as high as 20 percent.

26. Particularly interesting are the works of Erica Rand, including *Barbie's Queer Accessories* (Durham, NC: Duke University Press, 1995), and Marianne Debouzy's, "La poupée Barbie," *CLIO: Histoires, Femmes, Sociétés* 13, no. 4 (April 1996): 2–13.

27. For a very short time, Ken's place was taken by surfer Blaine, who quickly disappeared after a disappointing drop in sales.

28. Erich Fromm, "Sexuality and Sexual Perversions," in *The Revision of Psychoanalysis*, ed. Erich Fromm and Rainer Funk (Boulder, CO: Westview, 1992), 87.

29. Betty Friedan, *The Feminine Mystique* (New York: Norton, 1963).

30. Partially reproduced in Jonathan Beecher and Richard Bienvenu, tr. and ed., *The Utopian Vision of Charles Fourier: Selected Texts on Work, Love and Passionate Attraction* (Boston: Beacon Press: 1971).

31. Sigmund Freud, "'Civilized' Sexual Morality and Modern Nervous Illness," in *The Standard Edition of the Complete Psychological Works of Sigmund Freud*, Vol. 9 (London: The Hogarth Press and the Institute of Psycho-analysis, 1959), 187.

32. Michel Foucault, *Madness and Civilization* (London: Routledge, 2006); Thomas Szasz, *The Myth of Mental Illness* (New York: Hoeber-Harper, 1961).

33. Gilles Deleuze and Félix Guattari, *Anti-Oedipus, Capitalism and Schizophrenia*, tr. Robert Hurley, Mark Seem, and Helen R. Lane (New York: The Viking Press, 1982), 79, emphasis in original.

34. The part played by the clitoris in female sexual arousal had been frequently observed and noted by doctors. According to Freud, however, the clitoral pleasure experienced by young girls is taken over by vaginal pleasure as the woman matures.

35. Organizations such as The American Civil Liberty Union (ACLU), Advocates for Youth, and The Planned Parenthood Federation of America spoke out against this reactionary trend and outlined the dangers of its inevitable failure: the teen pregnancy rate in the United States is at least twice that of Canada, England, France, and Sweden, and ten times that of the Netherlands. "California, the only state that has not accepted federal abstinence-only money, has seen declines in teenage pregnancy similar to those in European countries. Over the last decade, the teenage pregnancy rate in California has dropped more than 40 percent." "California Reduces Teen Birth Rate Through Sex Education," *The Mercury News*, May 9, 2004. See also "Young People 15 to 24 Account for about Half the New Cases of Sexually Transmitted Diseases in the United States Each Year," *The Associated Press,* November 26, 2004.

36. The Ugandan government offers young girls chastity grants. Their school tuition fees will be paid for if they promise to remain virgins. The United States subsidizes this policy by sending eight million dollars per year to Uganda.

37. The French term *sexothérapeute* first appeared in the language in 1970.

38. "The building block of Western civilization has been the Nuclear Family. StraightPride.com staffers, like billions of others living out our 'life-style,' believe that family, morals, and procreation are the backbone of our well-being." See http://www.StraightPride.com/about.php.

39. Carrie L. Lukas, vice president for policy and economics for the Independent Women's Forum (IWF) published—through a small, extreme-right editing house—a book that summarizes the theoretical foundations of the movement: *The Politically Incorrect Guide to Women, Sex and Feminism* (Washington, DC: Regnery Publishing, 2006). On the cover she writes: "Most women want a husband and a strong family, but 'independent' feminists pine for a sugar daddy in Uncle Sam." Nancy Mitchell Pfotenhauer was nominated, in 2002, by President George W. Bush to serve as a delegate to the United Nations' Commission on the Status of Women and served during the 46th session of that commission. The Bush Administration also appointed her to the National Advisory Committee on Violence against Women. She was vice chairman of IWF's board of directors from 2005 to 2007. See also "Gun Control Hurts Women," *The Independent Women's Forum*, May 12, 2000.

40. E. G. Krug, et al., eds., *World Report on Violence and Health* (Geneva: World Health Organization, 2002), 89.

41. Examples of this thesis are found in the works of Elisabeth Badinter and Marcela Iacub. "But in fighting today for the extension of the definition of the sexual offence to prostitution and pornography, politically correct feminism, draped in its

offended dignity, unhesitatingly allies itself with the most traditional moral order." Elisabeth Badinter, *Dead End Feminism*, tr. Julia Borossa (Cambridge: Polity Press, 2006), 56. "It preaches an ever more severe cloistering of male sexuality that ricochets on women's sexuality. The gradual extension of the notion of sex crime and the repression of these last few years are helping to draw up a blueprint for a legalized, moralizing and sacralized sexuality radically opposed to the kind of sexual freedom that the newer generations make use of (some might say abuse)" (83).

42. "Until the early 1970s in France, almost everyone waited until marriage to live with their partner. ... Now marriage is frequently preceded by cohabitation, and more and more couples are not marrying at all. Unions also tend to be shorter-lived, as separation and divorce become more common. This new conjugal behaviour emerged in the late 1960s in Scandinavia, spearheaded by Sweden, and has gradually spread to the rest of Europe, but to varying degrees depending on the country. ... In the 35–59 age group, more than one woman in four in Sweden has already been in at least two cohabiting relationships. This is also the case for more than one woman in five in the United Kingdom, Latvia and Germany, and almost as many in Finland and Switzerland." France Prioux, "Cohabitation, Marriage and Separation: Contrasts in Europe," *Population and societies* 422 (April 2006): 1–4.

43. In France, the extramarital birth rate became the majority for the first time in 2006 (50.5%). In 1977, just one generation previous to this, it stood at just 10 percent.

Chapter 3

1. Martin Duberman, M. Vicinus, and G. Chauncey, eds., *Hidden from History: Reclaiming the Gay and Lesbian Past* (New York: NAL Books, 1989); Robert Aldrich, ed., *Gay Life and Culture: A World History* (London: Thames & Hudson, 2006).
2. Richard Krafft-Ebing, *Psychopathia Sexualis. Eine klinische-forensische Studie* (Stuttgart: Ferdinand Enke, 1886).
3. Magnus Hirschfeld, *Berlins drittes Geschlecht* (Berlin: H. Seemann, 1904).
4. Karl Heinrich Ulrichs, *Argonauticus* (Leipzig: A. Serbe's Verlag), 87.
5. Sigmund Freud, "Letter to an American Mother," *American Journal of Psychiatry* 107 (1951): 787.
6. George Chauncey, *Gay New York: Gender, Urban Culture, and the Making of the Gay Male World, 1890–1940* (New York: Basic Books, 1994).
7. Jens Rydström, *Sinners and Citizens: Bestiality and Homosexuality in Sweden, 1880–1950* (Chicago: University of Chicago Press, 2003).
8. Dan Healey, *Homosexual Desire in Revolutionary Russia: The Regulation of Sexual and Gender Dissent* (Chicago: University of Chicago Press, 2001).
9. Laura Doan, *Fashioning Sapphism: The Origins of a Modern English Lesbian Culture* (New York: Columbia University Press, 2001).
10. Florence Tamagne, *History of Homosexuality in Europe: Berlin, London, Paris: 1919–1939* (London: Algora Pub, 2004); Matt Houlbrook, *Queer London: Perils and Pleasures in the Sexual Metropolis, 1918–1957* (Chicago: The University of Chicago Press, 2005).

11. Michael Bollé, ed., *Eldorado: Homosexuelle Frauen und Männer in Berlin, 1850–1950: Geschichte, Alltag und Kultur* (Berlin: Frölich und Kaufmann, 1984); Monika Hingst et al., eds., *Goodbye to Berlin? 100 Jahre Schwulenbewegung* (Berlin: Verlag Rosa Winkel, 1997).

12. Hingst et al., *Goodbye to Berlin?*

13. Tamagne, *History of Homosexuality in Europe.*

14. Jeffrey Weeks, *Coming Out: Homosexual Politics in Britain from the Nineteenth Century to the Present* (London: Quartet Books, 1991).

15. Tamagne, *History of Homosexuality in Europe.*

16. Chauncey, *Gay New York.*

17. Tamagne, *History of Homosexuality in Europe.*

18. Doan, *Fashioning Sapphism*; Martha Vicinus, *Intimate Friends: Women Who Loved Women, 1778–1928* (Chicago: University of Chicago Press, 2004).

19. Lilian Faderman, *Surpassing the Love of Men: Romantic Friendship and Love between Women from the Renaissance to the Present* (New York: William Morrow, 1981).

20. Hingst, et al., *Goodbye to Berlin?*; Tamagne, *History of Homosexuality in Europe.*

21. Vito Russo, *The Celluloid Closet: Homosexuality in the Movies* (New York: Harper and Row, 1987).

22. Doan, *Fashioning Sapphism.*

23. Hingst, et al., *Goodbye to Berlin?*; Stefan Micheler, *Selbstbilder und Fremdbilder der "Anderen": eine Geschichte Männer begehrender Männer in der Weimarer Republik und der NS-Zeit* (Konstanz: UVK Verlag, 2005); Susanne zur Nieden, ed., *Homosexualität und Staatsräson: Männlichkeit, Homophobie und Politik in Deutschland 1900–1945* (Frankfurt: Campus Verlag, 2005).

24. Günther Grau, *Hidden Holocaust? Gay and Lesbian Persecution in Germany 1933–1945* (London: Cassell, 1995).

25. Grau, *Hidden Holocaust?*

26. Micheler, *Selbstbilder und Fremdbilder der "Anderen"*; zur Nieden, *Homosexualität und Staatsräson.*

27. Frédéric Martel, *The Pink and the Black: Homosexuals in France since 1968* (Stanford, CA: Stanford University Press, 1999).

28. Alan Berubé, *Coming Out Under Fire* (New York: The Free Press, 1990).

29. Houlbrook, *Queer London.*

30. Berubé, *Coming Out Under Fire.*

31. Robert J. Corber, *Homosexuality in Cold War America: Resistance and the Crisis of Masculinity* (Durham, NC: Duke University Press, 1997); David K. Johnson, *The Lavender Scare: The Cold War Persecution of Gays and Lesbians in the Federal Government* (Chicago: University of Chicago Press, 2004).

32. Weeks, *Coming Out.*

33. Aldrich, *Gay Life and Culture.*

34. John D'Emilio, *Sexual Politics, Sexual Communities: The Making of a Homosexual Minority in the United States, 1940–1970* (Chicago: The University of Chicago Press, 1998).

35. D'Emilio, *Sexual Politics, Sexual Communities.*

36. Lilian Faderman, *Odd Girls and Twilight Lovers: A History of Lesbian Life in Twentieth-Century America* (New York: Penguin, 1991).

37. D'Emilio, *Sexual Politics, Sexual Communities*.

38. Martel, *The Pink and the Black*; Julian Jackson, *Living in Arcadia: Homosexuality, Politics, and Morality in France from the Liberation to AIDS* (Chicago: University of Chicago Press, 2002).

39. Aldrich, ed., *Gay Life and Culture*.

40. Committee on Homosexual Offences and Prostitution, *Report of the Committee on Homosexual Offences and Prostitution* (London: Her Majesty's Stationery Office, 1957), 62.

41. Weeks, *Coming Out*; Houlbrook, *Queer London*.

42. D'Emilio, *Sexual Politics, Sexual Communities*.

43. Elizabeth Lapovsky Kennedy and Madeleine D. Davis, *Boots of Leather, Slippers of Gold: The History of a Lesbian Community* (New York: Penguin, 1993); Rebecca Jennings, *Tomboys and Bachelor Girls: A Lesbian History of Post-War Britain 1945–1971* (Manchester: Manchester University Press, 2007).

44. Russo, *The Celluloid Closet*.

45. Martin Duberman, *Stonewall* (New York: Penguin, 1993).

46. Hingst, et al., *Goodbye to Berlin?*; Martel, *The Pink and the Black*.

47. Radicalesbians, *The Woman-Identified Woman* (Pittsburgh, PA: Know, Inc., 1970).

48. Faderman, *Odd Girls and Twilight Lovers*.

49. Monique Wittig, "One Is Not Born a Woman," in *The Straight Mind and Other Essays* (Boston, MA: Beacon Press, 1992), 32.

50. Elizabeth A. Armstrong, *Forging Gay Identities: Organizing Sexuality in San Francisco 1950–1994* (Chicago: University of Chicago Press, 2002).

51. Martel, *The Pink and the Black*.

52. Faderman, *Odd Girls and Twilight Lovers*.

53. Russo, *The Celluloid Closet*.

54. Robert Violette and Hans-Ulrichs Obrist, eds., *The Words of Gilbert & George: With Portraits of the Artists from 1968 to 1997* (London: Thames & Hudson, 1997), 137.

55. Steven Epstein, *Impure Science: AIDS, Activism, and the Politics of Knowledge* (Berkeley: University of California Press, 1996).

56. Randy Shilts, *The Mayor of Castro Street: the Life and Times of Harvey Milk* (London: Altantic Books, 1982).

57. Epstein, *Impure Science*.

58. Annemarie Jagose, *Queer Theory: An Introduction* (Melbourne: Melbourne University Press, 1996).

59. Aldrich, *Gay Life and Culture*.

Chapter 4

1. Harry Oosterhuis, *Stepchildren of Nature: Krafft-Ebing, Psychiatry, and the Making of Sexual Identity* (Chicago: The University of Chicago Press, 2000); Volkmar Sigusch, *Geschichte der Sexualwissenschaft* (Frankfurt: Campus, 2008).

2. John Money, *Lovemaps* (Buffalo, NY: Prometheus, 1988); John Money, Gordon Wainwright, and David Hingsburger, *The Breathless Orgasm: A Lovemap Biography of Asphyxiophilia* (Buffalo, NY: Prometheus, 1991).

3. Brenda Love, *Encyclopedia of Unusual Sex Practices* (Fort Lee, NJ: Barricade Books, 1992); Katharina Gates, *Deviant Desires* (New York: Juno Books, 2000); Don Kulick and Anne Meneley, *Fat: The Anthropology of an Obsession* (New York: Penguin, 2005).

4. Sigmund Freud, *Drei Abhandlungen zur Sexualtheorie*, 5th ed. (Leipzig: Deuticke, 1915).

5. For overviews, see *Paidika: The Journal of Paedophilia*, 1987–1995; Theo Sandfort, Edward Brongersma, and Alex Van Naerssen, eds., *Male Intergenerational Intimacy* (New York: Haworth Press, 1991); Steven Angelides, "'Feminism, Child Sexual Abuse and the Erasure of Child Sexuality," *GLQ* 10 (2004): 141–77.

6. Linda Gordon, "The Politics of Child Sexual Abuse," *Feminist Review* 28 (1988): 57–65.

7. Jonathan Ned Katz, *The Invention of Heterosexuality* (New York: Dutton, 1995).

8. Wilhelm Stekel, *Psychosexueller Infantilismus* (Berlin: Urban & Schwarzenberg, 1922), 317–18.

9. Marjan Sax and Jules Deckwitz, eds., "On an Old Bicycle: Erotic and Sexual Relationships between Women and Minors," special issue, *Paidika* 2, no. 4 (1992).

10. Philip Jenkins, *Moral Panic: Changing Concepts of the Child Molester in Modern America* (New Haven, CT: Yale University Press, 1998), 80–93.

11. François-Paul Alibert, *Le Fils de Loth* [The Sons of Lot], 2nd ed. (Paris: Musardine, 2002).

12. Jean Danet et al., eds., "Fous d'enfance. Qui a peur des pédophiles?" special issue, *Recherches* 47 (1979).

13. Jenkins, *Moral Panic*; Judith Levine, *Harmful to Minors: The Perils of Protecting Children from Sex* (Minneapolis: University of Minnesota Press, 2002).

14. Philip Jenkins, *Pedophiles and Priests: Anatomy of a contemporary crisis* (Oxford: Oxford University Press, 1996).

15. Marcela Iacub and Patrice Maniglier, *Antimanuel d'éducation sexuelle* (Rosny: Breal, 2005).

16. Ronald Grassberger, *Die Unzucht mit Tieren* (Vienna: Springer, 1968).

17. Edward R. Dickinson, "Policing Sex in Germany, 1882–1982," *Journal of the History of Sexuality* 16, no. 2 (2007): 225.

18. For Sweden, see Jens Rydström, *Sinners and Citizens: Bestiality and Homosexuality in Sweden, 1880–1950* (Chicago: University of Chicago Press, 2003).

19. Alfred Kinsey, Wardell B. Pomeroy, and Clyde E. Martin, *Sexual Behavior in the Human Male* (Philadelphia: Saunders, 1948), 670–71; Alfred Kinsey, Wardell B. Pomeroy, Clyde E. Martin, and Paul H. Gebhard, *Sexual Behavior in the Human Female*, Philadelphia: Saunders, 1953), 505–6.

20. Love, *Encyclopedia of Unusual Sex Practices*, 299.

21. Jonathan Tisdall, "Animal Bordellos Draw Norwegians," *Aftenposten English Web Desk*, September 14, 2006.

22. Jean Sénac, *Ébauche du père* (Paris: Gallimard, 1989), 121.

23. Marie-Christine Anest, *Zoophilie, homosexualité: Rites de passage et initiation masculine dans la Grèce contemporaine* (Paris: L'Harmattan, 1994).

24. Midas Dekkers, *Lief Dier. Over bestialiteit* (Amsterdam: Contact, 1992), 164.

25. Joop Wilhelmus, *Bestialiteit* (Dordrecht: Chick, 1970).

26. CBS News, August 19, 2007.

27. Personal communication, Barbara Noske.

28. Mario Praz, *The Romantic Agony* (Oxford: Oxford University Press, 1970).

29. Andreas Spengler, *Sadomasochisten und ihre Subkulturen* (Frankfurt: Campus, 1979); Thomas S. Weinberg and G. W. Levi Kamel, eds., *S and M: Studies in Sadomasochism* (New York: Prometheus, 1983); Bill Thompson, *Sadomasochism: Painful Perversion or Pleasurable Play?* (London: Cassell, 1994); Mona Sammoun, *Tendance SM. Essai sur la représentation sadomasochiste* (Paris: La Musardine, 2004); Norbert Elb, *SM-Sexualität. Selbstorganisation einer sexuellen Subkultur* (Giessen: Psychosozial Verlag, 2006); Peggy Kleinplatz & Charles Moser, eds., *Sadomasochism: Powerful Pleasures* (Binghamton, NY: Harrington Park Press, 2006).

30. For essays on art, see Peter Weibel, ed., *Phantom of Desire: Visions of Masochism: Essays and Texts* (Graz: Neue Galerie, 2003).

31. Samois, *Coming to Power: Writings and Graphics on Lesbian S/M* (Boston: Alyson, 1981).

32. Robert Ruth Linden, et al., eds., *Against Sadomasochism: A Radical Feminist Analysis* (East Palo Alto, CA: Frog in the Well, 1982).

33. Lisa Duggan and Nan D. Hunter, *Sex Wars: Sexual Dissent and Political Culture* (New York: Routledge, 1995).

34. For a recent uneven overview, see Kleinplatz and Moser, *Sadomasochism*.

35. Joseph W. Bean, "L.A. Free Gay Slaves ... in 1976." *Leather Times* 24 (2005): 4–6.

36. Thompson, *Sadomasochism*, 1.

37. Thompson, *Sadomasochism*.

38. For details, see Kleinplatz and Moser, *Sadomasochism*.

39. Judith Squires, ed., "Perversity." Special issue, *New Formations* 19 (1993).

40. Paul Garnier, *Les Fétichistes, pervertis et invertis sexuels* (Paris: Baillière, 1896), 66–73.

41. E. L. McCallum, *Object Lessons: How to Do Things with Fetishism* (New York: State University of New York Press, 1999), 154.

42. Emily Apter, "Introduction," in *Fetishism as Cultural Discourse*, ed. Emily Apter and William Pietz (Ithaca, NY: Cornell University Press, 1993), 4.

43. Floor Bakker and Ine Vanwesenbeeck, eds., *Seksuele gezondheid in Nederland 2006* (Delft: Eburon, 2006).

44. Marcela Iacub, *Par le trou de la serrure. Une histoire de la pudeur publique XIX-XXIe siècle* (Paris: Fayard, 2008).

45. Ben van Weelden, *Pronken met jezelf* (Amsterdam: Candide, 1993).

46. Lisa Downing, *Desiring the Dead: Necrophilia and Nineteenth-Century Literature* (Oxford: Legenda, 2003).

Chapter 5

1. Igor S. Kon, *The Sexual Revolution in Russia: From the Age of the Czars to Today* (New York: Free Press, 1995).

2. Patrick Festy and France Prioux, "Le divorce en Europe depuis 1950," *Population French Edition* 30, no. 6 (1975): 975–1017.

3. Maria Clara Sottomayor, "The Introduction and Impact of Joint Custody in Portugal," *International Journal of Law, Policy and the Family* 13 (1999): 247–57.

4. In 1966 divorce (and both birth control and abortion) was rendered more difficult under Ceausescu in Romania in order to populate the country.

5. Patrizia Romito, ed., *Violenze alle donne e risposte delle istituzioni. Prospettive internazionali* (Milan: Franco Angeli, 2000); Daniela Danna, *Ginocidio. La violenza contro le donne nell'era globale* (Milan: Eleuthera, 2007).

6. Anika Rahman, Laura Katzive, and Stanley K. Henshaw, "A Global Review of Laws on Induced Abortion, 1985–1997," *International Family Planning Perspectives* 24 (1998): 56–64.

7. Tomas Frejka, "Induced Abortion and Fertility: A Quarter Century of Experience in Eastern Europe," *Population and Development Review* 9, no. 3 (1983): 494–520.

8. Incomplete information is available for Eastern Europe.

9. The diffuse commercialization of condoms and cervical caps started at the end of the nineteenth century.

10. N. Davis and J. Freier, eds., *Prostitution: An International Handbook on Trends, Problems, and Policies* (Westport CT: Greenwood Press, 1993); A. Cazals, *Prostitution et proxénétisme en Europe* (Paris: La documentation française, 1995); Daniela Danna, *Che cos'è la prostituzione? Le quattro visioni del commercio del sesso* (Trieste: Asterios, 2004); Daniela Danna, *Donne di mondo. Commercio del sesso e controllo statale* (Milan: Eleuthera, 2004); Daniela Danna, *Prostituzione e vita pubblica in quattro capitali europee* (Rome: Carocci, 2006); Joyce Outshoorn, ed., *The Politics of Prostitution: Women's Movements, Democratic States, and the Globalisation of Sex Commerce* (Cambridge: Cambridge University Press, 2004).

11. Laurie Essig, *Queer in Russia: A Study of Sex, Self, and the Other* (Durham, NC: Duke University Press, 1999), 24.

12. In Britain, same-sex relations were legalized in 1967 for men older than twenty-one, then in 1973 for men older than eighteen.

13. HOSI Wien/Auslandsgruppe, *Rosa Liebe unterm roten Stern. Zur Lage der Lesben und Schwulen in Osteuropa* (Vienna: Frülings Erwachen, 1984).

14. Lilian Faderman, *Surpassing the Love of Men: Romantic Friendship and Love between Women from the Renaissance to the Present* (New York: William Morrow & Co., 1981); Manfred Herzer, *Bibliographie zur Homosexualität. Verzeichnis des deutschsprachigen nichtbelletristischen Schriftums zur weiblichen und männlichen Homosexualität aus den Jahren 1466 bis 1975 in chronologischer Reihenfolge* (Berlin: Rosa Winkel, 1982); Martin Duberman, Martha Vicinus, and George Chauncey, Jr., eds., *Hidden from History: Reclaiming the Gay and Lesbian Past* (New York: Penguin, 1989); Florence Tamagne, *Histoire de l'homosexualité en Europe: Berlin, Londres, Paris 1919–1939* (Paris: Seuil, 2000); Daniela Danna, *Amiche, compagne, amanti. Storia dell'amore tra donne* (Trento: Uniservice, 2003).

15. Flora Leroy-Forgeot, *Histoire juridique de l'homosexualité en Europe* (Paris: PUF, 1997); Daniela Danna, *La gaia famiglia. Omogenitorialità: il dibattito e la ricerca* (Trieste: Asterios, 2005).

16. Daniela Danna, *Matrimonio omosessuale* (Rome: Erre Emme Edizioni, 1997).

Chapter 6

1. D. Jacquart and C. Thomasset, *Sexualité et savoir médical au moyen âge* (Paris: P.U.F., 1985).

2. A. Corbin, *L'harmonie des plaisirs. Les manières de jouir du siècle des Lumières à l'avènement de la sexologie* (Paris: Perrin, 2008).

3. A. Davidson, "Sex and the Emergence of Sexuality," *Critical Inquiry* 14 (1987): 16–48.

4. T. Laqueur, *Solitary Sex: A Cultural History of Masturbation* (New York: Zone Books, 2003).

5. A. Giami, "Sexual Health: The Emergence, Development and Diversity of a Concept," *Annual Review of Sex Research* 13 (2002): 1–33.

6. M. Foucault, *Les anormaux—Cours au Collège de France 1974–75* (Paris: Gallimard, Le Seuil, EHESS, 1999).

7. G. Lanteri Laura, *Lecture des perversions. Histoire de leur appropriation médicale* (Paris: Masson, 1979).

8. T. Szasz, *The Manufacture of Madness: A Comparative Study of the Inquisition and the Mental Health Movement* (New York: Harper & Row, 1970).

9. B. Dodson, *Liberating Masturbation: A Meditation on Self Love* (New York: Dodson, 1976).

10. R. Bayer, *Homosexuality and American Psychiatry: The Politics of Diagnosis* (New York: Basic Books, 1981).

11. J. Levine, *Harmful to Minors: The Perils of Protecting Children from Sex* (Minneapolis: University of Minnesota Press, 2002).

12. J. Rey-Debove and A. Rey, *Le nouveau Petit Robert* (Paris: Dictionnaires le Robert, 1994).

13. A. Moll, *Les perversions de l'instinct génital. Etude sur l'inversion sexuelle basée sur des documents officiels* (Paris: Georges Carré, 1893).

14. L. Bland and L. Doan, eds., *Sexology in Culture. Labelling Bodies and Desires* (Cambridge: Polity Press, 1999); H. Oosterhuis, *Stepchildren of Nature: Krafft-Ebing, Psychiatry and the Making of Sexual Identity* (Chicago: The University of Chicago Press, 2000).

15. P. Conrad and J. Schneider, *Deviance and Medicalization : From Badness to Sickness* (Saint Louis, MO: The C.V. Mosby Company, 1980).

16. L. Tiefer, "The Medicalization of Sexuality: Conceptual, Normative and Professional Issues," *Annual Review of Sex Research* 7 (1996): 252–82.

17. E. Kaschak and L. Tiefer, eds., *A New View of Women's Sexual Problems* (Binghamton, NY: Haworth Press, 2001).

18. A. Giami, "Fonction sexuelle masculine et sexualité féminine. Permanence des représentations du genre en sexologie et en médecine sexuelle," *Communications* 81 (2007): 135–51.

19. Lanteri Laura, *Lecture des perversions*.

20. T. H. Van de Velde, *Ideal Marriage: Its Physiology and Technique* (New York: Covici-Friede, 1933).

21. D. Lupton, *The Imperative of Health: Public Health and the Regulation of the Body* (London: Sage, 1995).

22. A. Giami and H. Leridon, eds., *Les enjeux de la stérilisation* (Paris: Éditions INSERM-INED, 2000); P. Reilly, *The Surgical Solution: A History of Involuntary Sterilization in the United States* (Baltimore, MD: The Johns Hopkins Press, 1991).

23. Alfred C. Kinsey, Wardell B. Pomeroy, and Clyde E. Martin, *Sexual Behavior in the Human Male* (Philadelphia: Saunders, 1948); W. Masters and V. Johnson, *Human Sexual Response* (Boston: Little Brown and Co., 1966).

24. P. Ariès and A. Béjin, eds., *Western Sexuality: Practice and Precept in Past and Present Times* (Oxford: Blackwell, 1985).

25. Bayer, *Homosexuality and American Psychiatry*.

26. W. Masters and V. Johnson, *Homosexuality in Perspective* (Boston: Little, Brown and Co., 1979).

27. Giami, "Sexual Health."

28. World Health Organization, "Education and Treatment in Human Sexuality: The Training of Health Professionals: Report of a WHO Meeting" (Technical Report Series No. 572), in *Sexology Today: A Brief Introduction,* ed. E. Haeberle and R. Gindorf (Dusseldorf: DGSS, 1993).

29. Lupton, *The Imperative of Health*.

30. M. North, *The Secular Priests: Psychotherapy in Contemporary Society* (London George Allen, 1972).

31. P. Robinson, *The Modernization of Sex* (New York: Harper & Row, 1976).

32. D. Teysseire, *Obèse et impuissant. Le dossier médical d'Elie de Beaumont* (Grenoble: Jérome Millon, 1995).

33. J. A. Belliol, *De l'impuissance ou perte de la virilité* (Paris: Chez l'auteur, ca. 1832).

34. J. Real, *Voronoff* (Paris: Stock, 2001).

35. A. McLaren, *Impotence: A Cultural History* (Chicago: Chicago University Press, 2007).

36. R. Virag, "Intracavernous Injection of Papaverine for Erectile Failure," *The Lancet* 2, no. 8304 (1982): 938.

37. I. Goldstein, et al., "Oral Sildenafil in the Treatment of Erectile Dysfunction," *The New England Journal of Medicine* 338, no. 20 (1998): 1397–404.

38. F. Dubois-Arber and B. Spencer, "Condom Use," in *Sexual Behaviour and HIV/AIDS in Europe*, ed. M. Hubert, N. Bajos, and T. Sandfort (London: UCL Press, 1998).

39. S. Gilman, *Disease and Representation* (Ithaca, NY: Cornell University Press, 1988).

40. A. Giami and M. A. Schiltz, "Representations of Sexuality and Relations between Partners: Sex Research in France in the Era of AIDS," *Annual Review of Sex Research* 7 (1996): 125–57.

41. S. Michaels and A. Giami, "Sexual Acts and Sexual Relationships: Asking about Sex in Surveys," *Public Opinion Quarterly* 63 (1999): 385–404.

42. B. Henriksson, *Risk Factor Love: Homosexuality, Sexual Interaction and HIV Prevention* (Goteborg: Goteborgs Universitets Skriftserien, 1995).

43. Giami and Schiltz, "Representations of Sexuality and Relations between Partners."

44. Conseil National du Sida, *Avis sur la pénalisation de la transmission sexuelle du VIH* (Paris: Conseil National du Sida, 2006).

45. G. W. Dowsett and M. Couch, "Roundtable: Male Circumcision and HIV Prevention: Is There Really Enough of the Right Kind of Evidence?" *Reproductive Health Matters* 15, no. 29 (2007): 33–44.

46. P. Darmon, *Le tribunal de l'impuissance* (Paris, Seuil, 1979).

47. W. Acton, *The Functions and Disorders of the Reproductive Organs in Childhood, Youth, Adult Age, and Advanced Life Considered in Their Physiological, Social and Moral Response* (Philadelphia, PA: Lindsay and Blakiston, 1865); Darmon, *Le tribunal de l'impuissance*; F. Roubaud, *Traité de l'impuissance et de la stérilité chez l'homme et chez la femme* (Paris: J.-B. Baillière, 1855).

48. W. Stekel, *L'homme impuissant* (Paris: Gallimard, 1950), p. 18.

49. W. Masters and V. Johnson, *Human Sexual Inadequacy* (Boston: Little, Brown and Co., 1970), 3.

50. R. Krane, I. Goldstein, and I. Saenz de Tejada, "Impotence," *The New England Journal of Medicine* 321, no. 24 (1989): 1656.

51. Krane, Goldstein, and Saenz de Tejada, "Impotence," 1656.

52. National Institute of Health Consensus Conference, "Impotence. NIH Consensus Development Panel on Impotence," *JAMA* 270: 1 (1993): 83–90.

53. Goldstein et al., "Oral Sildenafil in the Treatment of Erectile Dysfunction."

54. L. Garcia-Reboll, J. Mulhall, and I. Goldstein, "Drugs for the Treatment of Impotence," *Drugs Aging* 11, no. 2 (1997): 140–51.

55. H. Feldman, et al., "Impotence and Its Medical and Psychosocial Correlates: Results of the Massachusetts Male Aging Study," *The Journal of Urology* 151 (1994): 54–61.

56. A. Brandt, "The Cigarette, Risk and American Culture," *Daedalus* 119, no. 4 (1990): 155–76.

57. G. Oppenheimer, "In the Eye of the Storm: The Epidemiological Construction of AIDS," in *AIDS: The Burden of History*, ed. E. Fee and D. Fox (Berkeley: University of California Press, 1988).

58. Kinsey, Pomeroy, and Martin, *Sexual Behavior in the Human Male*.

59. E. Frank, C. Anderson, and D. Rubinstein, "Frequency of Sexual Dysfunctions in 'Normal' Couples," *New England Journal of Medicine* 299 (1978): 111.

60. I. P. Spector and M. P. Carey, "Incidence and Prevalence of the Sexual Dysfunctions: A Critical Review of the Literature," *Archives of Sexual Behavior* 19 (1990): 389–408.

61. Feldman et al., "Impotence and Its Medical and Psychosocial Correlates."

62. C. Johannes, et al., " Incidence of Erectile Dysfunction in Men 40 to 69 Years Old: Longitudinal Results from the Massachusetts Male Aging Study," *The Journal of Urology* 163 (2000): 460–63.

63. E. Laumann, et al. *The Social Organization of Sexuality: Sexual Practices in the United States* (Chicago: The University of Chicago Press, 1994), 368.

64. A. Spira, N. Bajos, and ACSF Group, *Sexual Behaviour and AIDS* (Aldershot, UK: Avebury, 1994).

65. Spira, Bajos, and ACSF Group, *Sexual Behaviour and AIDS*, 313.

66. O. Kontula and E. Haavio-Manila, *Sexual Pleasures: Enhancement of Sex Life in Finland* (Aldershot, UK: Dartmouth, 1995), 280.

67. A. R. Fugl-Meyer and K. Sjögren Fugl-Meyer, "Sexual Disabilities, Problems and Satisfaction in 18–74 Year Old Swedes," *Scandinavian Journal of Sexology* 2 (1999): 83.

68. J. Hitt, "The Second Sexual Revolution," *The New York Times Magazine*, February 20, 2000.

69. M. Boolell, S. Gepi-Attee, J. C. Gingell, and M. J. Allen, "Sildenafil, a Novel Effective Oral Therapy for Male Erectile Dysfunction," *British Journal of Urology* 78 (1996): 257.

70. G. Hart and K. Wellings, "Sexual Behaviour and Its Medicalisation: In Sickness and in Health," *British Medical Journal* 324, no. 7342 (2002): 896–900.

Chapter 7

1. Alfred Schütz and Thomas Luckmann, *Strukturen der Lebenswelt* (Konstanz: UVK Verlagsgesellschaft, 2003).

2. Harold E. Hinds, "A Holistic Approach to the Study of Popular Culture. Context, Text, Audience, and Recoding," in *Popular Culture Theory and Methodology: A Basic Introduction*, ed. Harold E. Hinds, Marilyn F. Motz, and Angela M. S. Nelson (Madison: University of Wisconsin Press, 2006), 163.

3. Ansley J. Coale and Susan Cotts Watkins, eds., *The Decline of Fertility in Europe: The Revised Proceedings of a Conference on the Princeton European Fertility Project* (Princeton, NJ: Princeton University Press, 1986); Simon Szreter, "Falling Fertilities and Changing Sexualities in Europe since c. 1850: Comparative Survey of National Demographic Patterns," in *Sexual Cultures in Europe: Themes in Sexuality*, ed. Franz X. Eder, Lesley Hall, and Gert Hekma (Manchester: Manchester University Press, 1999).

4. Bruno Wanrooij, "The 'Thorns of Love': Sexuality, Syphilis and Social Control in Modern Italy," in *Sex, Sin and Suffering: Venereal Disease and European Society Since 1870*, ed. Roger Davidson and Lesley A. Hall (London: Routledge), 152–53.

5. Ellen Chesler, *Woman of Valour: Margaret Sanger and the Birth Control Movement in America* (New York: Morrow, 1992).

6. Robert A. Peel, ed., *Marie Stopes: Eugenics and the English Birth Control Movement* (London: The Galton Institute, 1997).

7. Lesley A. Hall, *Sex, Gender and Social Change in Britain since 1880* (Houndmills, UK: Macmillan Press, 2000), 108.

8. Anne-Marie Sohn, "French Catholics between Abstinence and 'Appeasement of Lust', 1930–1950," in *Sexual Cultures in Europe: Themes in Sexuality*, ed. Franz X. Eder, Lesley A. Hall, and Gert Hekma (Manchester: Manchester University Press, 1999), 248.

9. Anne-Marie Sohn, "French Catholics," 235.

10. Roy Porter and Lesley Hall, *The Facts of Life: The Creation of Sexual Knowledge in Britain, 1650–1950* (New Haven, CT: Yale University Press, 1995), 182.

11. Gérard Lenne, *Érotisme et cinéma* (Paris: La Musardine, 1998); Luke Ford, *A History of X: 100 Years of Sex in Film* (Amherst, NY: Prometheus Books, 1999).

12. Michael Bollé, ed., *Eldorado: Homosexuelle Frauen und Männer in Berlin, 1850–1950: Geschichte, Alltag und Kultur* (Berlin: Frölich und Kaufmann, 1984).

13. George Chauncey, Jr., *Gay New York: Gender, Urban Culture and the Making of the Gay Male World, 1890–1940* (New York: Basic Books, 1994), 110–17.

14. Helmut Graupner, "Sexuelle Mündigkeit: Die Strafgesetzgebung in europäischen und außereuropäischen Ländern," *Zeitschrift für Sexualforschung* 10 (1997): 296–97.

15. Gert Hekma, Harry Oosterhuis, and James D. Steakley, eds., *Gay Men and the Sexual History of the Political Left* (New York: Harrington Park Press, 1995).

16. Kirsten von Sydow, "Female Sexuality and Historical Time: A Comparison of Sexual Biographies of German Women Born between 1895 and 1936," *Archives of Sexual Behaviour* 25 (1996): 473–93.

17. Alfred C. Kinsey, Wardell B. Pomeroy, and Clyde E. Martin, *Sexual Behavior in the Human Male* (Philadelphia: Saunders, 1948); Alfred C. Kinsey, Wardell B. Pomeroy, Clyde E. Martin, and Paul H. Gebhard, *Sexual Behavior in the Human Female* (Philadelphia: Saunders, 1953).

18. Maria Sophia Quine, *Population Politics in Twentieth-Century Europe: Fascist Dictatorships and Liberal Democracies* (London: Routledge, 1996).

19. Dagmar Herzog, *Sex after Fascism: Memory and Morality in Twentieth-Century Germany* (Princeton, NJ: Princeton University Press, 2005); Franz X. Eder, "The Nationalists' 'Healthy Sexuality' was Followed by America's Influence: Sexuality and Media from National Socialism to the Sexual Revolution," in *Sexuality in Austria,* ed. Günter Bischof, Anton Pelinka, and Dagmar Herzog (New Brunswick, NJ: Transaction Publishers, 2007).

20. Birgit Beck, *Wehrmacht und sexuelle Gewalt: Sexualverbrechen vor deutschen Militärgerichten 1939–1945* (Paderborn: Schöningh, 2004).

21. Hall, *Sex, Gender and Social Change in Britain,* 145.

22. Dian Hanson, ed., *The History of Men's Magazines: Vol. 1: From 1900 to Post-WW II* (Cologne: Taschen, 2004).

23. Liz Stanley, *Sex Surveyed, 1949–1994: From Mass-Observation's "Little Kinsey" to the National Survey and the Hite Reports* (London: Taylor and Francis, 1995).

24. L. R. England, "Little Kinsey: An Outline of Sex Attitudes in Britain," *The Public Opinion Quarterly* 13 (1949–1950): 591.

25. Geoffrey Gorer, *Exploring English Character* (New York: Criterion Books, 1955), 94.

26. Kinsey, Pomeroy, Martin, and Gebhard, *Sexual Behavior in the Human Female,* 315–16.

27. Michael Edward Melody and Linda M. Peterson, *Teaching America about Sex: Marriage Guides and Sex Manuals from the Late Victorians to Dr. Ruth* (New York: New York University Press, 1999), 135.

28. Michelle H. Martin, "No One Will Ever Know Your Secret! Commercial Puberty Pamphlets for Girls from the 1940s to the 1990s," in *Sexual Pedagogies: Sex Education in Britain, Australia, and America, 1879–2000*, ed. Claudia Nelson and Michelle H. Martin (New York: Palgrave Macmillan, 2003), 135–36.

29. John D'Emilio and Estelle B. Freedman, *Intimate Matters: A History of Sexuality in America* (New York: Perennial Library, 1988), 293.

30. Jan Löfström, "Sexuality and the Performance of Manliness: Sketching the Historical Trajectory of Male Fear," *Ethnologia Scandinavica* 27 (1997): 33.

31. Antony Copley, *Sexual Moralities in France, 1780–1980: New Ideas on the Family, Divorce and Homosexuality* (London: Routledge, 1989), 218.

32. Tom Reichert, *The Erotic History of Advertising* (Amherst, MA: Prometheus Books, 2003), 133–66.

33. Liliane Kerjan, "A Right to Personal Privacy," in *Sexualities in American Culture*, ed. Alfred Hornung (Heidelberg: Universitätsverlag Winter, 2004), 52.

34. Annette F. Timm and Joshua A. Sanborn, *Gender, Sex and the Shaping of Modern Europe: A History from the French Revolution to the Present Day* (Oxford: Berg, 2007), 190.

35. Jane F. Gerhard, *Desiring Revolution: Second-Wave Feminism and the Rewriting of American Sexual Thought, 1920 to 1982* (New York: Columbia University Press, 2001), 53.

36. Hera Cook, *The Long Sexual Revolution: Women, Sex, and Contraception in England 1800–1975* (Oxford: Oxford University Press, 2004), 281.

37. Gerhard, *Desiring Revolution*, 104–6.

38. Gunter Schmidt et al., "Veränderungen des Sexualverhaltens von Studentinnen und Studenten 1966–1981–1996," in *Sexualität und Spätmoderne. Über den kulturellen Wandel der Sexualität*, ed. Gunter Schmidt and Bernhard Strauß (Hamburg: Enke, 1998).

39. Reichert, *The Erotic History of Advertising*, 364.

40. Lisa Duggan and Nan D. Hunter, eds., *Sex Wars. Sexual Dissent and Political Culture* (New York: Routledge, 1995), 1.

41. Meika Loe, *The Rise of Viagra: How the Little Blue Pill Changed Sex in America* (New York: New York University Press, 2004), 185.

42. Gunter Schmidt, *Das Verschwinden der Sexualmoral: Über sexuelle Verhältnisse* (Hamburg: Klein, 1996).

43. Paul Sachdev, *Sex, Abortion, and Unmarried Women* (Westport, CT: Greenwood, 1993), 105.

44. Angus McLaren, *Twentieth-Century Sexuality: A History* (Oxford: Blackwell Publishers, 1999), 193–205.

45. Tom W. Smith, "Attitudes toward Sexual Permissiveness: Trend, Correlates, and Behavioral Connections," in *Sexuality across the Life Course*, ed. Alice S. Rossi, (Chicago: University of Chicago Press, 1994), 91.

46. Marty Klein, *America's War on Sex: The Attack on Law, Lust and Liberty* (Westport, CT: Praeger, 2006).

47. Janice M. Irvine, *Talk about Sex: The Battles Over Sex Education in the United States* (Berkeley: University of California Press, 2002).

48. Anthony Giddens, *The Transformation of Intimacy: Sexuality, Love, and Eroticism in Modern Societies* (Stanford, CA: Stanford University Press, 1992).

49. Alan Sinfield, *On Sexuality and Power* (New York: Columbia University Press, 2004).

50. Gert Hekma, "How Libertine is the Netherlands? Exploring Contemporary Dutch Sexual Cultures," in *Regulating Sex. The Politics of Intimacy and Identity,* ed. Elizabeth Bernstein and Laurie Schaffner (New York: Routledge, 2005), 220.

Chapter 8

1. Judith R. Walkowitz, *Prostitution and Victorian Society: Women, Class, and the State* (Cambridge: Cambridge University Press, 1980).

2. The armies of Napoleon started to regulate prostitution to protect soldiers against venereal diseases. Sex workers were forced to register and were subjected to medical examinations. Registered women were handed a red card, which was a sort of work permit. When they appeared to be infected, they got a white card and were hospitalized. The introduction of these medical regulations meant more regulation and supervision of prostitution.

3. Walkowitz, *Prostitution and Victorian Society.*

4. Roger Davidson, "The Culture of Compulsion: Venereal Disease, Sexuality and the State in Twentieth-Century Scotland," in *Sexual Cultures in Europe. Themes in Sexuality,* vol. 2, ed. Franz X. Eder, Lesley A. Hall, and Gert Hekma (Manchester: Manchester University Press, 1999).

5. Davidson, "The Culture of Compulsion," 66.

6. Ibid., 67.

7. Petra de Vries, "'The Shadow of Contagion': Gender, Syphilis and the Regulation of Prostitution in the Netherlands, 1870–1914," in *Sex, Sin And Suffering: Venereal Disease and European Society since 1870,* ed. Roger Davidson and Lesley A. Hall (London: Routledge, 2001).

8. Marieke van Doorninck and Margot Jongedijk, *In het Leven. Vier eeuwen Prostitutie in Nederland* (Apeldoorn: Historisch Museum Apeldoorn, 1997).

9. In 1909, the Dutch Ministry of Justice collected information and counted in Amsterdam almost three times more free sex workers than in other cities with a Ban on Brothels, such as Rotterdam and The Hague. In 1920, according to the municipal statistics of Amsterdam, the number of sex workers doubled. In 1936 there are about 4,000 sex workers in Amsterdam.

10. Sietske Altink, *Huizen van Illusies. Bordelen en Prostitutie van Middeleeuwen tot Heden* (Utrecht: Veen uitgevers, 1983).

11. van Doorninck and Jongedijk, *In het Leven.*

12. Annemarie de Wildt and Paul Arnoldussen, *Liefde te koop. Vier eeuwen prostitutie in Amsterdam* (Amsterdam: Uitgeverij Bas Lubberhuizen, 2002).

13. de Wildt and Arnoldussen, *Liefde te koop,* 31.

14. International Convention on Human Trafficking, "Article 1 of the International Agreement for the Suppression of the White Slave Traffic," http://www.oas.org/juridico/MLA/en/traites/en_traites-inter-wst.pdf (accessed May 8, 2007).

15. Elizabeth Waters, "Restructuring the 'Woman Question': Perestroika and Prostitution," *Feminist Review* 33 (1989): 3–19.

16. Ralf Dose, "The World League for Sexual Reform: Some Possible Approaches," in *Sexual Cultures in Europe: National Histories*, Vol. 1, ed. Franz X. Eder, Lesley A. Hall, and Gert Hekma (Manchester: Manchester University Press, 1999).

17. During the 1980s and the early 1990s, the U.S. feminist movement was polarized by the sex wars—sharp debates around pornography and other issues. Some feminists consider pornography to be a central aspect of the oppression of women and one of the most widespread and effective mechanisms through which sexism is enforced and reproduced. Most defenders of this perspective have supported some form of censorship as a means of protecting women from pornography. This has certainly been the case of writers such as Robin Morgan, Catherine MacKinnon, and Andrea Dworkin, the most influential feminist critics of pornography.

18. Robin Morgan, *Going Too Far: The Personal Chronicle of a Feminist* (New York: Random House, 1977), 174.

19. Kerwin Kaye, "Male Prostitution in the Twentieth Century: Pseudohomosexuals, Hoodlum Homosexuals, and Exploited Teens," *Journal of Homosexuality* 46, no. 1/2 (2003): 2.

20. Trumbach in Kaye, "Male Prostitution in the Twentieth Century," 7.

21. Kaye, "Male Prostitution in the Twentieth Century," 23.

22. Chauncey in Kaye, "Male Prostitution in the Twentieth Century," 19.

23. Minton in Kaye, "Male Prostitution in the Twentieth Century," 20.

24. Peg houses took their name from British India where the term referred to brothels that provided adolescent boys to male customers. Allegedly, the youths sat on pegs in order to dilate their anuses between clients. Minton Kaye, "Male Prostitution in the Twentieth Century," 58.

25. Kaye, "Male Prostitution in the Twentieth Century," 20.

26. Ibid., 34.

27. Julia Roos, "Backlash against Prostitutes' Rights: Origins and Dynamics of Nazi Prostitution Policies," *Journal of the History of Sexuality* 11, no. 1/2 (2002): 67–94, 70.

28. Roos, "Backlash against Prostitutes' Rights," 81.

29. Ibid.

30. Ibid., 82.

31. Altink, *Huizen van Illusies*.

32. Roos, "Backlash against Prostitutes' Rights," 69.

33. Ibid., 93.

34. Ibid.

35. Ibid., 90.

36. Ibid., 91.

37. Ibid., 91–92.

38. Michel Hubert, Nathalie Bajos, and Theo Sandfort, eds., *Sexual Behaviour and HIV/AIDS in Europe* (London: UCL Press, 1998).

39. Hubert, Bajos, and Sandfort, *Sexual Behaviour and HIV/AIDS in Europe,* 410.

40. Alfred C. Kinsey, Wardell B. Pomeroy, and Clyde E. Martin, *Sexual Behavior in the Human Male* (Philadelphia: Saunders, 1948).

41. Valerie Jenness, *Making It Work: The Prostitutes' Right Movement in Perspective* (New York: Aldine de Gruyter, 1993), 2.

42. Claude Jaget, ed., *Prostitutes, Our Life* (Bristol: Falling Wall Press, 1980), 46.

43. Jaget, *Prostitutes, Our Life,* 46.

44. With thanks to Florence Tamagne.

45. However, thirty years later, the conditions of work and living for sex workers have not changed a lot in France. On the pretext of fighting against trafficking and insecurity, a law called the Sarkozy Bill hardened the situation of sex workers, especially for street prostitution. This shows the fragility of sex workers' rights in France. Since the Sarkozy interior security law of March 13, 2003, France punishes both active and passive soliciting, which means that the simple fact of waiting on the pavement, wearing a mini-skirt, or exposing cleavage can be taken as a proof that an individual is a sex worker. The penalty is two months prison and a fine. The purpose of the law is to clean inner cities of sex workers; on the other side, the law strengthens penalties against procuring and trafficking.

46. Valentino and Johnson in Jaget, *Prostitutes, Our Life,* 17.

47. Jaget, *Prostitutes, Our Life,* 24, 25.

48. Jenness, *Making It Work,* 62–63.

49. Lilian Mathieu, "The Emergence and Uncertain Outcomes of Prostitutes' Social Movements," *The European Journal of Women's Studies* 10, no. 1 (2003): 32.

50. Gail Pheterson, ed., *A Vindication of the Rights of Whores* (Seattle, WA: The Seal Press, 1989), 40.

51. In this context, *the sex industry* refers to all kinds of different forms of sexual economic exchange. Sex work can be part-time or incidental or can also consist of a complete working week. The work can take place in brothels, clubs, bars, discos and cabarets, erotic phone lines, in sex shops with private rooms, massage parlors and saunas, escort services, via marriage agencies, in pornographic cinemas, erotic restaurants, on the street, and on Internet.

52. Licia Brussa, "The Tampep Project in Western Europe," in *Global Sex Workers: Rights, Resistance, and Redefinition,* ed. Kamala Kempadoo and Jo Doezema (New York: Routledge, 1998); Kamala Kempadoo, "Women of Color and the Global Sex Trade: Transnational Feminist Perspectives," *Meridians: Feminism, Race, Transnationalism* 1, no. 2 (2001): 28–51.

53. Diana van Bergen, *Een gedoogde schemerwereld binnen de prostitutie. De werk- en leefsituatie van jongensprostitués in Amsterdam* (Amsterdam: Vrije Universiteit, 2002); Paul van Gelder, *Kwetsbaar, Kleurig en Schaduwrijk. Jongens in de prostitutie: Een verschijnsel in meervoud* (Amsterdam: Thela Thesis, 1998); Dirk J. Korf, Ton Nabben, and Madelon Schreuders, *Roemeense trekvogels. Nieuwkomers in de jongensprostitutie* (Amsterdam: Thesis Publishers, 1996); M. S. van Roosmalen, et al., *Hiv-Infectie en riskant gedrag onder travestieten en transseksuelen in de Rotterdamse straatprostitutie* (Bilthoven: Rijksinstituut voor Volksgezondheid en Milieu, 1996). Following the Dutch sexologist and researcher Paul Vennix, *Travestie,*

een serieuze (nood)zaak (Delft: Eburon, 2001), I am using here the term "transgender" as an umbrella term for transvestites, transgenders, and transsexuals. In the European sex industry the term "transgender" refers mainly to male transvestites who identify themselves with or behave as a woman during work or to male transsexuals who identify themselves as a woman in work and also in daily life. With hormone treatments and medical surgery, this last group wants to adapt themselves as much as possible to the female gender. A great part uses silicon implants and does the final genital operation. Many transsexuals finance the costs of their hormone treatments and the sex operation with the earnings from their work in the sex industry.

54. Bridget Anderson and Julia O'Connell Davidson, *Trafficking—a Demand Led Problem?* (Stockholm: Save the Children, 2002); Licia Brussa, *Health, Migration, Sex Work: The Experience of Tampep: Transnational Aids/STD Prevention among Migrant Prostitutes in Europe* (Amsterdam: TAMPEP International Foundation, 1999).

55. Transnational Aids/STD Prevention Among Migrant Prostitutes in Europe/Project (TAMPEP), *Final Report 6. June 2002-June 2004* (Amsterdam: TAMPEP, 2004).

56. Marie-Louise Janssen, *Reizende Sekswerkers. Latijns-Amerikaanse vrouwen in de Europese prostitutie* (Amsterdam: Het Spinhuis, 2007).

57. Ibid.

58. Nederlands Instituut voor Sociaal Seksuologisch Onderzoek (NISSO). *Aard en omvang van (Gedwongen) prostitutie onder Minderjarige (Allochtone) Meisjes* (Utrecht: NISSO, 1998); van Roosmalen, et al., *Hiv-Infectie*; Pheterson, *A Vindication of the Rights of Whores*.

59. In 2000, two protocols were added to the U.N. convention from 1949 against transnational organized crime. These protocols contain two concepts, namely: the smuggling of migrants and trafficking.

60. Barbara Sullivan, "Trafficking in Women. Feminism and New International Law," *International Feminist Journal of Politics* 5, no. 1 (2003): 67–91.

61. Janice Raymond, "The New UN Trafficking Protocol," *Women's Studies International Forum* 25, no. 5 (2002): 496.

62. Don Kulick, "Four Hundred Thousand Swedish Perverts," *GLQ* 11, no. 2 (2005): 225.

63. In 1988 the Dutch foundation Man & Prostitution was created in Amsterdam, a foundation that looks after the interests of the clients of sex workers. Its primary objective was breaking the taboo on prostitution and the use of the services of sex workers. Later on the name was changed in Man/Women & Prostitution.

64. According to the *National Reporter of Human Trafficking* in the Netherlands a group of sex workers, by estimation 1,500 to 3,000 of the total amount of sex workers, is victim of human trafficking. Despite the fact that immigrants form a great part of the total amount of victims, human trafficking is not specifically related to migrants. Generally, there are more Dutch women who become victims of forced prostitution in the Netherlands. In 2004, 405 persons were officially

registered as victims of human trafficking. Fifty-nine of the women were Dutch, which put the Dutch nationality at number one within victims of trafficking in Dutch prostitution.

65. International Committee on the Rights of Sex Workers in Europe, *Declaration of the Rights of Sex Workers in Europe* (2005), http://www.sexworkeurope.org/site/images/PDFs/dec_brussels2005.pdf (accessed August 12, 2007).

Chapter 9

1. Michel Foucault, *History of Sexuality*, vol. 1, trans. Robert Hurley (New York: Random House, 1980).
2. Richard Meyer, *Outlaw Representation: Censorship and Homosexuality in Twentieth-Century American Art* (Boston: Beacon Press, 2002), 17.
3. Kelly Dennis, "The Hegelian Implications of the Museum of Sex; or, Does MoSex Mean No Sex?" *Art Journal* 65, no. 2 (2006): 13.
4. Jane Fletcher, "The Uncanny Effect of Sally Mann's *Immediate Family*," *n.paradoxa* 7 (1998).
5. Meyer, *Outlaw Representation*, 37–56.
6. Klaus Theweleit, *Male Fantasies*, vol. 1 (Minneapolis: University of Minnesota Press, 1987); Dagmar Herzog, *Sex after Fascism: Memory and Morality in Twentieth-Century Germany* (Princeton, NJ: Princeton University Press, 2005).
7. Max Horkheimer and Theodor W. Adorno, *Dialectic of Enlightenment* (New York: Continuum, 1947).
8. Gen Doy, *Claude Cahun: A Sensual Politics of Photography* (London: I. B. Taurus, 2008), 16.
9. James Smalls, *The Homoerotic Photography of Carl Van Vechten: Public Face, Private Thoughts* (Philadelphia: Temple University Press, 2006), 38.
10. Smalls, *The Homoerotic Photography of Carl Van Vechten*, 6.
11. Thomas Waugh, *Hard to Imagine: Gay Male Eroticism in Photography and Film from Their Beginnings to Stonewall* (New York: Columbia University Press, 1996).
12. Kelly Dennis, *Art/Porn: A History of Seeing and Touching* (Oxford: Berg Publishers, 2009), 136–58.
13. Gavin Butt, *Between You and Me: Queer Disclosures in the New York Art World, 1948–1963* (Durham, NC: Duke University Press, 2005), 9.
14. Butt, *Between You and Me*.
15. Lynda Boose, "Techno-Muscularity and the 'Boy Eternal,'" in *Cultures of U.S. Imperialism*, ed. Amy Kaplan and Donald E. Pease (Durham, NC: Duke University Press, 1993).
16. Ricardo Ortíz, "L.A. Women: Jim Morrison with John Rechy," in *The Queer Sixties*, ed. Patricia Smith (New York: Routledge, 1999).
17. Boose, "Techno-Muscularity."
18. Gertrud Koch, "The Body's Shadow Realm," *October* 50 (1989): 3–30.

19. Shelley Stamp, *Movie-Struck Girls: Women and Motion Picture Culture after the Nickelodeon* (Princeton, NJ: Princeton University Press, 2000).

20. Richard Dyer, *Now You See It: Studies on Lesbian and Gay Film* (London: Routledge, 1990), 149.

21. Ara Osterweil, "Andy Warhol's *Blow Job*: Toward the Recognition of a Pornographic Avant-Garde," in *Porn Studies*, ed. Linda Williams (Durham, NC: Duke University Press, 2004).

22. David. E. James, *Allegories of Cinema: American Film in the Sixties* (Princeton, NJ: Princeton University Press, 1989), 318.

23. John Di Stefano, "How Men Look: On the Masculine Ideal and the Body Beautiful," *Art Journal* 2 (1997): 18–23.

24. Kathleen M. Vernon and Barbara Morris, eds., *Post-Franco, Postmodern: The Films of Pedro Almodóvar* (Westport, CT: Greenwood Press, 1995), 175.

25. Barbara Wilinsky, *Sure Seaters: The Emergence of Art House Cinema* (Minneapolis: University of Minnesota Press, 2001).

26. Obsterweil, "Andy Warhol's *Blow Job*," 432.

27. Linda Williams, *Hard Core: Power, Pleasure, and the "Frenzy of the Visible"* (Berkeley: University of California Press, 1999).

28. Dennis, *Art/Porn*, 135–158.

29. Bob Adelman, *Art and Wit in America's Forbidden Funnies* (New York: Simon & Schuster, 2004).

30. David Hajdu, *The Ten-Cent Plague: The Great Comic-Book Scare and How It Changed America* (New York: Farrar, Straus and Giroux, 2008).

31. Hajdu, *The Ten-Cent Plague*.

32. Douglas Crimp, *Melancholia and Moralism: Essays on AIDS and Queer Politics* (Cambridge, MA: The MIT Press, 2004).

33. Bad Object Choices, ed. *How Do I Look? Queer Film and Video* (Seattle, WA: Bay Press, 1991), 50–51.

34. Christie, Ian. " 'Gentlemen, Start Your Joysticks': An X-rated Tour through the Early Days of Porn Video Games." Salon.com, 6 December 1999. Available online http://www.salon.com/tech/feature/1999/12/06/atarisex.

35. Steven Nelson, "Transgressive Transcendence in the Photographs of Rotimi Fani-Kayode," *Art Journal* 64, no. 1 (2005): 5–19.

36. Wilinsky, *Sure Seaters*, 125–26.

37. Theweleit, *Male Fantasies*.

38. Joseba Gabilondo, "Like Blood for Chocolate, Like Queers for Vampires: Border and Global Consumption in Rodríguez, Tarantino, Arau, Esquivel, and Troyano (Notes on Baroque, Camp, Kitsch, and Hybridization)," in *Queer Globalizations: Citizenship and the Afterlife of Colonialism*, ed. Arnaldo Cruz-Malavé and Martin F. Manalansan IV (New York: New York University Press, 2002), 236.

39. Eithne Luibhéid, *Entry Denied: Controlling Sexuality at the Border* (Minneapolis: University of Minnesota Press, 2002).

40. Dennis Altman, *Global Sex* (Chicago: University of Chicago Press, 2001).

41. Stephen F. Eisenman, *The Abu Ghraib Effect* (London: Reaktion Books, 2007), 35.

42. Eisenman, *The Abu Ghraib Effect*.
43. Dennis, *Art/Porn*.
44. Dorelies Kraakman, "Pornography in Western European Culture," in *Sexual Cultures in Europe: Themes in Sexuality*, ed. Franz X. Eder, Lesley A. Hall, and Gert Hekma (Manchester: Manchester University Press, 1999), 104.

BIBLIOGRAPHY

For more literature on this topic, see the following database: Franz X. Eder, "Bibliography of the History of Western Sexuality," http://www.univie.ac.at/Wirtschaftsgeschichte/Sexbibl, with over 25,000 entries.

Acton, W. *The Functions and Disorders of the Reproductive Organs in Childhood, Youth, Adult Age, and Advanced Life Considered in Their Physiological, Social and Moral Response.* Philadelphia, PA: Lindsay and Blakiston, 1865.

Adelman, Bob. *Art and Wit in America's Forbidden Funnies.* New York: Simon & Schuster, 2004.

Agustín, Laura María. "Helping Women Who Sell Sex: The Construction of Benevolent Identities." *Rhizomes* 10 (2005).

Aldrich, Robert, ed. *Gay Life and Culture: A World History.* London: Thames & Hudson, 2006.

Alexander, Priscilla. "Feminism, Sex Workers and Human Rights." In *Whores and Other Feminists,* edited by J. Nagle. New York: Routledge, 1997.

Alibert, François-Paul. *Le Fils de Loth* [The Sons of Lot], 2nd ed. Paris: Musardine, 2002.

Allyn, David. *Make Love Not War: The Sexual Revolution: An Unfettered History.* Boston: Little, Brown & Co., 2000.

Altink, Sietske. *Huizen van Illusies. Bordelen en Prostitutie van Middeleeuwen tot Heden.* Utrecht: Veen, 1983.

Altman, Dennis. *Global Sex.* Chicago and London: University of Chicago Press, 2001.

Anderson, Bridget, and Julia O'Connell Davidson. *Trafficking—a Demand Led Problem?* Stockholm: Save the Children, 2002.

Anest, Marie-Christine. *Zoophilie, homosexualité: Rites de passage et initiation masculine dans la Grèce contemporaine.* Paris: L'Harmattan, 1994.

Angelides, Steven. "Feminism, Child Sexual Abuse and the Erasure of Child Sexuality." *GLQ* 10, no. 2 (2004): 141–77.

Apter, Emily. "Introduction." In *Fetishism as Cultural Discourse*, ed. Emily Apter and William Pietz. Ithaca, NY: Cornell University Press, 1993.

Ariès, Philippe, and André Béjin, eds. *Western Sexuality: Practice and Precept in Past and Present Times*. Oxford, New York: Blackwell, 1985.

Bad Object Choices, eds. *How Do I Look? Queer Film and Video*. Seattle, WA: Bay Press, 1991.

Badinter, Elisabeth. *Dead End Feminism*. Translated from French by Julia Borossa. Cambridge: Polity Press, 2006.

Bakker, Floor, and Ine Vanwesenbeeck, eds. *Seksuele gezondheid in Nederland 2006*. Delft: Eburon, 2006.

Barry, Kathleen. *The Prostitution of Sexuality*. New York: New York University Press, 1995.

Bayer, Ronald. *Homosexuality and American Psychiatry: The Politics of Diagnosis*. New York, Basic Books, 1981.

Bean, Joseph W. "L.A. Police Free Gay Slaves ... in 1976." *Leather Times* 24 (2005): 4–6.

Beauvoir, Simone de. 1949. *Le Deuxième Sexe*. Translated from French as *The Second Sex* by H. M. Parshley. New York: Knopf, 1952.

Beck, Birgit. *Wehrmacht und sexuelle Gewalt: Sexualverbrechen vor deutschen Militärgerichten 1939–1945*. Paderborn: Schöningh, 2004.

Beetz, Andrea M., and Anthony L. Podberscek, eds. *Bestiality and Zoophilia: Sexual Relations with Animals*. West Lafayette, IN: Purdue University Press, 2005.

Belliol, J. A. *De l'impuissance ou perte de la virilité*. Paris: Chez l'auteur, ca. 1832.

Bergen, Diana van. *Een gedoogde schemerwereld binnen de prostitutie. De werk- en leefsituatie van jongensprostitués in Amsterdam*. Amsterdam: Vrije Universiteit, 2002.

Bernstein, Elizabeth. "The Meaning of the Purchase: Desire, Demand and the Commerce of Sex." *Ethnography* 2, no. 3 (2001): 389–420.

Bérubé, Alan. *Coming Out Under Fire: The History of Gay Men and Women in World War Two*. New York: The Free Press, 1990.

Bland, Lucy, and Laura Doan, eds. *Sexology in Culture: Labelling Bodies and Desires*. Cambridge, UK: Polity Press, 1999.

Blessing, Jennifer. *Rrose Is a Rrose: Gender Performance in Photography*. New York: Guggenheim Museum, 2006.

Bollé, Michael, ed. *Eldorado: Homosexuelle Frauen und Männer in Berlin, 1850–1950: Geschichte, Alltag und Kultur*. Berlin: Frölich und Kaufmann, 1984.

Boolell, M., S. Gepi-Attee, J. C. Gingell, and M. J. Allen. "Sildenafil, a Novel Effective Oral Therapy for Male Erectile Dysfunction." *British Journal of Urology* 78 (1996): 257–61.

Boose, Lynda. "Techno-Muscularity and the 'Boy Eternal.'" In *Cultures of U.S. Imperialism*, edited by Amy Kaplan and Donald E. Pease. Durham, NC: Duke University Press, 1993.

Brandt, A. "The Cigarette, Risk and American Culture." *Daedalus* 119, no. 4 (1990): 155–76.

Bright, Deborah. *The Passionate Camera: Photography and Bodies of Desire*. New York: Routledge, 1998.

Brussa, Licia. *Health, Migration, Sex Work: The Experience of Tampep: Transnational Aids/STD Prevention among Migrant Prostitutes in Europe.* Amsterdam: TAMPEP International Foundation, 1999.

Brussa, Licia. "The Tampep Project in Western Europe." In *Global Sex Workers: Rights, Resistance, and Redefinition*, edited by Kamala Kempadoo and Jo Doezema. New York: Routledge, 1998.

Butt, Gavin. *Between You and Me: Queer Disclosures in the New York Art World, 1948–1963.* Durham, NC: Duke University Press, 2005.

Carleton, Gregory. *Sexual Revolution in Bolshevik Russia.* Pittsburgh, PA: University of Pittsburgh Press, 2005.

Cazals, A. *Prostitution et proxénétisme en Europe.* Paris: La documentation française, 1995.

Chauncey, George. *Gay New York. Gender, Urban Culture, and the Making of the Gay Male World, 1890–1940.* New York: Basic Books, 1994.

Chesler, Ellen. *Woman of Valour: Margaret Sanger and the Birth Control Movement in America.* New York: Morrow, 1992.

Christie, Ian. "'Gentlemen, Start Your Joysticks': An X-Rated Tour through the Early Days of Porn Video Games." Salon.com, December 6, 1999, http://www.salon.com/tech/feature/1999/12/06/atarisex.

Coale, Ansley J., and Susan Cotts Watkins, eds. *The Decline of Fertility in Europe: The Revised Proceedings of a Conference on the Princeton European Fertility Project.* Princeton, NJ: Princeton University Press, 1986.

Cocks, Harry G., and Matt Houlbrook, eds. *Palgrave Advances in the Modern History of Sexuality.* Basingstoke, UK: Palgrave, 2006.

Committee on Homosexual Offences and Prostitution. *Report of the Committee on Homosexual Offences and Prostitution.* London: Her Majesty's Stationery Office, 1957.

Conrad, P., and J. Schneider, *Deviance and Medicalization: From Badness to Sickness.* Saint Louis, MO: The C.V. Mosby Company, 1980.

Conseil National du Sida. *Avis sur la pénalisation de la transmission sexuelle du VIH.* Paris: Conseil National du Sida, 2006.

Cook, Hera. *The Long Sexual Revolution: Women, Sex, and Contraception in England 1800–1975.* Oxford: Oxford University Press, 2004.

Copley, Antony. *Sexual Moralities in France, 1780–1980: New Ideas on the Family, Divorce and Homosexuality.* London: Routledge, 1989.

Corber, Robert J. *Homosexuality in Cold War America. Resistance and the Crisis of Masculinity.* Durham, NC: Duke University Press, 1997.

Corbin, A. *L'harmonie des plaisirs. Les manières de jouir du siècle des Lumières à l'avènement de la sexologie.* Paris: Perrin, 2008.

Cornell, Drucilla. *Feminism and Pornography.* New York: Oxford University Press, 2000.

COYOTE. http://www.walnet.org/csis/groups/coyote.html, July 26, 2007.

Crimp, Douglas. *Melancholia and Moralism: Essays on AIDS and Queer Politics.* Cambridge, MA: The MIT Press, 2004.

Danet, Jean, et al., eds. "Fous d'enfance. Qui a peur des pédophiles?" Special issue, *Recherches* 47 (1979).

Danna, Daniela. *Amiche, compagne, amanti. Storia dell'amore tra donne.* Trento: Uniservice, 2003.

Danna, Daniela. *Che cos'è la prostituzione? Le quattro visioni del commercio del sesso.* Trieste: Asterios, 2004.

Danna, Daniela. *Donne di mondo. Commercio del sesso e controllo statale.* Milan: Eleuthera, 2004.

Danna, Daniela. *Ginocidio. La violenza contro le donne nell'era globale.* Milan: Eleuthera, 2007.

Danna, Daniela. *La gaia famiglia. Omogenitorialità: il dibattito e la ricerca.* Trieste: Asterios, 2005.

Danna, Daniela. *Matrimonio omosessuale.* Rome: Erre Emme Edizioni, 1997.

Danna, Daniela. *Prostituzione e vita pubblica in quattro capitali europee.* Rome: Carocci, 2006.

Darmon, P. *Le tribunal de l'impuissance.* Paris: Seuil, 1979.

Davidson, A. "Sex and the Emergence of Sexuality." *Critical Inquiry* 14 (1987): 16–48.

Davidson, Roger. "The Culture of Compulsion: Venereal Disease, Sexuality and the State in Twentieth-Century Scotland." In *Sexual Cultures in Europe. Themes in Sexuality,* edited by F. X. Eder, L. A. Hall, and G. Hekma. Vol. 2. Manchester: Manchester University Press, 1999.

Davis, Katherine Bement. *Factors in the Sex Life of Twenty-Two Hundred Women.* New York: Harper & Brothers Publishers, 1929.

Davis, Nanette J., ed. *Prostitution: An International Handbook on Trends, Problems, and Policies.* Westport, CT: Greenwood Press, 1993.

Debouzy, Marianne. "La poupée Barbie." *CLIO: Histoires, Femmes, Sociétés* 13, no. 4 (April 1996): 2–13.

De Grazia, Victoria. *How Fascism Ruled Women: Italy, 1922–1945.* Berkeley: University of California Press, 1992.

Dekkers, Midas. *Lief Dier. Over bestialiteit.* Amsterdam: Contact, 1992. Translated from Dutch as *Dearest Pet. On Bestiality.* London: Verso, 1994.

Deleuze, Gilles, and Félix Guattari. *Anti-Oedipus, Capitalism and Schizophrenia.* Translated from the French by Robert Hurley, Mark Seem, and Helen R. Lane. New York: The Viking Press, 1982.

D'Emilio, John. *Sexual Politics, Sexual Communities: The Making of a Homosexual Minority in the United States, 1940–1970.* Chicago: University of Chicago Press, 1983.

D'Emilio, John, and Estelle B. Freedman. *Intimate Matters. A History of Sexuality in America.* New York: Harper & Row, 1988.

Dennis, Kelly. *Art/Porn: A History of Seeing and Touching.* Oxford: Berg Publishers, 2009.

Dennis, Kelly. "The Hegelian Implications of the Museum of Sex; or, Does MoSex Mean No Sex?" *Art Journal* 65, no. 2 (2006): 8–22.

Dickinson, Edward R. "Policing Sex in Germany, 1882–1982." *Journal of the History of Sexuality* 16, no. 2 (2007): 204–250.

Dickinson, R. L., and L. Beam. *The Single Woman: A Medical Study in Sex Education.* Baltimore, MD: Williams & Wilkins, 1934.

Dickinson, R. L., and L. Beam. *A Thousand Marriages: A Medical Study of Sex Adjustment.* Baltimore, MD: Williams & Wilkins, 1932.

Di Stefano, John. "How Men Look: On the Masculine Ideal and the Body Beautiful." *Art Journal* 2 (1997): 18–23.

Doan, Laura. *Fashioning Sapphism: The Origins of a Modern English Lesbian Culture.* New York: Columbia University Press, 2001.

Dodson, B. *Liberating Masturbation: A Meditation on Self Love.* New York: Bodysex Designs, 1974.

Doezema, Jo. "Forced to Choose. Beyond the Voluntary v. Forced Prostitution Dichotomy." In *Global Sex Workers: Rights, Resistance and Redefinitions,* edited by Kamala Kempadoo and Jo Doezema. New York: Routledge, 1998.

Doorninck, Marieke van, and Margot Jongedijk. *In het Leven. Vier eeuwen Prostitutie in Nederland.* Apeldoorn: Historisch Museum Apeldoorn, 1997.

Dose, Ralf. "The World League for Sexual Reform: Some Possible Approaches." In *Sexual Cultures in Europe: National Histories,* edited by Franz X. Eder, Lesley A. Hall, and Gert Hekma. Vol. 1. Manchester: Manchester University Press, 1999.

Downing, Lisa. *Desiring the Dead. Necrophilia and Nineteenth-Century Literature.* Oxford: Legenda, 2003.

Dowsett, Gary W., and M. Couch. "Roundtable: Male Circumcision and HIV Prevention: Is There Really Enough of the Right Kind of Evidence?" *Reproductive Health Matters* 15, no. 29 (2007): 33–44.

Doy, Gen. *Claude Cahun: A Sensual Politics of Photography.* London: I. B. Taurus, 2008.

Duberman, Martin, Martha Vicinus, and George Chauncey, eds. *Hidden from History: Reclaiming the Gay and Lesbian Past.* New York: NAL Books, 1989.

Duberman, Martin. *Stonewall.* New York: Penguin, 1993.

Dubois-Arber, F., and B. Spencer. "Condom Use." In *Sexual Behaviour and HIV/AIDS in Europe,* edited by M. Hubert, N. Bajos, and T. Sandfort,. London: UCL Press, 1998.

Duggan, Lisa, and Nan D. Hunter. *Sex Wars: Sexual Dissent and Political Culture.* New York: Routledge, 1995.

Dyer, Richard. *Now You See It: Studies on Lesbian and Gay Film.* London: Routledge, 1990.

Eder, Franz X. *Kultur der Begierde: Eine Geschichte der Sexualität.* München: C.H. Beck, 2002.

Eder, Franz X. "The Nationalists' 'Healthy Sexuality' Was Followed by America's Influence: Sexuality and Media from National Socialism to the Sexual Revolution." In *Sexuality in Austria,* edited by Günter Bischof, Anton Pelinka, and Dagmar Herzog. New Brunswick, NJ: Transaction Publishers, 2007.

Eder, Franz X. "Sexual Cultures in Germany and Austria, 1700–2000." In *Sexual Cultures in Europe: National Histories,* edited by Franz X. Eder, Lesley A. Hall, and Gert Hekma. Manchester: Manchester University Press, 1999.

Eder, Franz X., Lesley A. Hall, and Gert Hekma, eds. *Sexual Cultures in Europe.* 2 Vols. Manchester: Manchester University Press, 1999.

Eisenman, Stephen F. *The Abu Ghraib Effect*. London: Reaktion Books, 2007.

Elb, Norbert. *SM-Sexualität. Selbstorganisation einer sexuellen Subkultur*. Giessen: Psychosozial Verlag, 2006.

Elsaesser, Thomas. *Fassbinder's Germany: History, Identity, Subject*. Amsterdam: Amsterdam University Press, 1996.

England, L. R. "Little Kinsey: An Outline of Sex Attitudes in Britain." *The Public Opinion Quarterly* 13 (1949–50): 587–600.

Epstein, Steven. *Impure Science: AIDS, Activism, and the Politics of Knowledge*. Berkeley: University of California Press, 1996.

Essig, Laurie. *Queer in Russia: A Study of Sex, Self, and the Other*. Durham, NC: Duke University Press, 1999.

Faderman, Lilian. *Odd Girls and Twilight Lovers: A History of Lesbian Life in Twentieth-Century America*. New York: Penguin, 1991.

Faderman, Lilian. *Surpassing the Love of Men: Romantic Friendship and Love between Women from the Renaissance to the Present*. New York: Willam Morrow, 1981.

Feldman, H., I. Goldstein, D. Hatzichristou, R. Krane, and J. McKinlay. "Impotence and its Medical and Psychosocial Correlates: Results of the Massachusetts Male Aging Study." *The Journal of Urology* 151 (1994): 54–61.

Festy, Patrick, and Prioux, France. "Le divorce en Europe depuis 1950." *Population French Edition* 30, no. 6 (1975): 975–1017.

Fletcher, Jane. "The Uncanny Effect of Sally Mann's *Immediate Family*." *n.paradoxa* 7 (July 1998).

Ford, Luke. *A History of X: 100 Years of Sex in Film*. Amherst, NY: Prometheus Books, 1999.

Foucault, Michel. 1976. *History of Sexuality*. Vol. 1. Translated from French by Robert Hurley. New York: Random House, 1980.

Foucault, Michel. *Les anormaux—Cours au Collège de France 1974–75*. Paris: Gallimard, Le Seuil & EHESS, 1999.

Foucault, Michel. *Madness and Civilization*. Translated from French. London: Routledge, 2006.

Fourier, Charles. *The Utopian Vision of Charles Fourier: Selected Texts on Work, Love and Passionate Attraction*. Translated and edited by Jonathan Beecher and Richard Bienvenu. Boston: Beacon Press, 1971.

Frank, E., C. Anderson, and D. Rubinstein. "Frequency of Sexual Dysfunctions in 'Normal' Couples." *New England Journal of Medicine* 299 (1978): 111–15.

Frejka, Tomas. "Induced Abortion and Fertility: A Quarter Century of Experience in Eastern Europe." *Population and Development Review* 9, no. 3 (1983): 494–520.

Freud, Sigmund. "'Civilized' Sexual Morality and Modern Nervous Illness." In *The Standard Edition of the Complete Psychological Works of Sigmund Freud*. Vol. 9. London: The Hogarth Press, 1959.

Freud, Sigmund. 1905. *Drei Abhandlungen zur Sexualtheorie*. 5th ed. Leipzig: Deuticke, 1915.

Freud, Sigmund. "Letter to an American Mother." *American Journal of Psychiatry* 107 (1951): 787.

Freud, Sigmund. "The Taboo of Virginity." In *Collected Papers*. Vol. 4. Translated by Joan Riviere. New York: Basic Books, 1959.

Friedan, Betty. *The Feminine Mystique*. New York: Norton, 1963.

Fromm, Erich. "Sexuality and Sexual Perversions." In *The Revision of Psychoanalysis*, edited by Erich Fromm and Rainer Funk. Boulder, CO: Westview, 1992.

Fugl-Meyer, A. R., and K. Sjögren Fugl-Meyer. "Sexual Disabilities, Problems and Satisfaction in 18–74 Year Old Swedes." *Scandinavian Journal of Sexology* 2 (1999): 79–105.

Gabilondo, Joseba. "Like Blood for Chocolate, Like Queers for Vampires: Border and Global Consumption in Rodríguez, Tarantino, Arau, Esquivel, and Troyano." In *Queer Globalizations: Citizenship and the Afterlife of Colonialism*, edited by Arnaldo Cruz-Malavé and Martin F. Manalansan IV. New York: New York University Press, 2002.

Garcia-Reboll, L., J. Mulhall, and I. Goldstein. "Drugs for the Treatment of Impotence." *Drugs Aging* 11, no. 2 (1997): 140–51.

Garnier, Paul. *Les Fétichistes, pervertis et invertis sexuels*. Paris: Baillière, 1896.

Gates, Katharina. *Deviant Desires*. New York: Juno Books, 2000.

Gelder, Paul van. *Kwetsbaar, Kleurig en Schaduwrijk. Jongens in de prostitutie: Een verschijnsel in meervoud*. Amsterdam: Thela Thesis, 1998.

Gerhard, Jane F. *Desiring Revolution: Second-Wave Feminism and the Rewriting of American Sexual Thought, 1920 to 1982*. New York: Columbia University Press, 2001.

Giami, Alain. "Fonction sexuelle masculine et sexualité féminine. Permanence des représentations du genre en sexologie et en médecine sexuelle." *Communications* 81 (2007): 135–51.

Giami, Alain. "Sexual Health: The Emergence, Development and Diversity of a Concept." *Annual Review of Sex Research* 13 (2002): 1–33.

Giami, A., and H. Leridon, eds. *Les enjeux de la stérilisation*. Paris: Éditions INSERM-INED, 2000.

Giami, Alain, and M. A. Schiltz. "Representations of Sexuality and Relations between Partners: Sex Research in France in the Era of AIDS." *Annual Review of Sex Research* 7 (1996): 125–57.

Giddens, Anthony. *The Transformation of Intimacy. Sexuality, Love and Eroticism in Modern Societies*. London: Polity, 1992.

Gilman, Sander. *Disease and Representation*. Ithaca, NY: Cornell University Press, 1988.

Goldstein, I., T. Lue, H. Padma-Nathan, R. Rosen, W. Steers, and P. Wicker, for the Sildenafil Study Group. "Oral Sildenafil in the Treatment of Erectile Dysfunction." *The New England Journal of Medicine* 338, no. 20 (1998): 1397–404.

Gordon, Linda. "The Politics of Child Sexual Abuse." *Feminist Review* 28 (1988): 57–65.

Gorer, Geoffrey. *Exploring English Character*. New York: Criterion Books, 1955.

Grassberger, Ronald. *Die Unzucht mit Tieren*. Vienna: Springer, 1968.

Grau, Günther. *Hidden Holocaust? Gay and Lesbian Persecution in Germany 1933–1945*. London: Cassell, 1995.

Graupner, Helmut. "Sexuelle Mündigkeit: Die Strafgesetzgebung in europäischen und außereuropäischen Ländern." *Zeitschrift für Sexualforschung* 10 (1997): 281–310.

"Gun Control Hurts Women." *The Independent Women's Forum*, May 12, 2000.

Haavio-Mannila, Elina, Osmo Kontula, and Anna Rotkirch. *Sexual Lifestyles in the Twentieth Century: A Research Study*. Basingstoke, UK: Palgrave, 2002.

Hajdu, David. *The Ten-Cent Plague: The Great Comic-Book Scare and How It Changed America*. New York: Farrar, Straus and Giroux, 2008.

Hall, Lesley A. *Sex, Gender and Social Change in Britain since 1880*. Houndmills, UK: Macmillan Press, 2000.

Hanson, Dian, ed. *The History of Men's Magazines: Vol. 1: From 1900 to Post-WW II*. Cologne: Taschen, 2004.

Hart, G., and K. Wellings. "Sexual Behaviour and its Medicalisation: In Sickness and in Health." *British Medical Journal* 324, no. 7342 (2002): 896–900.

Havelock Ellis, Henry. *Little Essays of Love and Virtue*. New York: George H. Doran Company, 1922.

Healey, Dan. *Homosexual Desire in Revolutionary Russia: The Regulation of Sexual and Gender Dissent*. Chicago: University of Chicago Press, 2001.

Hekma, Gert. "Amsterdam." In *Queer Sites. Gay Urban Histories since 1600*, edited by David Higgs. London: Routledge, 1999.

Hekma, Gert. "The Drive for Sexual Equality." *Sexualities* 11, no. 1 (2008): 51–55.

Hekma, Gert. "How Libertine is the Netherlands? Exploring Contemporary Dutch Sexual Cultures." In *Regulating Sex: The Politics of Intimacy and Identity*, edited by Elizabeth Bernstein and Laurie Schaffner. New York: Routledge, 2005.

Hekma, Gert, Harry Oosterhuis, and James D. Steakley, eds. *Gay Men and the Sexual History of the Political Left*. New York: Harrington Park Press, 1995.

Henriksson, B. *Risk Factor Love: Homosexuality, Sexual Interaction and HIV Prevention*. Goteborg: Goteborgs Universitets Skriftserien, 1995.

Herzer, Manfred. *Bibliographie zur Homosexualität. Verzeichnis des deutschsprachigen nichtbelletristischen Schriftums zur weiblichen und männlichen Homosexualität aus den Jahren 1466 bis 1975 in chronologischer Reihenfolge*. Berlin: Rosa Winkel, 1982.

Herzer, Manfred. "Kertbeny and the Nameless Love." *Journal of Homosexuality* 12, no. 1 (1985): 1–25.

Herzog, Dagmar. *Sex after Fascism: Memory and Morality in Twentieth-Century Germany*. Princeton, NJ: Princeton University Press, 2005.

Herzog, Dagmar. *Sex in Crisis: The New Sexual Revolution and the Future of American Politics*. New York: Basic Books, 2008.

Herzog, Dagmar, ed., *Sexuality and German Fascism*. Oxford: Berghahn Books, 2005.

Herzog, Dagmar, ed. "Sexuality and Nazism." Special issue, *Journal of the History of Sexuality* 11, no. 1/2 (2002).

Hinds, Harold E. "A Holistic Approach to the Study of Popular Culture. Context, Text, Audience, and Recoding." In *Popular Culture Theory and Methodology: A Basic Introduction*, edited by Harold E. Hinds, Marilyn F. Motz, and Angela M. S. Nelson. Madison: University of Wisconsin Press, 2006.

Hingst, Monika, Manfred Herzer, Karl-Heinz Steinle, Andreas Sternweiler, and Wolf-
    gang Theis, eds. *Goodbye to Berlin? 100 Jahre Schwulenbewegung*. Berlin: Ver-
    lag Rosa Winkel, 1997.

Hirschfeld, Magnus. *Berlins drittes Geschlecht*. Berlin: H. Seemann, 1904.

Hitt, J. "The second sexual revolution." *The New York Times Magazine*, February 20,
    2000.

Hooven III, F. Valentine. *Beefcake: The Muscle Magazines of America, 1950–1970*.
    Cologne: Taschen, 2002.

Horkheimer, Max, and Theodor W. Adorno. *Dialectic of Enlightenment*. New York:
    Continuum, 1947.

HOSI Wien/Auslandsgruppe. *Rosa Liebe unterm roten Stern. Zur Lage der Lesben und
    Schwulen in Osteuropa*. Vienna: Frülings Erwachen, 1984.

Houlbrook, Matt. *Queer London. Perils and Pleasures in the Sexual Metropolis, 1918–
    1957*. Chicago: University of Chicago Press, 2005.

Hubert, Michel, Nathalie Bajos, and Theo Sandfort, eds. *Sexual Behaviour and HIV/
    AIDS in Europe*. London: UCL Press, 1998.

Iacub, Marcela. *Par le trou de la serrure. Une histoire de la pudeur publique XIX-XXIe
    siècle*. Paris: Fayard, 2008.

Iacub, Marcela, and Patrice Maniglier. *Antimanuel d'éducation sexuelle*. Rosny: Breal,
    2005.

International Committee on the Rights of Sex Workers in Europe. *Declaration of the
    Rights of Sex Workers in Europe*. 2005. http://www.sexworkeurope.org/site/
    images/PDFs/dec_brussels2005.pdf.

International Convention on Human Trafficking. "Article 1 of the International Agree-
    ment for the Suppression of the White Slave Traffic." http://www.oas.org/juridico/
    MLA/en/traites/en_traites-inter-wst.pdf (accessed May 8, 2007).

Irvine, Janice M. *Talk about Sex. The Battles over Sex Education in the United States*.
    Berkeley: University of California Press, 2002.

Jackson, Julian. *Living in Arcadia: Homosexuality, Politics, and Morality in France
    from the Liberation to AIDS*. Chicago: University of Chicago Press, 2000.

Jacquart, D., and C. Thomasset. *Sexualité et savoir médical au moyen âge*. Paris: P.U.F.,
    1985.

Jaget, Claude, ed. *Prostitutes, Our Life*. Bristol: Falling Wall Press, 1980.

Jagose, Annemarie. *Queer Theory: An Introduction*. Melbourne: Melbourne University
    Press, 1996.

James, David. E. *Allegories of Cinema: American Film in the Sixties*. Princeton, NJ:
    Princeton University Press, 1989.

Janssen, Marie-Louise. *Reizende Sekswerkers. Latijns-Amerikaanse vrouwen in de
    Europese prostitutie*. Amsterdam: Het Spinhuis, 2007.

Jay, Karla. *The Amazon and the Page: Natalie Clifford Barney and Renée Vivien*.
    Bloomington: Indiana University Press, 1988.

Jenkins, Philip. *Moral Panic: Changing Concepts of the Child Molester in Modern
    America*. New Haven and London: Yale University Press, 1998.

Jenkins, Philip. *Pedophiles and Priests: Anatomy of a Contemporary Crisis*. Oxford:
    Oxford University Press, 2001.

Jenness, Valerie. *Making It Work: The Prostitutes' Right Movement in Perspective.* New York: Aldine de Gruyter, 1993.

Jennings, Rebecca. *Tomboys and Bachelor Girls: A Lesbian History of Post-War Britain 1945–1971.* Manchester: Manchester University Press.

Johannes, C., A. Araujo, H. Feldman, C. Derby, K. Kleinman, and J. McKinlay. "Incidence of Erectile Dysfunction in Men 40 to 69 Years Old: Longitudinal Results from the Massachusetts Male Aging Study." *The Journal of Urology* 163 (2000): 460–63.

Johnson, David K. *The Lavender Scare: The Cold War Persecution of Gays and Lesbians in the Federal Government.* Chicago: University of Chicago Press, 2004.

Kaplan, E. Ann. *Women in Film Noir.* London: British Film Institute, 2008.

Kaschak, Ellyn, and Leonore Tiefer, eds. *A New View of Women's Sexual Problems.* Binghamton, NY: Haworth Press, 2001.

Katz, Jonathan Ned. *The Invention of Heterosexuality.* New York: Dutton, 1995.

Kaye, Kerwin. "Male Prostitution in the Twentieth Century: Pseudohomosexuals, Hoodlum Homosexuals, and Exploited Teens." *Journal of Homosexuality* 46, no. 1/2 (2003): 1–77.

Kempadoo, Kamala. "Women of Color and the Global Sex Trade: Transnational Feminist Perspectives." *Meridians: Feminism, Race, Transnationalism* 1, no. 2 (2001): 28–51.

Kennedy, Elizabeth Lapovsky, and Madeleine D. Davis. *Boots of Leather, Slippers of Gold: The History of a Lesbian Community.* New York: Penguin, 1993.

Kerjan, Liliane. "A Right to Personal Privacy." In *Sexualities in American Culture,* edited by Alfred Hornung. Heidelberg: Universitätsverlag Winter, 2004.

Kiernan, James G. "Responsibility in Sexual Perversion." *Chicago Medical Recorder* 3 (1892): 185–210.

Kinsey, Alfred C., Wardell B. Pomeroy, Clyde E. Martin, and Paul H. Gebhard. *Sexual Behavior in the Human Female.* Philadelphia: Saunders, 1953.

Kinsey, Alfred C., Wardell B. Pomeroy, and Clyde E. Martin. *Sexual Behavior in the Human Male.* Philadelphia: Saunders, 1948.

Kissack, Terence. *Free Comrades: Anarchism and Homosexuality in the United States, 1895–1917.* Oakland, CA: AK Press, 2008.

Klein, Marty. *America's War on Sex: The Attack on Law, Lust and Liberty.* Westport, CT: Praeger, 2006.

Kleinplatz, Peggy, and Charles Moser, eds. *Sadomasochism: Powerful Pleasures.* Binghamton, NY: Harrington Park Press, 2006.

Koch, Gertrud. "The Body's Shadow Realm." *October* 50 (1989): 3–30.

Kon, Igor S. *The Sexual Revolution in Russia: From the Age of the Czars to Today.* New York: Free Press, 1995.

Kontula, Osmo, and Elina Haavio-Manila. *Sexual pleasures. Enhancement of sex life in Finland.* Aldershot, UK: Dartmouth, 1995.

Korf, Dirk J., Ton Nabben, and Madelon Schreuders. *Roemeense trekvogels. Nieuwkomers in de jongensprostitutie.* Amsterdam: Thesis Publishers, 1996.

Kraakman, Dorelies. "Pornography in Western European Culture." In *Sexual Cultures in Europe: Themes in Sexuality,* edited by Franz X. Eder, Lesley A. Hall, and Gert Hekma. Manchester: Manchester University Press, 1999.

Krafft-Ebing, Richard. *Psychopathia Sexualis. Eine klinische-forensische Studie*. Stuttgart: Ferdinand Enke, 1886.

Krane, R., I. Goldstein, and I. Saenz de Tejada. "Impotence." *The New England Journal of Medicine* 321, no. 24 (1989): 1648–59.

Krug, E. G., Linda L. Dahlberg, James A. Mercy, Anthony B. Zwi, and Rafael Lozano, eds. *World Report on Violence and Health*. Geneva: World Health Organization, 2002.

Kulick, Don. "Four Hundred Thousand Swedish Perverts." *GLQ* 11, no. 2 (2005): 205–35.

Kulick, Don, and Anne Meneley, eds. *Fat: The Anthropology of an Obsession*. New York: Penguin, 2005.

Kunzel, Regina. *Criminal Intimacy: Prison and the Uneven History of Modern American Sexuality*. Chicago: University of Chicago Press, 2008.

Lanteri Laura, G. *Lecture des perversions. Histoire de leur appropriation médicale*. Paris: Masson, 1979.

Laqueur, Thomas W. *Making Sex: Body and Gender from the Greeks to Freud*. Cambridge MA: Harvard University Press, 1990.

Laqueur, Thomas W. *Solitary Sex: A Cultural History of Masturbation*. New York: Zone Books, 2003.

Laumann, Edward O., John H. Gagnon, Robert T. Michael, and Stuart Michaels. *The Social Organization of Sexuality. Sexual Practices in the United States*. Chicago: University of Chicago Press, 1994.

Lenne, Gérard. *Érotisme et cinéma*. Paris: La Musardine, 1998.

Lennerhed, Lena. *Friheten att njuta. Sexualdebatten i Sverige på 1960-talet*. Stockholm: Norstedts, 1994.

Leroy-Forgeot, Flora. *Histoire juridique de l'homosexualité en Europe*. Paris: PUF, 1997.

Levine, Judith. *Harmful to Minors: The Perils of Protecting Children from Sex*. Minneapolis: University of Minnesota Press, 2002.

Levy, Ariel. *Female Chauvinist Pigs: Women and the Rise of Raunch Culture*. New York: Free Press, 2005.

Linden, Robert Ruth, et al., eds. *Against Sadomasochism: A Radical Feminist Analysis*. East Palo Alto, CA: Frog in the Well, 1982.

Loe, Meika. *The Rise of Viagra: How the Little Blue Pill Changed Sex in America*. New York: New York University Press, 2004.

Löfström, Jan. "Sexuality and the Performance of Manliness: Sketching the Historical Trajectory of Male Fear." *Ethnologia Scandinavica* 27 (1997): 21–40.

Love, Brenda. *Encyclopedia of Unusual Sex Practices*. Fort Lee, NJ: Barricade Books, 1992.

Luibhéid, Eithne. *Entry Denied: Controlling Sexuality at the Border*. Minneapolis: University of Minnesota Press, 2002.

Lukas, Carrie L. *The Politically Incorrect Guide to Women, Sex and Feminism*. Washington, DC: Regnery Publishing, 2006.

Lupton, D. *The Imperative of Health: Public Health and the Regulation of the Body*. London: Sage, 1995.

Macciocchi, Maria A. *La donna nera. Consenso femminile al fascismo*. Milan: Feltrinelli, 1976.

Mahoon, James, and Christine Wenburg, eds. *The Mosher Survey: Sexual Attitudes of 45 Victorian Women.* New York: Arno Press, 1980.

Mann, Sally. *Immediate Family.* New York: Aperture, 2005.

Marcuse, Herbert. *Eros and Civilization: A Philosophical Inquiry into Freud.* Boston: The Beacon Press, 1955.

Martel, Frédéric. *The Pink and the Black: Homosexuals in France since 1968.* Stanford: Stanford University Press, 1999.

Martin, Michelle H. "No One Will Ever Know Your Secret! Commercial Puberty Pamphlets for Girls from the 1940s to the 1990s." In *Sexual Pedagogies: Sex Education in Britain, Australia, and America, 1879–2000,* edited by Claudia Nelson and Michelle H. Martin. New York: Palgrave Macmillan, 2003.

Masters, William H., and Virginia E. Johnson. *Homosexuality in Perspective.* Boston: Little Brown & Co., 1979.

Masters, William H., and Virginia E. Johnson. *Human Sexual Inadequacy.* Boston: Little Brown & Co., 1970.

Masters, William H., and Virginia E. Johnson. *Human Sexual Response.* Boston: Little Brown & Co., 1966.

Mathieu, Lilian. "The Debate on Prostitution in France: A Conflict between Abolitionism, Regulation and Prohibition." *The Journal of Contemporary European Studies* 12, no. 2 (2004): 153–63.

Mathieu, Lilian. "The Emergence and Uncertain Outcomes of Prostitutes' Social Movements." *The European Journal of Women's Studies* 10, no. 1 (2003): 29–50.

McCallum, E. L. *Object Lessons: How to Do Things with Fetishism.* New York: State University of New York Press, 1999.

McLaren, Angus. *Impotence: A Cultural History.* Chicago: Chicago University Press, 2007.

McLaren, Angus. *Twentieth-Century Sexuality: A History.* Oxford: Blackwell Publishers, 1999.

Melody, Michael Edward, and Linda M. Peterson. *Teaching America about Sex: Marriage Guides and Sex Manuals from the Late Victorians to Dr. Ruth.* New York: New York University Press, 1999.

Meyer, Richard. *Outlaw Representation: Censorship and Homosexuality in Twentieth-Century American Art.* Boston: Beacon Press, 2002.

Michaels, Stuart, and Alain Giami. "Sexual Acts and Sexual Relationships: Asking about Sex in Surveys." *Public Opinion Quarterly* 63 (1999): 385–404.

Micheler, Stefan. *Selbstbilder und Fremdbilder der "Anderen": eine Geschichte Männer begehrender Männer in der Weimarer Republik und der NS-Zeit.* Konstanz: UVK Verlag, 2005.

Moll, Albert. *Les perversions de l'instinct génital. Etude sur l'inversion sexuelle basée sur des documents officiels.* Translated from German. Paris: Georges Carré, 1893.

Money, John. *Lovemaps.* Buffalo, NY: Prometheus, 1988.

Money, John, J. G. Hampson, and J. L. Hampson. "An Examination of Some Basic Sexual Concepts: Evidence of Human Hermaphroditism." *Bulletin of the Johns Hopkin's Hospital* 97 (1955): 301–19.

Money, John, Gordon Wainwright, and David Hingsburger. *The Breathless Orgasm: A Lovemap Biography of Asphyxiophilia.* Buffalo, NY: Prometheus, 1991.

Morgan, Robin. *Going Too Far: The Personal Chronicle of a Feminist.* New York: Random House, 1977.

Morgan, Robin. "Theory and Practice: Pornography and Rape." In *Take Back the Night,* edited by L. J. Lederer. New York: William Morrow, 1980.

Mossuz-Lavau, Janine. *Les lois de l' amour: Les politiques de la sexualité en France (1950–2002).* Paris: Petite bibliothèque Payot, 1991.

Nakamura, Lisa. "Race in/for Cyberspace: Identity Tourism and Racial Passing on the Internet." In *Reading Digital Culture,* editcd by David Trend. Malden, MA: Blackwell, 2001.

National Institute of Health Consensus Statement Online 1992 Dec 7–9 ;10(4): 1–31.

Nederlands Instituut voor Sociaal Seksuologisch Onderzoek (NISSO). *Aard en omvang van (Gedwongen) prostitutie onder Minderjarige (Allochtone) Meisjes.* Utrecht: NISSO, 1998.

Nelson, Steven. Transgressive Transcendence in the Photographs of Rotimi Fani-Kayode. *Art Journal* 64, no. 1 (2005): 5–19.

Nieden, Susanne zur, ed. 2005. *Homosexualität und Staatsräson: Männlichkeit, Homophobie und Politik in Deutschland 1900–1945.* Frankfurt: Campus Verlag, 2005.

North, M. *The Secular Priests: Psychotherapy in Contemporary Society.* London: George Allen, 1972.

Oosterhuis, Harry. *Stepchildren of Nature: Krafft-Ebing, Psychiatry, and the Making of Sexual Identity.* Chicago: University of Chicago Press, 2000.

Oppenheimer, G. "In the Eye of the Storm: The Epidemiological Construction of AIDS." In *AIDS: The Burden of History,* edited by E. Fee and D. Fox. Berkeley: University of California Press, 1988.

Ortíz, Ricardo. "L.A. Women: Jim Morrison with John Rechy." In *The Queer Sixties,* edited by Patricia Smith. New York: Routledge, 1999.

Osterweil, Ara. "Andy Warhol's *Blow Job*: Toward the Recognition of a Pornographic Avant-Garde." In *Porn Studies,* edited by Linda Williams. Durham, NC: Duke University Press, 2004.

Outshoorn, Joyce. "The Political Debates on Prostitution and Trafficking of Women." *Social Politics: International Studies in Gender, State and Society* 12, no. 1 (2005): 141–55.

Outshoorn, Joyce, ed. *The Politics of Prostitution: Women's Movements, Democratic States, and the Globalisation of Sex Commerce.* Cambridge: Cambridge University Press, 2004.

Paasonen, Susanna, Kaarina Nikunen, and Laura Saarenmaa, eds. *Pornification: Sex and Sexuality in Media Culture.* Oxford: Berg, 2007.

Pascoe, C. J. *"Dude, You Are a Fag": Adolescent Masculinity and the Fag Discourse.* Berkeley: University of California Press, 2007.

Peel, Robert A., ed. *Marie Stopes: Eugenics and the English Birth Control Movement.* London: The Galton Institute, 1997.

Perkins, Roberta. "A Decade and a Half of Struggle: The Prostitutes' Movement." In *Working Girls: Prostitutes, their Life and Social Control.* Canberra, Australia: Australian Institute of Criminology, 1991.

Pheterson, Gail. *The Prostitution Prism.* Amsterdam: Amsterdam University Press, 1996.

Pheterson, Gail. ed. *A Vindication of the Rights of Whores*. Seattle: The Seal Press, 1989.

Physique Pictorial. *The Complete Reprint of* Physique Pictorial. Cologne: Taschen, 1997.

Pierre, José, ed. *Investigating Sex*. London: Verso, 1992.

Poplaski, Peter. *The R. Crumb Handbook*. London: MQ Publications, 2005.

Porter, Roy, and Lesley Hall. *The Facts of Life: The Creation of Sexual Knowledge in Britain, 1650–1950*. New Haven, CT: Yale University Press, 1995.

Praz, Mario. *The Romantic Agony*. Translated from the Italian by Angus Davidson. Oxford: Oxford University Press, 1970.

Prioux, France. "Cohabitation, Marriage and Separation: Contrasts in Europe." *Population and societies* 422 (April 2006): 1–4.

Quine, Maria Sophia. *Population Politics in Twentieth-Century Europe: Fascist Dictatorships and Liberal Democracies*. London: Routledge, 1996.

Radicalesbians. *The Woman-Identified Woman*. Pittsburgh, PA: Know, Inc., 1970.

Raffalovich, Marc-André. "L'éducation des invertis." *Archives d'anthropologie criminelle de médecine légale et de psychologie normale et pathologique* 9 (November 1894): 738–40.

Rahman, Anika, Laura Katzive, and Stanley K. Henshaw. "A Global Review of Laws on Induced Abortion, 1985–1997." *International Family Planning Perspectives* 24, no. 2 (1998): 56–64.

Ramakers, Micha. *Dirty Pictures: Tom of Finland, Masculinity, and Homosexuality*. New York: St. Martin's Press, 2000.

Rand, Erica. *Barbie's Queer Accessories*. Durham, NC: Duke University Press, 1995.

Raymond, Janice. "The New UN Trafficking Protocol." *Women's Studies International Forum* 25, no. 5 (2002): 491–502.

Real, J. *Voronoff*. Paris: Stock, 2001.

Reich, Wilhelm. *Die Massenpsychologie des Faschismus*. Copenhagen, Prague, and Zurich: Verlag für Sexual politik, 1933. Translated from German as *The Mass Psychology of Fascism*. New York: Orgone Institute Press, 1946.

Reich, Wilhelm. *The Sexual Revolution*. New York: Orgone Institute Press, 1945.

Reichert, Tom. *The Erotic History of Advertising*. Amherst, MA: Prometheus Books, 2003.

Reilly, P. *The Surgical Solution: A History of Involuntary Sterilization in the United States*. Baltimore, MD: The Johns Hopkins Press, 1991.

Rey-Debove, J., and A. Rey. *Le nouveau Petit Robert*. Paris: Dictionnaires le Robert, 1994.

Roberts, Nickie. *Whores in History: Prostitution in Western Society*. London: HarperCollins, 1992.

Robinson, P. *The Modernization of Sex*. New York: Harper & Row, 1976.

Romito, Patrizia. ed. *Violenze alle donne e risposte delle istituzioni. Prospettive internazionali*. Milan: Franco Angeli, 2000.

Roos, Julia. "Backlash against Prostitutes' Rights: Origins and Dynamics of Nazi Prostitution Policies." *Journal of the History of Sexuality* 11, no. 1/2 (2002): 67–94.

Roosmalen, M. S. van, L. G. Wiessing, J. van der Meer, P. Koedijk, and H. Houweling. *Hiv-Infectie en riskant gedrag onder travestieten en transseksuelen in de Rotterdamse straatprostitutie*. Bilthoven: Rijksinstituut voor Volksgezondheid en Milieu, 1996.

Roth-Bettoni, Didier. *L'Homosexualité au cinema*. Paris: La Musardine, 2007.

Roubaud, F. *Traité de l'impuissance et de la stérilité chez l'homme et chez la femme*. Paris: J.-B. Baillière, 1855.

Russo, Vito. *The Celluloid Closet. Homosexuality in the Movies*. New York: Harper and Row, 1987.

Rydström, Jens. *Sinners and Citizens: Bestiality and Homosexuality in Sweden, 1880–1950*. Chicago: University of Chicago Press, 2003.

Sachdev, Paul. *Sex, Abortion, and Unmarried Women*. Westport, CT: Greenwood, 1993.

Sammoun, Mona. *Tendance SM. Essai sur la représentation sadomasochiste*. Paris: La Musardine, 2004.

Samois. *Coming to Power: Writings and Graphics on Lesbian S/M*. Boston: Alyson, 1981.

Sandfort, Theo, Edward Brongersma, and Alex van Naerssen, eds. *Male Intergenerational Intimacy*. New York: Haworth Press, 1991.

Sax, Marjan, and Jules Deckwitz, eds. "On an Old Bicycle: Erotic and Sexual Relationships between Women and Minors." Special issue, *Paidika* 2, no. 4 (1992).

Schérer, René. *Emile perverti ou des rapports entre l'éducation et la sexualité*. Paris: Laffont, 1974.

Schmidt, Gunter. *Das Verschwinden der Sexualmoral: Über sexuelle Verhältnisse*. Hamburg: Klein, 1996.

Schmidt, Gunter, et al. "Veränderungen des Sexualverhaltens von Studentinnen und Studenten 1966–1981–1996." In *Sexualität und Spätmoderne. Über den kulturellen Wandel der Sexualität*, edited by Gunter Schmidt and Bernhard Strauß. Hamburg: Enke, 1998.

Schütz, Alfred, and Thomas Luckmann. *Strukturen der Lebenswelt*. Konstanz: UVK Verlagsgesellschaft, 2003.

Sénac, Jean. *Ébauche du père*. Paris: Gallimard, 1989.

Sigusch, Volkmar. *Geschichte der Sexualwissenschaft*. Frankfurt: Campus, 2008.

Sigusch, Volkmar. *Karl Heinrich Ulrichs. Der erste Schwule der Weltgeschichte*. Berlin: Rosa Winkel, 2000.

Sinfield, Alan. *On Sexuality and Power*. New York: Columbia University Press, 2004.

Smalls, James. *The Homoerotic Photography of Carl Van Vechten: Public Face, Private Thoughts*. Philadelphia: Temple University Press, 2006.

Smith, Tom W. "Attitudes toward Sexual Permissiveness: Trend, Correlates, and Behavioral Connections." In *Sexuality across the Life Course*, edited by Alice S. Rossi. Chicago: University of Chicago Press, 1994.

Sohn, Anne-Marie. "French Catholics between Abstinence and 'Appeasement of Lust,' 1930–1950." In *Sexual Cultures in Europe: Themes in Sexuality*, edited by Franz X. Eder, Lesley A. Hall, and Gert Hekma. Manchester: Manchester University Press, 1999.

Sottomayor, Maria Clara. "The Introduction and Impact of Joint Custody in Portugal." *International Journal of Law, Policy and the Family* 13 (1999): 247–57.

Spector, I. P., and M. P. Carey. "Incidence and Prevalence of the Sexual Dysfunctions: A Critical Review of the Literature." *Archives of Sexual Behavior* 19 (1990): 389–408.

Spengler, Andreas. *Sadomasochisten und ihre Subkulturen.* Frankfurt: Campus, 1979.

Spira, Alfred, Nathalie Bajos, and ACSF Group. *Sexual Behaviour and AIDS.* Aldershot, UK: Avebury, 1994.

Squires, Judith, ed. "Perversity." Special issue, *New Formations* 19 (1993).

Stamp, Shelley. *Movie-Struck Girls: Women and Motion Picture Culture after the Nickelodeon.* Princeton, NJ: Princeton University Press, 2000.

Stanley, Liz. *Sex Surveyed, 1949–1994: From Mass-Observation's "Little Kinsey" to the National Survey and the Hite Reports.* London: Taylor and Francis, 1995.

Stekel, Wilhelm. *Der Fetischismus.* Berlin: Urban & Schwarzenberg, 1923.

Stekel, Wilhelm. *L'homme impuissant.* Paris: Gallimard, 1950.

Stekel, Wilhelm. *Psychosexueller Infantilismus.* Berlin: Urban & Schwarzenberg, 1922.

Sullivan, Barbara. "Rethinking Prostitution and 'Consent.'" Conference Paper, 2000, http://apsa2000.anu.edu.au/confpapers/sullivan.rtf.

Sullivan, Barbara. "Trafficking in Women. Feminism and New International Law." *International Feminist Journal of Politics* 5, no. 1 (2003): 67–91.

Sydow, Kirsten von. "Female Sexuality and Historical Time: A Comparison of Sexual Biographies of German Women Born between 1895 and 1936." *Archives of Sexual Behaviour* 25 (1996): 473–93.

Szasz, Thomas. *The Manufacture of Madness: A Comparative Study of the Inquisition and the Mental Health Movement.* New York: Harper & Row, 1970.

Szasz, Thomas. *The Myth of Mental Illness.* New York: Hoeber-Harper, 1961.

Szreter, Simon. "Falling Fertilities and Changing Sexualities in Europe since c. 1850. Comparative Survey of National Demographic Patterns." In *Sexual Cultures in Europe: Themes in Sexuality,* edited by Franz X. Eder, Lesley Hall, and Gert Hekma. Manchester: Manchester University Press, 1999.

Tamagne, Florence. *Histoire de l'homosexualité en Europe. Berlin, Londres, Paris 1919–1939.* Translated as *History of Homosexuality in Europe: Berlin, London, Paris 1919–1939.* London: Algora Pub, 2000.

Teysseire, D. *Obèse et impuissant. Le dossier médical d'Elie de Beaumont.* Grenoble: Jérome Millon, 1995.

Theweleit, Klaus. *Male Fantasies.* Vol. 1. Translated from German. Minneapolis: University of Minnesota Press, 1987.

Thompson, Bill. *Sadomasochism: Painful Perversion or Pleasurable Play?* London: Cassell, 1994.

Thurber, James, and E. B. White. *Is Sex Necessary?* New York: Blue Ribbon, 1929.

Tiefer, Leonor. "The Medicalization of Sexuality: Conceptual, Normative and Professional Issues." *Annual Review of Sex Research* 7 (1996): 252–82.

Timm, Annette F., and Joshua A. Sanborn. *Gender, Sex and the Shaping of Modern Europe: A History from the French Revolution to the Present Day*. Oxford: Berg, 2007.

Tin, Louis-Georges. *L'Invention de la culture hétérosexuelle*. Paris: Éditions Autrement, 2008.

Tisdall, Jonathan. "Animal Bordellos Draw Norwegians." *Aftenposten English Web Desk*, September 14, 2006.

Transnational AIDS/STD Prevention Among Migrant Prostitutes in Europe/Project (TAMPEP). *Final Report 6. June 2002-June 2004*. Amsterdam: TAMPEP, 2004.

Ulrichs, Karl Heinrich. *Argonauticus*. Leipzig, Germany: A. Serbe's Verlag, 1869.

Velde, T. H. van de. *Ideal Marriage: Its Physiology and Technique*. Translated from Dutch. New York: Random House, 1930.

Velde, Theodor H. van de. *Die vollkommene Ehe: Eine Studie über ihre Physiologie und Technik*. Leipzig: Montane, 1926.

Vennix, Paul. *Travestie, een serieuze (nood)zaak*. Delft: Eburon, 2001.

Vernon, Kathleen M., and Barbara Morris. *Post-Franco, Postmodern: The Films of Pedro Almodóvar*. Westport, CT: Greenwood Press, 1995.

Vicinus, Martha. *Intimate Friends. Women Who Loved Women, 1778–1928*. Chicago: University of Chicago Press, 2004.

Violette, Robert, and Hans-Ulrichs Obrist, eds. *The Words of Gilbert & George: With Portraits of the Artists from 1968 to 1997*. London: Thames & Hudson, 1997.

Virag, R. "Intracavernous Injection of Papaverine for Erectile Failure." *The Lancet* 2, no. 8304 (1982): 938.

Vries, Petra de. "'The Shadow of Contagion': Gender, Syphilis and the Regulation of Prostitution in the Netherlands, 1870–1914." In *Sex, Sin and Suffering. Venereal Disease and European Society since 1870*, edited by Roger Davidson and Lesley A. Hall. London: Routledge, 2001.

Wagner, Hans, Kasper König, and Jula Friedrich, eds. *Das achte Feld / The Eighth Square: Geschlechter, Leben und Begehren in der Kunst seit 1960 / Gender, Life, and Desire in the Arts Since 1960*. Cologne: Hatje Cantz Verlag, 2006.

Walkowitz, Judith R. *Prostitution and Victorian Society: Women, Class, and the State*. Cambridge: Cambridge University Press, 1980.

Wanrooij, Bruno. "The 'Thorns of Love': Sexuality, Syphilis and Social Control in Modern Italy." In *Sin and Suffering: Venereal Disease and European Society since 1870*, edited by Roger Davidson and Lesley A. Hall. London: Routledge, 2001.

Waters, Elizabeth. "Restructuring the 'Woman Question': Perestroika and Prostitution." *Feminist Review* 33 (1989): 3–19.

Watkins, Elizabeth S. *On the Pill: A Social History of Oral Contraceptives, 1950–1970*. Baltimore, MD: Johns Hopkins University Press, 1998.

Waugh, Thomas. *Hard to Imagine: Gay Male Eroticism in Photography and Film from Their Beginnings to Stonewall*. New York: Columbia University Press, 1996.

Weeks, Jeffrey. *Coming Out: Homosexual Politics in Britain from the Nineteenth Century to the Present*. London: Quartet Books, 1991.

Weelden, Ben van. *Pronken met jezelf*. Amsterdam: Candide, 1993.

Weibel, Peter, ed. *Phantom of Desire: Visions of Masochism: Essays and Texts*. Graz, Austria: Neue Galerie, 2003.

Weinberg, Thomas S., and G. W. Levi Kamel. *S and M: Studies in Sadomasochism*. New York: Prometheus, 1995.

West, Jackie. "Prostitution: Collectives and the Politics of Regulation." *Gender, Work and Organization* 7, no. 2 (2000): 106–18.

Wildt, Annemarie de, and Paul Arnoldussen. *Liefde te koop. Vier eeuwen prostitutie in Amsterdam*. Amsterdam: Bas Lubberhuizen, 2002.

Wilhelmus, Joop. *Bestialiteit*. Dordrecht: Chick, 1970.

Wilinsky, Barbara. *Sure Seaters: The Emergence of Art House Cinema*. Minneapolis, MN: University of Minnesota Press, 2001.

Williams, Linda. *Hard Core: Power, Pleasure, and the "Frenzy of the Visible."* Berkeley: University of California Press, 1999.

Williams, Linda, ed. *Porn Studies*. Durham, NC: Duke University Press, 2004.

Wittig, Monique. "One Is Not Born a Woman." In *The Straight Mind and Other Essays*. Boston, MA: Beacon Press, 1992.

World Health Organization. "Education and Treatment in Human Sexuality: The Training of Health Professionals: Report of a WHO Meeting" (Technical Report Series No. 572). In *Sexology Today: A Brief Introduction*, edited by E. Haeberle and R. Gindorf. Dusseldorf: DGSS, 1993.

CONTRIBUTORS

Daniela Danna is research fellow in sociology at the Università degli studi in Milan, Italy. She has researched and published on homosexuality, prostitution, and violence against women. Her books are mainly available in Italian, among others: *Ginocidio. La violenza contro le donne nell'era globale* (2007), *Donne di mondo. Commercio del sesso e controllo statale* (2004), *Amiche, compagne, amanti. Storia dell'amore tra donne* (2003). She edited *Prostitution policy in Four European Capitals* (2007), which is available in English at her Web site: http://www.danieladanna.it.

Kelly Dennis is the author of *Art/Porn: A History of Seeing and Touching* (Berg Publishers, 2009), as well as numerous essays on pornography, photography, and performance art. She has consulted on films and theatrical productions about pornography and sexuality, and, in 2009, she was a keynote speaker at the first international conference on pornography in Latin America. A 2009 fellow at the Ansel Adams Center for Creative Photography in Tucson, Arizona, her next book project concerns Western landscape photography. She teaches modern and contemporary art and history of photography at the University of Connecticut, Storrs.

Franz X. Eder is professor at the Department of Economic and Social History, University of Vienna. He has carried out research on quantitative methods and discourse analysis, on the history of labor organization, the history of family, consumption, and sexuality. His current research projects are on the history of sexuality and consumption in the twentieth century; he is finishing an introduction to the history of sexuality. He is co-editor of *Österreichis-che Zeitschrift für Geschichtswissenschaften* and of *Studien zur Sozial- und Wirtschaftsgeschichte*; he is on the editorial board of *Sexuality and Culture*; and is editor of *Bibliography of the History of Western Sexuality* (3rd ed., http://www.univie.ac.at/wirtschaftsgeschichte/Sexbibl/). His last publication on the history of sexuality is *Kultur der Begierde. Eine Geschichte der Sexualität* (2009).

Alain Giami coordinates, at the French National Institute of Health and Medical Research, the group Sexual Health and the Medicalisation of Sexuality. He obtained his PhD in 1978 (Sorbonne, Paris). His scientific interests have focused on sex research from a multidisciplinary perspective including psychology, sociology, history, and public health. He has carried out numerous international projects using qualitative and quantitative methods. His major study on attitudes toward the sexuality of people with cognitive disabilities became a book (1983). Between 1990 and 1994, he served in the French task force on HIV/AIDS in the field of social sciences and public health. He carried out research on the representations and attitudes of nurses toward AIDS and HIV patients. He participated in the French national survey on sexual behavior and was a senior editor of two of the books that were published following this study. He is now finalizing a book on the evolution of sexology into sexual health, sexual medicine, and sexual rights.

Gert Hekma teaches gay and lesbian studies and sexuality and gender studies within the BA/MA program Gender, Sexuality and Society at the Department of Sociology and Anthropology, University of Amsterdam. His research is on the sociology and history of (homo)sexuality. He wrote numerous articles on those subjects and co-edited with Kent Gerard *The Pursuit of Sodomy* (1989), with Harry Oosterhuis and James D. Steakley *Gay Men and the Sexual History of the Political Left* (1995), and with Franz Eder and Lesley Hall *Sexual Cultures in Europe* (2 volumes, 1999). He published *Homoseksualiteit in Nederland van 1730 tot de moderne tijd* (2004) and *ABC van perversies* (2009) and contributed to *Gewoon doen* (2006), a report on acceptance of homosexuality in the Netherlands.

Marie-Louise Janssen studied cultural anthropology at the University of Amsterdam. After finishing her study she has worked extensively with Latin American sex workers and trafficked persons. She is the cofounder of the foundation Esperanza, a Colombian/Dutch organization for the prevention and combating of human trafficking from Latin America to Europe. In 2007 she obtained her PhD at the University of Amsterdam with a thesis titled *Sex Workers on the Move: Latin American Women in the European Sex Industry*. The fieldwork for this research was conducted in Colombia, the Dominican Republic, and the Netherlands. At the moment she is teaching in the areas of gender and sexuality studies and research methods at the Department of Sociology and Anthropology of the University of Amsterdam. Her research interests currently include the Dutch sex industry and human trafficking.

Francis Ronsin is professor emeritus, Department of Contemporary History, at the Université de Bourgogne (Dijon). He has published several books and numerous articles that focus on the relationship between political struggles and private life: *La Grève des ventres—Propagande néo-malthusienne et baisse de la natalité en France 19ème-20ème siècles* (1980); *Le Contrat sentimental—Débats sur le mariage, l'amour, le divorce, de l'Ancien Régime à la Restauration* (1990); *Les Divorciaires—Affrontements politiques et conceptions du mariage dans la France du XIXème siècle* (1992); *Le Sexe apprivoisé -Jeanne Humbert et la lutte pour le contrôle des naissances* (1990); and *La population de la France de 1789 à nos jours. Données démographiques et affrontements idéologiques* (1997). He is also the principal organizer of the international research seminar Socialism and Sexuality.

Florence Tamagne is associate professor at the University of Lille 3. A specialist of the history of homosexuality, she has published in English *A History of Homosexuality in Europe: Berlin, London, Paris, 1919–1939* (2004), and has also contributed to Robert Aldrich, ed., *Gay Life and Culture: A World History* (2006) and Louis-Georges Tin, ed., *The Dictionary of Homophobia: A Global History of Gay and Lesbian Experience* (2008).

INDEX